ABOUT THE AUTHOR

JEFFREY BERNSTEIN, PHD, is a licensed psychologist specializing in child and family therapy in the Philadelphia area. He has helped more than one thousand children and their families restore their relationships. A nationally known expert, he is the author of *10 Days to a Less Defiant Child* and *Why Can't You Read My Mind?* Bernstein lives outside Philadelphia, Pennsylvania.

10 Days *to a* Less Distracted Child

10 Days
to a
Less Distracted Child

The Breakthrough Program That Gets Your Kids to Listen, Learn, Focus and Behave

JEFFREY BERNSTEIN, PhD

MARLOWE & COMPANY
NEW YORK

10 Days to a Less Distracted Child:
The Breakthrough Program that Gets Your Kids to Listen, Learn, Focus and Behave

Copyright © 2007 by Jeffrey Bernstein

Published by
Marlowe & Company
An Imprint of Avalon Publishing Group, Incorporated
245 West 17th Street • 11th floor
New York, NY 10011

AVALON
publishing group incorporated

ISBN-10: 1-60094-019-6
ISBN-13: 978-1-60094-019-4

9 8 7 6 5 4 3 2 1

Book design by Neuwirth & Associates, Inc.

Printed in the United States of America

To Alissa, Sam, and Gabby: You are the most enjoyable
and fulfilling distractions I could ever wish for. I have learned
so many valuable insights about life by being your dad.
I am so proud of each of you.

To my loving parents, who have infused me with strength and
self-determination. Thanks so much for all you have done for me.

Lastly, I dedicate this book to all of those who struggle
and strive to better themselves. I continue to draw strength
from your collective resilient spirit.

CONTENTS

INTRODUCTION

O dds are you've picked up this book because you're fed up with your child's distracted behavior. You're tired of the missed homework, failed quizzes and tests, and hassles at home. It worries you that your child's impulsive outbursts are putting a strain on his friendships. And it seems like no matter how many times you ask your child to do something, it doesn't get done. Even though you know you're nagging, you just can't help it.

Your child's distractibility is causing you both a lot of tension and grief. Yet nothing you do to remedy the situation seems to work. Every punishment you've tried—such as taking away the computer, withholding other privileges, or grounding—either has no effect or makes things worse. You may even be wondering if your child has a legitimate problem, or if she is just plain lazy and unmotivated. If this sounds familiar, rest assured that you are not alone. An enormous number of parents are also struggling to understand and meet the challenges of parenting distracted children.

I really do get it. Distractible children are difficult and very challenging to manage. However, as you'll learn in detail in "Day 1", your child *is* struggling with a legitimate problem, and she needs your help to manage it. If problematic distractibility is not properly identified and dealt with, it can damage your child's life. I know that sounds scary, but the good news is that by simply reading this book and putting this ten-day program into action, you will be doing something about the problem. That takes strength and guts, and your determination to make things better for your child will pay off.

Why This Program Is So Effective

This book and its companion book, *10 Days to a Less Defiant Child*, are both loaded with powerful strategies, tips, and techniques that will help you target your child's problematic behavior quickly and easily. In both books, I heavily emphasize the need for empathy and for creating emotional safety when trying to improve your child's behavior. These important components help to make the strategies and tips in these programs "stick," as opposed to being rejected by your child if she becomes resistant or defensive. I also encourage parents to be understanding and calm, firm, and non-controlling with their children, which, according to the feedback I received from readers of *10 Days to a Less Defiant Child*, creates a very effective formula for delivering the strategies in the ten-day program. While *10 Days to a Less Distracted Child* has a different focus than *10 Days to a Less Defiant Child*, these two books share a commitment to helping parents help kids who have a tough time helping themselves.

It's important to note that children who are plagued with distraction can also end up becoming defiant if their distraction is not managed. If you're also contending with defiance issues in your child—such as frequent arguing, blaming others for her mistakes, or defying rules—*10 Days to a Less Defiant Child* can provide you with support and many helpful strategies.

As you will see when you begin Day 1, I address the issue of distractibility as a whole. There can be situational, emotional, and neurological causes that drive the problem. In some cases, the specific causes of distractibility may not be easy to identify. For instance, a child of recently divorced parents who has ADHD or learning disabilities and anxiety issues likely has more than one factor fueling her distractibility problem Regardless of the underlying causes of distractibility, I am confident that the interventions in this book will be valuable and applicable to the vast majority of families.

You *Can* Lower Your Child's Distractibility

Distracted kids are resistant to help. They pretend they know answers when they don't. They give answers that may not make sense. Distracted kids often lie as a way to cope, when they feel confused or scared. Sometimes it seems to their parents—and to the kids—that there is no way out of the situation, no way to find focus. I am here to tell you that there absolutely *is* a way to manage this problem. Over and over during my twenty years of practice in the field of psychology, I have seen the tears, the anger, the disappointment, and the motivational shutdowns firsthand. I have also seen so many distracted children—including those with ADHD and other conditions—break through barriers and powerfully reemerge. I am highly confident that by following this groundbreaking ten-day program, you will significantly reduce your child's distractibility and improve your child's social skills and self-esteem. Your child will also gain the confidence she needs to tackle everyday challenges at school, at home, and with peers. You too can achieve positive results, just like so many of the parents and children I have worked with.

You may be wondering if perhaps your child will grow out of her attention deficit problems. While it's possible that your child's distractibility will lessen somewhat as she grows up, I can tell you that when distractibility occurs at problematic levels for children, it typically won't go away on its own. It takes the right interventions to help these children become well-adjusted in school, with peers, in the family, and in the community.

This book shows you step-by-step how to reduce distraction problems and improve your relationship with your child. The program is designed for children ages four to eighteen. For clarity and easy reading, I use the term "child" to represent this entire age group, throughout the text. Most of the examples I provide are from cases in my own psychology practice. I have changed names and other identifying information to protect confidentiality. Please realize that this book is not intended as a substitute for professional help. I encourage you to seek out a trained medical and mental heath professional if problems persist.

I've Had Distractibility Issues, Too

As a distracted child and young adult, I have had my own challenges. My determination to work through my own obstacles has helped me succeed in ways I never would have imagined. I am very grateful for the accomplishments I have been able to achieve.

However, I also know firsthand what it's like to fall short and feel lost. Distractibility definitely played a role in my struggle through chemistry class and my failing grades in trigonometry during high school. I had to repeat the latter. In college, my distractibility spurred me to seek more fun than study time. This led me to academic probation after my first semester, and I had to scramble to catch up. Let's just say that transitions were not easy for me in those earlier years. Let me be clear that I do not blame my distractibility for my past difficulties. In fact, learning to overcome my personal challenges has helped me be empathetic to the many children I see with similar struggles.

I was also fortunate to have supportive parents who always believed in me. They did not have a book to tell them how to help me, but they always gave me words of encouragement. While my parents have chuckled, over the years, about fishing my lost car keys out of the trash when I was younger (one of my many absent-minded moments), they never stopped believing in me.

Distractibility is not all bad. It has helped me think outside the box and become creative in new ways. At the same time, if distractibility is not compensated for and the problems it creates are not overcome, it can truly shortchange a child's life.

Seize This New Opportunity

As you follow this program of ten life-changing days, I ask that you think of yourself as a coach. Of course, you're always first and foremost your child's parent, but I also encourage you to put on your coaching hat and help your child attain success in her educational, social, and emotional experiences.

As you will learn, it's crucial for you to understand your distracted child in a whole new way. I realize you have probably tried everything you could think of to improve your child's distractibility. Many parents are perplexed because distracted kids seem to be able to focus when *they* want to. You may wonder how she can watch TV for so long, or how she can stay focused on saving up money for that new dance leotard. Your child can focus quite well on things that are important to her, but not so well in situations in her normal everyday life, such as listening to a teacher's lecture, interacting with peers, or doing homework. It is in these situations I am asking you to coach her.

How to Get the Most from This Book

I recommend that you go through each of the ten days consecutively. If circumstances prevent you from following the program on consecutive days, don't get discouraged. Just go through this entire program in the most doable way possible.

Each day is a step where you will learn powerful distraction-lowering strategies that build on one another. I recommend that you read each chapter in the morning and then use the strategies throughout the day. Please realize that it will certainly take more than one day for you and your child to get used to each new step/set of strategies, but you don't need to stop after each day and master all of the strategies it provided. Figure out which ones work best for you and your child as you keep moving forward.

In addition, please give yourself and your distracted child time to get used to your new approach. Please don't give up after the first day. Too many parents give up way too easily when trying to manage their distracted children. Sticking to the changes you make is key. If you don't quit on this program, it won't quit on you. Most parents I have worked with see appreciable decreases in their child's distraction-related problems within ten days.

I recommend that you keep a log of positive changes you see in yourself and in your child. The log does not have to be formal or elaborate. Any format that records your positive breakthroughs and successes with your child will be helpful. The main point is to stay mindful of and encouraged by specific improvements and the overall progress you have made.

If you follow it, my ten-day plan will work for you. But it's only the beginning of your journey. You must continue using the strategies and principles outlined throughout these chapters in order to coach your child to lessen and manage her distractibility over time. I strongly encourage you to keep using the strategies in this book as an ongoing effort. Trust me, your effort will pay off, and your child will be less distracted—much less than you could have imagined.

A Note about Language

When referring to your child, I have alternated the words "he" and "she" with each chapter of this book for easy readability. Male children and teens are more frequently diagnosed with distraction problems than females, but it's important to keep in mind that both genders suffer significantly from this problem.

Grasping the Devastating Distractibility Problem

You have been trying your best to be patient and supportive of your distracted child, but he is driving you up the wall. Nothing seems to be working. You've had enough of his incomplete schoolwork, missed homework assignments, and declining grades. You're tired of your requests going in one ear and out the other. Parenting a distracted child can be very overwhelming, and your growing frustration level is affecting both you and your child. (Trust me, your child is also quite frustrated, whether he admits it or not.)

Welcome to Day 1 of this new and exciting program to reduce your child's distractibility. Today you will learn about the causes, implications, and costs of this serious problem. Sadly, there are record numbers of children whose lives have been turned upside down because of attention-deficit problems. The harsh reality is that distractibility in children can make life equally difficult for families and educators. However, your child's distractibility can be vastly minimized, and this ten-day program will give you the powerful, specialized skills and tools you need to do just that.

Distractibility Means Poor Attention, Not Laziness

When I refer to a child as distracted or distractible, I mean that he has trouble paying attention, especially if he is not interested.

Children with distractibility have trouble with one or more parts of the attention process. Some children have difficulty concentrating on tasks (particularly tasks that are routine or boring). Other kids have trouble knowing where or how to begin a task. Still others zone in and out of attention and get lost along the way. As you will see below, there is no single cause for distractibility, and the very broadness of this problem has exacted a huge emotional, educational, and financial price from our families and our society.

It's important to realize that your child's distractibility does not mean that he is intentionally forgetful, irresponsible, or absent-minded. And, although it may seem this way, your child's distractibility definitely does not mean that he is lazy. The "lazy" label is hard for many parents to let go of, but it's important that you do so. It's a destructive label that can cause deep feelings of inadequacy in your child and negatively shape his destiny.

Your Child May Have ADHD

The most common cause of distractibility in children is a neurological disorder called attention-deficit hyperactivity disorder (ADHD). Distractibility can be a big problem for kids with ADHD. Theresa, age eleven, was brought to me by her very concerned and exasperated parents—with Theresa in tears. I took a thorough history of Theresa's pattern of not paying attention in class, forgetting to write down assignments, problematic peer interactions, and lack of follow-through on chores at home. After interviewing her teachers and consulting with her school psychologist, I determined that Theresa had ADHD. Educational modifications were put in place, and Theresa was prescribed medication by her pediatrician (I discuss the use of medications in "Day 9"). With her diagnosis, Theresa's parents were better able to understand her limitations and support her in working through her challenges.

This story has a happy ending—but without proper intervention, many don't.

Many children who struggle with distractibility have ADHD tendencies but do not meet the full criteria for an ADHD diagnosis. In these cases, the interventions may be different, but the need for us to understand that these children are not choosing to be distracted remains crucial. Knowing that distractibility is unintentional plays a key role in finding coping strategies and solutions.

Other children diagnosed with ADHD are hyperactive and impulsive rather than distracted. These kids are constantly fidgeting or blurting out comments that get them into trouble. To make matters even more complicated, there are children diagnosed with ADHD who have the symptoms of *both* distractibility and hyperactivity/impulsivity.

In this ten-day program, my focus is on the concerns related to distractibility, but it's important to realize that a hyperactive or impulsive child faces considerable challenges as well. Many parents have reported to me that the strategies in this ten-day program also reduce hyperactivity and impulsivity, but you should also seek out more focused help for your hyperactive and impulsive child.

Recognizing Distractibility

To get a better understanding of how distractible your child really is, take a look at the list below. While this list is borrowed from the diagnostic criteria for the inattentive type of ADHD, the behaviors below are also representative of distractibility as seen in children with no formal ADHD diagnosis.

Using the space next to each description, rate the impact of your child's behaviors from 1 (most problematic) to 5 (least problematic).

_____ Does not seem to listen when spoken to.
_____ Does not reliably finish his chores or homework.

_____ Finds it hard to keep his mind on what he's doing for very long, unless he finds it interesting or stimulating.

_____ Makes a lot of careless mistakes due to poor attention. Note: Many parents think that extended video game use (a few hours) means their child can pay attention if he really wants to. However, video games are an exception because they have multimodal input (visual, auditory, and tactile) and give immediate feedback, which makes them exciting, fun, and attention grabbing/sustaining.

_____ Is really disorganized. A kid with poor attention may take hours to finally finish homework, then "lose" it at school (but the whole time it's in his backpack), or forget to turn it in.

_____ Tries to avoid doing homework or chores.

_____ Gets distracted easily, or pays attention to the wrong things.

_____ Is forgetful and needs frequent reminders.

Now look carefully at how you rated your child's behaviors. It should be clear which distractibility behaviors present the biggest problems for you. Now ask yourself the following questions:

- When did these behaviors start?
- In what settings do they occur?
- Are negative events in my child's past influencing these behaviors?
- What, if anything, has helped my child manage these distractible behaviors in the past?
- How have I tended to respond to these behaviors?

As I mentioned above, ADHD can also involve hyperactivity and impulsivity, which could accompany your child's distractibility, if he does have the condition. Consider whether your child exhibits any of the following behaviors:

- Feeling restless, often fidgeting with hands or feet, or squirming while seated
- Running, climbing, or leaving a seat, in situations where sitting or quiet behavior is expected
- Difficulty playing or engaging in leisure activities quietly
- Talking excessively
- Blurting out answers before hearing the whole question
- Having difficulty waiting in line or taking turns

If your child's distractibility or hyperactivity as described above occurs on a frequent basis, make an appointment to see your child's pediatrician or other qualified health-care professional to discuss the possibility of an ADHD diagnosis.

Your Child May Not Have ADHD

The reason distractibility is such a widespread problem is that there are several possible underlying causes, not just ADHD. The following is a description of other conditions and factors that can cause distractibility in children. I discuss these in more detail in "Day 7: Conquering Coexisting Conditions."

Anxiety

Children with anxiety are often internally preoccupied with worries, which can lead them to be distractible. For instance, anxious children and teens often feel particularly uptight or stressed on the first day in a new school, or when they have problems with their friends. As they repeatedly think about concerns (obsessing is a big part of anxiety), their hearts beat faster and they have "butterfly feelings" in their stomachs. Some children may meet the criteria for anxiety disorders, which are much, much stronger versions of anxiety. Children with anxiety disorders have intense fear and worry. They also may develop problems sleeping and have physical symptoms such as headaches, stomachaches, and nausea.

Eight-year-old Erica was brought in to see me by her parents because she was "being spacey" at school, and her grades were declining. Erica's teacher had taken her mother, Joyce, aside and suggested that Erica had distractibility problems. When she spoke to me privately "off the record" on the phone, this teacher said she firmly believed Erica had ADHD.

However, Joyce and Erica's teacher were unaware of the extent to which Erica had been harboring worries about her father, who had recently been diagnosed with a major medical condition. Bearing this in mind, I helped Erica share and work through her fears about her father's health. Fortunately, Erica's father's health gradually improved. Erica continued to see me for follow-up counseling to help her manage her lingering anxiety about her father. Not surprisingly, Erica became less distractible as she worked through and managed her anxiety. Fortunately, her teacher also saw this improvement.

While frustrating to many parents, anxiety is challenging for children to control by will power alone. Anxiety in children often comes and goes in unpredictable ways. It robs them of performing and enjoying their usual activities. In fact, without the necessary coping skills, controlling anxiety is next to impossible for children, and the condition doesn't fade with time. I have worked with many anxious adults who've shared stories of untreated anxiety that they've lived with most of their lives.

Anxiety is the most common mental health concern in the United States. About 13 percent of American children and adolescents are affected by anxiety disorders each year, and many more are plagued with anxiety that does not qualify as an actual anxiety disorder. They may worry about school pressures, home life, peer relationships, or other miscellaneous concerns. Even a moderate amount of anxious feelings can lead a child to be distractible.

Depression

Depression is another mental health problem that can cause distraction. Depression, like anxiety, is an emotional problem, whereas ADHD is generally recognized as a neurologically based problem. In less frequent cases, depression can occur with manic cycles, which is a condition known as bipolar disorder.

In children, depression may have a more insidious onset than in adults. It may be characterized more by irritability than sadness, and it occurs more often in association with other conditions such as anxiety, oppositional defiant disorder, and learning problems. The term *major depression* is used to distinguish discrete episodes of depression from mild, chronic (one year or longer) low mood, or irritability (also known as dysthymia).

Thirteen-year-old Kevin came to see me because he, too, was presumed to have ADHD. Kevin's family history revealed that his maternal grandmother had struggled with depression all of her life. In the course of my evaluation, Kevin scored significantly on an inventory (test) measuring depression in children. As I worked with him, he revealed a lot of self-defeating thoughts (e.g., "I can never get anyone to like me" and "I'm stupid"), which left him unable to focus in school and with peers. Fortunately, through counseling, Kevin learned to overcome his negative self-perceptions, and he also became far less distractible.

Learning Disabilities

Fourteen-year-old Terrell saw me for counseling during the early fall of his eighth-grade year. In order to get to know Terrell, I took turns with him, reading question cards designed to let us discover interesting information about one another. While I am not a certified reading instructor, I could soon see that Terrell had a difficult time reading the questions. I referred him to his school psychologist, who determined that Terrell had dyslexia, a reading disability.

Learning disabilities, like ADHD, have a neurological basis; they are disorders that affect the ability to understand or use spoken or written language, do mathematical calculations, coordinate movements, or direct attention. Making matters worse, learning disabilities can shatter the self-confidence of many children and also cause distractibility. They can exist alone or with the other conditions discussed here. Educators estimate that between 5 and 10 percent of kids between six and seventeen have learning disabilities, and that more than half of the kids receiving special education in the United States have them. (Please note: The term *learning differences,* which sounds less judgmental and less negative than the term *learning disabilities,* is the one I prefer. However, I'm using the term *learning disability* in this book because it's still more common, and it's the language found in the law and the regulations.)

Eighty percent of students with learning disabilities have dyslexia, making this reading problem the most common learning disability. However, any child struggling with a learning process that is different from the mainstream is likely to face distraction that further interferes with his learning. Below is a list of common learning disabilities:

Dyslexia: This is a language-based disability. Children with dyslexia have trouble understanding words, sentences, or paragraphs.

Dyscalculia: This is a mathematical disability that causes a child to have a very difficult time solving arithmetic problems and grasping math concepts.

Dysgraphia: A child with this writing disability finds it hard to form letters correctly or write within a defined space.

Nonverbal learning disabilities: These include any learning disability that is not language-related, such as difficulty in recognizing and interpreting nonverbal communication and difficulties with reasoning.

Auditory and visual processing disabilities: These are sensory disabilities that cause a child to have difficulty understanding language, despite normal hearing and vision.

Children with learning disabilities often require services available through the special education system. These children can be highly distractible, and special education is specially designed instruction designed to meet their unique needs. This instruction may include intensive remediation in reading, math, or other areas of need. It also may include services such as psychological counseling, physical and occupational therapy, speech and language services, transportation, and medical diagnosis. Most children receiving special education are considered to have some form of learning disability.

Learning disabilities and the consequent distractibility can be a lifelong challenge. Some children may have several overlapping learning disabilities. Other children may have a single, isolated learning problem that has little impact on their lives. The good news is that there are many educational recommendations and resources to help address learning disabilities (see the Resources section for more information).

Autism/Asperger's Disorder

While he was outwardly flat in his emotions, when twelve-year-old Sean walked into his first session with me, I sensed that he had a unique, private, rich inner world. Sean has Asperger's disorder, a higher-functioning form of autism. Sean had a relatively solid level of intelligence, but he had difficulties negotiating successful social relationships.

The functioning levels of children with autism vary widely, but for most of them, paying attention proves to be highly challenging. This is because they focus on sensations, which to them are highly intriguing and important. These children often switch attention rapidly from one sensation to another, which distracts them from the comments of peers, their parents' requests, or their teachers' lectures.

Often the sources of the distraction for children with autism are visual. For example, when a teacher puts a paper on the desk, the child may be so distracted by the paper that he does not attend to his work. Or the student sees something in the hallway and is so distracted that he stops working in order to watch more closely. Auditory stimuli such as outside voices can also be very distracting.

Whatever the source of the distraction, children with autism have great difficulty ignoring it as irrelevant and refocusing on what needs to be attended to. Some get swept up in sensations that always seem new and exciting. Others deal with sensory bombardment by shutting out much of the stimulation around them and becoming preoccupied with a very limited array of objects.

Other Conditions That Cause Distractibility

There are several other possible causes for distractibility in children. I will briefly mention some to keep in mind. Tourette's disorder is a neurological disorder characterized by involuntary body movements and vocal outbursts that last for at least twelve months. Tourette's is known to cause children to have poor attention. Substance abuse and its related psychosocial stress can also disrupt attention for children, particularly the teen population.

Vision and hearing problems, which can make a child appear inattentive, are important considerations to rule out with appropriate testing. Children with undetected vision problems can exhibit symptoms similar to those of ADHD. The same parallel symptoms may be seen in children with head trauma and petit mal seizures, as well as children who are victims of physical or emotional abuse.

There is also evidence that gifted children show enhanced sensory activation and awareness, with distractibility. Consider a former client of mine, ten-year-old Keith. In class, he was spacey and off in another world. Tests conducted by the school psychologist showed that he was highly intelligent. But, as the expression goes, Keith would have "lost his own head if it was not attached." If Keith remembered to bring home assignments, he usually did them (with a little parental reminding). However, Keith often neglected to turn in the homework, which earned him C's and D's for school grades. I have worked with many frustrated parents dealing with gifted kids like Keith. Fortunately, in Keith's case, the interventions in this book helped to raise his focus and lower his distractibility.

Oppositional defiant disorder is another problem that can lead to distractibility in some children. When children "flip a switch" and act defiant, they tend to get distracted in the process. My previous book, *10 Days to a Less Defiant Child*, offers an effective program for parents dealing with this issue.

Stress

Many children not diagnosed with any major emotional or physical disorder may become distracted in response to stresses in their environment. Death of a loved one, divorce, relocation, and the arrival of a new child are just a few of the stresses that can lead to distractibility in children. I have also seen a fair share of overscheduled children overwhelmed by the stress of trying to keep up with school, after-school sports, religious activities, and community-based activities. Sometimes, too much of too many good things can cause stress overload.

Media

Research suggests that children in the United States are exposed to eight and a half hours of TV, video games, computers, and other media each day—often at the same time. The problem intensifies after third grade, when harder course work requires children to concentrate more. Let's also not forget about phone calls, instant messaging on the computer, and text messaging on the phone. The difference between today and even a few years ago is that video games and televisions have invaded children's bedrooms for even greater exposure.

Many children are seemingly addicted to media. Befuddled parents find it hard to understand how their child can struggle with distractibility yet be able to sit for hours glued to the television. Obviously, television and computer screens offer bright sounds and sights that are more stimulating to a distractible child than a teacher's drone while giving a lecture or Mom's request for help with the dishes.

The sad news is that television, computers, and all this techie stuff interfere with a child's ability to control distractibility. For most children, it's impossible to watch TV or listen to a favorite song and at the same time give sufficient attention to schoolwork.

That being said, I have found in a few cases that some kids benefit from background noise such as television or music. For these children, the background noise offers a soothing, calming presence that augments rather than compromises their ability to focus their attention where it is needed (e.g., on their homework).

For this to be effective, however, make sure favorite television shows or songs are not competing with your child's need to maintain focus elsewhere.

Power struggles between parents and children over television viewing often just make kids yearn for the "idiot box" even more. I advocate a calm, firm, and noncontrolling parenting philosophy, and I advise parents not to try to keep the media away from distractible children, but to teach them how to make good choices (see "Day 5" for more information on being calm, firm, and noncontrolling).

Ten-year-old Bob's parents calmly yet assertively set a boundary of no TV on school days and only an hour a day on weekends. Although Bob would on occasion wake up around 7:00 AM on the weekends to watch cartoons as his parents slept, for the most part the boundary worked.

Take a Breath

All of these diagnostic classifications and conditions can be overwhelming, so take a moment now and catch your breath. (Note that I address many of these conditions further in "Day 7".) All you need to remember right now is that your child is a living, breathing human being who may not fit neatly into any one of these categories. Because there are many possible causes of distractibility and no single assessment process that can identify it with full accuracy, understanding the reasons for your child's distractibility can be challenging. The good news is that approaching your child's distractibility problem with the tools and strategies in the ten-day plan *will* help him, regardless of what is driving him to be distracted. You'll be equipped to help your child manage his distractibility more successfully than you may ever have imagined.

Focusing on Yourself

Clearly, managing a child struggling with distractibility can be very taxing for any parent. I see so many burnt-out parents at their wits' end in my practice. The next section provides you with guidance on taking care of yourself while taking care of your distracted child's needs.

THOUGHTS THAT DISTRACT YOU FROM YOUR DISTRACTED CHILD

Parenting a distracted child can have a big effect on your ability to focus on yourself and the rest of your family. You probably have experienced some or all of the feelings listed below. Please put a check next to any that you can identify with.

_____ You are conflicted about how much to help your child versus letting him sink or swim.

_____ You struggle to determine how much your child cannot or chooses not to pay attention.

_____ You feel guilty for getting impatient with your child's distractibility.

_____ You feel as if you are failing as a parent.

_____ You try to put your concerns aside, but you find yourself consumed by your child's distractibility-related issues.

_____ You feel exhausted.

_____ You feel alone.

_____ You resent the drain of time and energy that your child's distractibility causes your family.

Making Changes

Distractibility reduces motivation in your child because it's unpleasant for him to attempt to focus when it's so challenging to do so. Many distraction-prone children become reluctant to participate in discussions or conversations because experience has taught them that they have missed a key piece, and they don't want to appear stupid. There is a fine line between having empathy for your child's challenges and becoming mired in your own consequent negativity.

The first step in making life better for your child is for you to realize that you have already done many good things to motivate your child. The better you feel about what you have done well, the more able you will be to help your child.

Identifying Your Positive Motivational Behaviors

To help you stop blaming yourself for your child's distractibility and gain more control over the situation, consider all of the positive actions you've taken for your child. Read the list of the following positive motivating behaviors, and put a check next to those you have done.

_____ Give compliments.

_____ Hug him.

_____ Help with schoolwork.

_____ Attend Back to School Night.

_____ Say "I love you."

_____ Compliment his positive behaviors.

_____ Buy school supplies.

_____ Offer selective and appropriate incentives.

_____ Contact his teachers about school concerns.

_____ Communicate with him about school concerns.

These are just a few of the positive actions you have taken to support your distracted child. I hope that you will allow yourself to feel good about them. These behaviors alone will not lower your child's distractibility, but they will be a big help to you as you apply the strategies in this program.

Identifying Your Negative Motivational Behaviors

This is the necessary but not-so-fun part. As you're checking off the behaviors listed below that may have demotivated your distracted child, remember that no parent is perfect.

Following this list is a brief discussion of the negative motivational behaviors that are particularly problematic. At this point, you are identifying your negative behaviors so you can be more mindful of them. In "Day 3", I provide you with further explanation of negative parenting behaviors and coach you on how to best react to your distracted child.

_____ Yell.

_____ Lose sight of your child's feelings.

_____ Use sarcasm.

_____ Tease him.

_____ Hit him.

_____ Ignore him.

_____ Lecture him.

_____ Shame him.

_____ Criticize.

_____ Act impatient.

_____ Have unrealistic expectations.

_____ Nag.

_____ Interrupt him.

_____ Make him feel guilty.

_____ Lie to him or about him.

_____ Make threats.

_____ Put him down.

_____ Deny his feelings.

Nagging

Children who are prone to distraction tend to get constantly nagged by their parents. Eleven-year-old Elizabeth was disorganized, forgetful, and easily distracted in the middle of a task. Her mother, Jill, was an office manager with superb focus and organizational skills. Jill tried to manage Elizabeth's distractibility at home by nagging her to get things done, which just made the situation worse. I worked with both mother and daughter. As Jill stopped her nagging, Elizabeth became more open to letting her mother help her get organized.

Shaming by Predicting Ruination

Parents who are upset and at their wits' end tend to say demotivating things to their children, such as "You'll end up on the streets unless you start paying attention." This approach just leads to demoralized feelings and does not foster motivation.

Ignoring the Problem

Julia's twelve-year-old son, Ian, had consistently achieved 99 percent composite scores on standardized tests and had been in the gifted program since kindergarten. Their home, however, was in turmoil because of Ian's "constant distraction" problem. Julia had ignored the problem for the first two quarters of school because she was "sick and tired of nagging." Julia and Ian had seen a counselor in the past who told Julia to quit harping on Ian's behavior and to let him fail—he needed to learn responsibility on his own. Unable to focus and finding that his intellectual muscle alone could not carry him, Ian began to fail miserably at school. The situation improved dramatically when Julia became reinvolved and used the strategies in this program.

Yelling

Yelling at your child will only serve to demotivate him. My recent book, *10 Days to a Less Defiant Child,* provides twenty-five ways to help parents stop yelling. They include using active listening skills, recognizing your anger as a signal to act constructively versus destructively, being concise and clear with directions (this is very important for children prone to distraction), and managing your expectations of your child. Yelling at your child will just make him more distracted and further bruise his already banged-up self-esteem.

Making Threats

Parents often erroneously believe that they can motivate their children by threatening them. This is a recipe for disaster. Threatening your distracted child will only alienate him and encourage lying and other avoidance behaviors.

Lecturing

Remember that if your child knew how to be less distracted, he would fix the problem himself. Avoid lecturing him about why he should be focused, and remember to empathize with him—he did not choose to be distractible in the first place.

Losing Sight of Your Child's Feelings

As I will discuss in Day 2, distractible children are highly misunderstood. Onions have many layers, and so do children. Children may act as if their distractibility does not bother them. I can tell you firsthand, however, that once you peel away a few layers of denial, most distracted children are flooded with feelings of low self-esteem and angst about their distractibility. Too often, parents lose sight of this.

Hitting

Studies have shown that physical punishment, such as hitting and slapping, is not effective. Distracted children do not choose to be distracted, and hitting them just leads to disaster. Physical punishment can humiliate and discourage children and can cause them to think of themselves as bad. Showing children that violence is acceptable will tear down their self-esteem and can even promote physical aggression in children. If you have hit your kids in the past, don't beat yourself up about it now. No one is perfect. However, I strongly encourage you to stop using physical punishment with your child from this point forward. Instead, use the tools in this program to lower your child's distractibility and build a positive relationship with him.

More than he will ever likely admit, your child desperately needs your help to overcome his distractibility problem. Your distracted child needs to learn that there are effective ways for him to improve his attention span and to compensate for his distractibility. Most strategies fail because they are given up on too quickly. This ten-day plan works because I not only coach you on what to do, I also show you how to set up the right relationship conditions in which to do it. If you apply my suggestions in earnest, your child will become less distractible and more focused on taking care of himself.

DAY 1: SUMMING IT UP

Today you have already come a long way in learning about why your child is distractible. You have begun a highly effective ten-day program that will make a wonderful difference in your child's life by lowering his distractibility. Keep the following points in mind as you continue on this important journey:

- There is no single cause of distractibility.
- Your distracted child is not lazy. Whether or not he meets the full criteria for ADHD or another disorder, you must take action to help him be less prone to distractibility.
- The strategies in this ten-day program generally work for all distracted children, no matter what is causing their distractibility or the degree to which it is present.
- Your parenting and motivational methods have a huge impact on your child's distractibility.
- Value yourself and your efforts. This will help your distractible child do the same for himself.

Understanding Your Distracted Child

In order to help your child overcome her attention problems, you must truly understand what she struggles with on a daily basis. In "Day 1," I stressed that there is a reason (or reasons) for your child's distractibility. Today, I focus on getting you to see the world through your child's eyes. By the end of this day, you will see that your child has a legitimate problem that must be solved, and that she is not purposefully acting distracted.

Because most parents view distractibility as a problem their children can control, they often speak to their kids with a frustrated tone or angry voice. It makes perfect sense—of course you are frustrated and angry if you think your child is willfully defying you. One of my own children has struggled with distraction issues (prone to forgetting homework materials), and I, too, fell prey to using an irritated tone more often than I care to admit. I discovered, however, as you may already have done, that getting upset over distractibility defeats our purpose of supporting and motivating our children. If you act angry or irritated, your child will respond negatively to your emotion, rather than positively to your suggestions.

Today you will make a tremendous, positive difference in your child's life by learning to understand her mind and her perspective. This may sound easy, but believe me, it takes discipline and skill to look beyond your frustrations and other negative feelings. All the effort in the world will not help your child decrease her distractibility unless you understand where she's coming from.

Your Child Feels Misunderstood

The better you understand what it's like for your child to combat distraction on a daily basis, the better armed you will be to help her work through it. Years ago, a colleague of mine shared a helpful metaphor that illustrates what it's like to struggle with distraction. Given my own problems with distractibility, I really like this metaphor. Imagine a traffic cop directing cars at the scene of an accident. If this police officer can't sustain his attention properly, what will happen? More accidents will occur. Similar to misdirected cars at the scene of a traffic accident, speedy and misdirected thoughts frequently collide in the minds of distracted children.

Distracted children usually feel very misunderstood by others, but they also don't really understand themselves. They don't know why they are so absent-minded, and they don't know how to fix things. So, when they are urged by their parents, their teachers, or anyone else to pay attention, they justifiably feel as if their heads are going to explode. Understanding your distracted child is the most effective way you can help her through the strategies in this ten-day program. In fact, being understanding of your child is in and of itself a strategy to help. The more your child feels like you see her perspective, the more open and honest she will be with you.

Common Symptoms

As you now know, our main purpose today is to heighten your awareness and understanding of the struggles your distracted child faces. The following is an overview of common daily struggles, as well as a few glimpses of how parents or teachers have effectively helped children deal with them. In the days that follow, I give you many more strategies and suggestions for dealing with each aspect of your child's distractibility problem. As you read through the problems listed below, stay mindful of how they can weigh down your child's motivation and her spirit.

Being Easily Distracted

This is an obvious one, but let's take a really close look. Children prone to distraction are often overwhelmed with thoughts and signals that are bombarding them from all angles. For instance, when a distractible child is talking with someone in a crowded room, she is often aware of all the other conversations going on in the area—her brain is taking in all the other stimuli in the room at the same time, even if they are irrelevant. Not only does she have trouble concentrating on her own conversation, she may be mistakenly considered nosy by her friends and family. She is "tuning out" of her conversation against her own wishes, and on top of that, she is misunderstood for it.

Distractible children often feel helpless when they have trouble filtering out the relevant from the irrelevant. It really gets in the way of the conversation or task they are trying to attend to and make sense of. This feeling of helplessness is crucial for you to understand because it lowers your child's overall sense of self-worth and leads her to avoid required tasks and responsibilities.

Janis, age fifteen, was a client of mine whose father, Robert, was bewildered and upset by his daughter's distractibility. Robert initially came in to see me complaining about how Janis often, while in the middle of doing something important (e.g., homework), would suddenly shift to doing something else. For instance, Janis would stop working on her homework to talk to a friend on the phone. Consequently, the tensions between Robert (a full-time single dad) and Janis were very high. Janis, not surprisingly, was frustrated, sad, and angry about her own distractibility. She was also boiling over with anger in response to her father's strong negative reactions. Fortunately, once Robert and I spoke, he gained a better understanding of the situation. He realized that what Janis was doing was common for distracted children, and he was better able to understand her struggles. This was the crucial first step to managing Janis's distractibility.

Having a Short Attention Span (but Not Always)

Based on what you have read so far, it will come as no shock to you that it's very difficult for distracted children to stay focused on one subject for long, without their minds jumping to something else. Yet, equally baffling to parents and teachers is that, at select times, the opposite can be true. In some cases, distracted children may find that they cannot stop from focusing on one project for hours. They literally can't relax or do anything else until the project is completed. As I mentioned in Day 1's list of behaviors (see pages 3–4), distractible children can often focus very well on things they find particularly interesting. In short, there is usually no happy medium between the two extremes in a distracted child's life.

Being Disorganized

Distracted children tend to be chronically disorganized. Their rooms are often in shambles, and, to make matters worse, this chaos in their living environment exacerbates their distractibility. Much to the chagrin of parents, this cycle of chaos becomes a living nightmare of chronic disarray for the distracted child.

For most distractible children, it takes all of their strength and energy just to get started cleaning their rooms, and once they start, the room becomes a disaster area all over again. Most distractible children cave in under the organizational demands of everyday life. They are told over and over by caring parents to "just put things down where they are supposed to go" so there won't be so much clutter. The problem with this advice is that distractible kids often can't think of what should go where, or what they should do with what is presently in their hands. They feel overwhelmed by what they perceive as the monumental task of cleaning and organizing their rooms on their own.

I, like so many others who struggle with distraction, find that I can be in the middle of one project when all of a sudden I think of another task that needs doing. This other task screams for my attention, so I leave the first task, thinking that I'll get back to it later. The phone may ring, or someone may come to my door, and the next thing I know the first task is forgotten. This is not good, especially if that first task was to, say, pick up one of my children. (Thankfully, that has not happened—yet. As you can imagine, however, given my own struggles with distractibility, writing a self-help book on distraction had some amusing ironies.)

I encourage you to help your child get started cleaning her room, cleaning out her backpack, or straightening out her desktop. Your willingness to jump-start your child's motivation for organization will help her internalize the good feelings that come from gaining order and balance. Helping your child help herself is far better than letting her get overwhelmed by her own inertia.

Losing Track of Time

Over and over, I have seen that distracted children have trouble with sensing time. They usually wait until the last minute to get ready. They are often late and have no real sense of how long a task or project will take. Parents like Tony, the father of thirteen-year-old Sam, find themselves ready to pull their hair out in frustration after hounding their children to hurry up. Tony, like so many frustrated parents of distracted kids, convinced himself that Sam was being defiant instead of being unintentionally distracted.

Once I helped Tony stop misinterpreting Sam's poor sense of time as defiance, we were able to improve the situation. After the quarreling between Tony and Sam had stopped, Sam felt safe enough to express his idea for a solution. Sam asked his father if his strivings for time diligence could be rewarded with breakfast at Sam's favorite bagel shop. Tony agreed to do this twice a week (Tuesdays and Fridays). While the problem did not completely disappear, Sam significantly improved his morning time-management skills and felt more understood by his father.

Having Trouble Following Directions

I can recall opening up many "assembly required" boxes and, erroneously trusting my instincts, setting aside (and eventually misplacing) the directions on the closest table, chair, or whatever item happened to be there. I not only had trouble following directions, I also had trouble remembering where I put them in the first place!

Distractible children are often misperceived as being defiant because they do not do what is asked of them. The reality is that many distracted children *cannot* do what is asked of them. Their failure to do things the "right way" (due to their distraction) leaves them feeling extremely frustrated and, again, very misunderstood.

The bottom line is that distractible children have difficulty understanding directions, or quickly start to lose the details of directions. At school, many distractible children look like the proverbial deer caught in the headlights when they are being given directions. I recall helping the teacher of ten-year-old José come up with a more concise strategy for giving him directions. When José used to hear multiple directions such as "Please sit down, take out your pencil and your ruler, and open your math folder," he would zone out. To improve the situation, the teacher made it a point to stand close to José and repeat the directions to him in a low-key, reassuring manner. Teachers who demonstrate patience and understanding are a huge help to their distracted students.

Being Easily Frustrated and Impatient

Most people wrestle with frustrations on occasion. But frustration comes readily to distracted children. They are often not able to do things that they think they should be able to do. I know many distracted children who can describe how to do a task, yet cannot do it themselves. For instance, a distractible child may be able to tell you exactly how to organize her school work, even though she needs her parents to help her do so. This type of frustration reminds them of past failures and can cause anger and a tendency to withdraw.

Distractible children find themselves feeling impatient because of their need for stimulation and also because they want so much to be able to do the things they can't. Nine-year-old Celine so wrestled with this dilemma that she became tearful when speaking to me. In Celine's case, her distractibility interfered with her keeping up in her dance class. She was perceived by her peers, and even by the instructor, as clumsy, overemotional, and immature. Fortunately, Celine's parents moved her to a different dance school with a more empathetic instructor, where she flourished. While it may not be in the cards for Celine to become a professional dancer, she at least found a supportive setting that helped her make progress and have fun while doing so.

Procrastinating

Distractible children fear that they won't do something "right," so they put it off, which only adds to their stress. I helped Monica and her husband, David, work with their twelve-year-old son, Joey, on his procrastination. Monica and David became more aware and understanding of how Joey got overwhelmed when facing a new task. After I coached them on showing Joey how to break a task into smaller segments, good things started to happen. For example, David stopped lecturing and shared with Joey how it wasn't so easy for him to tackle the onerous task of paying bills. He also modeled to Joey how he kept his papers organized and how to complete tasks in a timely fashion to avoid "paying late fees."

Having Trouble with Multitasking

In our fast-paced world, the ability to multitask is often seen as a virtue. For distractible children, however, several activities and projects going on at the same time can spell disaster. Many times projects are left unfinished. I worked with fifteen-year-old Bonnie, who tearfully shared how she became lost in multiple activities. Bonnie repeatedly shifted back and forth from her school assignments to her church youth group projects, and at the end of the day, neither would be complete. I helped Bonnie and her parents devise a mutually agreeable schedule (with mutually agreeable break times). Progress was made when Bonnie began working for shorter, more concentrated time intervals. Her parents' calm, firm, and noncontrolling approach made things even better.

As with Bonnie's case, doing too much at the same time causes distracted children to feel mixed up and confused. Children like Bonnie, unless shown another way, lose track of the requirements of each project and fall woefully behind.

Suffering from Impaired Coordination

Many distractible children are prone to difficulties with eye-hand coordination. They are often told that if they just practice and keep trying, they will be able to overcome their coordination problems. Frustratingly, no matter how hard distracted kids may try to work at some movement-oriented tasks, such tasks still may be difficult for them. Many of these children have difficulty with sports such as baseball and tennis, which demand serious focus and eye-hand coordination. They are often the last ones picked for games with peers. Some distracted children may also have a tendency to walk into walls or doors.

Blurting Out Whatever Comes to Mind

When I was a teenager, my mother used to say to me, "Jeff, think about time and place." This was her loving reminder for me to resist the urge to blurt out what I wanted—or, as I thought then, needed—to say at the moment. Distractible children often get very carried away by enthusiasm. When an idea comes to their minds, like a swelling rush of water that bursts the dam, they believe that it must be spoken right away. One reason for this may be that they know they may forget it later, if they don't speak it immediately. Unless distracted children learn strategies for appropriate conversational give and take, this tendency can end up being a problem for them. It's very important that they learn to contain their impulses and be able to listen to peers, parents, teachers, and others in their lives.

Acting Out Impulsively

Some distracted children can be frequently impulsive. The impulsiveness may be verbal, as discussed above, or it may come in the form of impulsive actions. For example, distracted teens may be prone to impulsive spending. Their distractibility leaves them swirling and confused when it comes to determining whether what they see is a want or a need. In their minds, everything feels like a need.

To help control her impulsivity, calmly encourage your child to express what she is feeling. For example, airing her anger about the girl who snubbed her may help reduce her urge to lash out harshly in return. Share with your child that acting impulsively might feel good in the moment, but that it can lead to poor choices, which will leave her feeling even worse than she does now.

Searching for High Levels of Stimulation

In my years of working with distracted children, I've come to see them as having whirlwinds in their minds. Always striving for more stimulation, they are usually on the lookout for something new and exciting to match or surpass the force of the whirlwind, and they often cannot find it. This means that distractible children tend to get bored very easily, because they are unable to sustain interest in less stimulating material or situations. This can lead them into trouble at home and at school. Twelve-year-old Carl was sent to see me because he told his teacher to "screw off." Carl had urges to get attention from others, and in this case, his desire for attention bought him a trip to the principal's office and an apology to his teacher.

When talking with your child about coping with boredom, encourage her to take a deep breath, count to ten, and visualize something that makes her happy, such as learning new moves for dance class. While this strategy may seem to encourage distraction, it actually helps your child soothe herself and refocus in a more productive way on what is relevant and necessary.

Being Tempted by Addictive Behavior

The desire for stimulation goes hand in hand with the possibility of developing addictive behaviors. I don't mean to scare you and imply that your distracted child will definitely abuse drugs. In fact, by being as involved a parent as you are, you are making this less likely to be the case. At the same time, distractible teenagers tend to feel high levels of stress from peer pressures, school demands, and expectations of them at home. To soothe themselves, they may seek relief by engaging in addictive behaviors. This can include alcohol, drugs, eating, gambling, overwork, shopping, relationships, and codependency. Addictive behaviors may begin as coping mechanisms, to deal with underachievement, self-doubt, poor self-esteem, and depression, but then spiral out of control. In the words of Andrew, a seventeen-year-old client of mine, "Getting high helped me deal with all the crap, but then I learned it just made things even more crappy."

As children, distracted teens were often labeled as lazy, unmotivated, or disruptive. Remember that I earlier mentioned how destructive the "lazy" label is? Tragically, I have seen many cases of parents and teachers who so rigidly perceived distracted children as underachievers that they lost sight of their obvious intelligence and capability. Again, this is another case of how misunderstanding leads to missed opportunities to help a distractible child. Guiding children to soothe themselves by talking it out, rather than drugging themselves to escape, is crucial.

Having Sleep Problems

A lot of distractible children struggle to shut their minds down at night. Their minds are such a whirlwind of thoughts that they won't shut off. Distracted kids often try all sorts of strategies to help them go to sleep. Some kids rock themselves to sleep. One child told me that he did somersaults in his bed to try to wear out his mind and body, so he could sleep. I have had kids report that they made up stories and talked themselves to sleep. Unfortunately, lack of sleep can cause distractible children to be very unproductive the following day.

To help relieve sleep problems, make sure your child has a consistent bedtime and a predictable night routine. Consult your child's medical doctor to rule out a serious sleep disorder, if her sleep problems worsen or become unmanageable.

Being Inflexible

Distracted children tend to lack flexibility and resilience. Transitions in life often create emotional turbulence. For example, I have seen distractible children have great difficulty transitioning between one house and another, in the early stages of divorce situations. Other challenging transitions can be relocation to a new school or a new home.

Distracted kids can get emotionally short-circuited (i.e., stressed out) unless someone warns them ahead of time when a change is coming their way. When feeling overwhelmed by sudden changes, it's not uncommon for distractible children to involuntarily tense up. The more you prime the pump by preparing your child for any impending changes, the better she will be able to adjust to them.

Experiencing Short-Term Memory Problems

The mind of a distractible child is pulled in so many directions that she often cannot remember doing something immediately after she has done it. Alicia, a fourteen-year-old client of mine, came to see me for school-related issues. In speaking to her, I realized how her memory problems impacted her not only at school but also at home. Alicia found herself struggling to answer questions such as: Did I brush my teeth? Did I brush my hair? Did I take my medicine? Did I turn out the light? Did I lock the door?

I have found that checklists can help distraction-prone children to remember things more clearly.

Being Poor Self-Observers

Distractible children tend to be poor self-observers. They do not accurately gauge the impact and effect they have on other people. This lack of self-observation also causes many distractible children to have low emotional intelligence. Emotional intelligence refers to a child's or teen's ability to control impulses, delay gratification, motivate herself, tune in to her own feelings, read other people's social cues, and cope with life's ups and downs. It is no shock that a lack of emotional intelligence can lead distractible kids to struggle with low self-esteem.

Distracted Kids Have Chronic Self-Esteem Issues

Distracted kids usually come up short in the self-esteem department. Their self-esteem suffers greatly in response to years of hearing negative feedback. They have been told by peers and adults that they are a burden, different, a failure, in the way, lazy, out of it, a slob, a space cadet, stupid, an underachiever, and weird. This is not a flattering foundation on which a distracted child can build her self-esteem. Distractible children often eventually come to believe that they truly possess these negative qualities. It takes a long time for distracted kids to change their perceptions of themselves after years of being told something negative.

The irony is that many distractible children are highly accomplished, but don't think they have accomplished anything. I have marveled at the artistic and musical ability of many distracted children. No matter how sincerely effusive I have been with praise, most of these kids trivialized their talents prior to sustained counseling.

Low self-esteem often leaves distracted kids struggling with depression. They feel they have failed so many times already that they are afraid of becoming a failure again. Or they are afraid to take risks and put themselves in a situation where they might be ridiculed. This can lead to social withdrawal.

Social Withdrawal

Low self-esteem can cause children to withdraw socially. Many distraction-prone children become reluctant to participate in discussions or conversations. Experience has taught them that they are "missing something," and they don't want to appear stupid.

At age seventeen, Deborah still struggled to pay attention and act appropriately. She had a long, hard road dealing with her distractibility. I recall a session where Deborah told me how she became embarrassed one night when her parents took her to a restaurant to celebrate her tenth birthday. She had gotten so distracted by the waitress's bright purple hair that her mother called her name three times before she remembered to order. Then before she could stop herself, she blurted, "Your hair dye looks awful!"

In her elementary and junior high school days, Deborah was quiet and cooperative, but often seemed to be daydreaming. She was smart, yet couldn't improve her grades, no matter how hard she tried. Several times, she failed exams. Even though she knew most of the answers, she couldn't keep her mind on the test. Initially, her parents responded to her low grades by taking away privileges and scolding, "You're just lazy. You could get better grades if you only tried." Deborah gave up trying.

One day, after Deborah had failed yet another exam, her teacher found her sobbing, "What's wrong with me?" Fortunately, this led Deborah to be examined, diagnosed, and treated for ADHD, giving her the help she so desperately needed. Still, the years of struggling left an indelible mark on her self-esteem.

Creativity Can Offset Poor Self-Esteem

Many parents and teachers are amazed at how creative distractible children can be, even in the midst of all their disorganization. While it has not been unequivocally proven, research suggests that distractible kids may score higher on measures of creativity.

Contrary to the stereotype of being "spacey," distractible children also are often very intelligent. In some cases, they may not be classically "book smart," but may demonstrate their intellect in some other manner, such as discerning spatial relationships. It's important for you to praise these abilities in your child. Later in this program ("Day 8"), you will learn how to use positive reinforcement to foster other positive qualities within your child, to help boost self-esteem.

Six Obstacles to Understanding Your Distracted Child

By now, you have gained a solid understanding of how a child's distractibility impacts her, you, and her teachers. I have covered a lot of what goes on in the minds of distractible children. Your goal for today is to see your child's difficulties openly and honestly, keeping frustrations and negative feelings from getting in the way. In order to do this, you must give up trying to make sense of your child's struggles in the usual ways (e.g., attributing her distractibility problems to laziness or indifference). It's time to look at the common obstacles to understanding your distracted child.

1. Blaming Yourself for Your Child's Problems

Parents often unfairly blame themselves for their children's struggles. This is particularly the case with parents of distractible children, and it's highly unproductive for both you and your child.

I have also been astonished to hear from parents that they have encountered mental health or education professionals who have unfairly blamed them for their child's attention problems. Having been blessed with many wonderful colleagues, my hope is that this rarely happens. I believe that, more often, parents of distracted children can be hypersensitive to any feedback about their children from others. Consequently, it's possible that some parents misinterpret this feedback and perceive themselves as blamed when that may not be the intention. I will say that anyone (particularly a professional) who blames a parent for a child's distractibility is seriously ignorant. And any parents who are determined to blame themselves are wasting precious time and energy that could be better spent helping their child.

2. Confusing Distraction with Disinterest at School

Distressed parents and drained teachers often misperceive distracted kids as being "uninterested in everything." This point is critically important. I have never met a distractible child who was uninterested in learning new things. Granted, some distractible children may appear uninterested in school. Yet, the fact that a traditional classroom learning situation does not work well for them does not mean that they can't be motivated to learn in other ways.

To remain committed to understanding your child, you must stay mindful of your child's academic challenges, caused by her distractibility problems. The clearer you are about how your child's distractibility impacts her at school, the more you can effectively advocate for her. For example, some distractible kids may not be able to focus well in class or remember their homework. Others may focus well in class but forget to turn in their homework. Some distractible kids may do well in some subjects but not others. I discuss school-related concerns further in "Day 4."

3. Believing That Distractibility Can Be Fixed with Punishment

Unfortunately, many parents and health professionals still believe that a good swift kick in the backside will improve a child's focus. Disciplining your child is one thing; punishing her is another. Discipline means teaching your child, and punishment means presenting her with a negative consequence—obviously there is a huge difference between the two. Anyone who's read *10 Days to a Less Defiant Child* knows that I am a much bigger fan of discipline than of punishment.

Research has shown that parents of children with ADHD in fact enforce more disciplinary measures than other parents. I realize that distracted kids can challenge many more boundaries, but staying discipline-minded instead of punishment-minded will help you stay meaningfully connected to your child.

Keep in mind that there's a difference between what your child cannot do and what she chooses not to do. Punishing a child for something that she has no control over is cruel. Distractible kids don't enjoy being in trouble, and I can assure you, based on the tears I have seen, that they do not bring further aggravation upon themselves for amusement. Anyone who says distraction can be cured by punishment is seriously misguided. Discipline can help, but punishment will only make matters worse. In "Day 8", I offer some positive reinforcement strategies.

4. Saying "Just Pay Attention"

The worst three words you can say to a distracted child are "just pay attention." The reasons for this are obvious. You are asking your child to do something she may not be able to do, depending on the circumstances. All you will accomplish by saying this to her is demoralizing her. This is such a big concern that I have devoted a day of this program to addressing it. In "Day 3: Avoiding the 'Demanding Attention' Trap," I discuss ways to avoid falling into this destructive parenting pattern, and what you should say to your child instead.

5. Not Looking through Your Child's Eyes

Think about how you feel when your boss or partner tells you, "That's ridiculous," or insists that you really like something you know you hate. You probably feel that what you had to say was dismissed, and that your feelings were not taken seriously. Kids feel the same way when their parents say, "You shouldn't feel that way!" or "I can't believe you said that!" It's important for you to stop and try to see things through your child's eyes before responding to her. Distracted children are even more likely than others to view their feelings as negated, because they have a hard time focusing on what they feel. So when you invalidate what your child may not be sure of in the first place, she ends up feeling even more unsure of herself and her feelings.

6. Thinking That a Child Who Can Focus Sometimes Can't Really Be Distractible

As I mentioned earlier, some distractible children who can't concentrate on mundane, boring, or repetitive tasks can actually hyper-focus on something that really interests them. Computer games, for example, are very stimulating to the distractible child.

The ever-alluring video game console provides a one-on-one situation, and there's usually plenty of action to keep a child's interest. Captivating sounds, bright lights, and sleek control knobs and buttons also help engage distractible children. Keep in mind, however, that just because they can concentrate on something that *really* interests them, that doesn't mean they are readily able to focus on less exciting things, such as the drone of a teacher's voice after lunchtime.

Twenty-Two Ways to Understand Your Distracted Child

Here are twenty-two powerful ways to understand and stay connected to your distractible child. Remember, understanding your distracted child is the first step to helping her.

1. Hold back your negative gut reaction.

If your gut reaction to what your child has done or said is negative, try to hear your child out before reacting. If your distractible child says, "I don't want to go to school anymore," instead of immediately saying, "You have to go," you might ask, "What's the worst thing about it?" It's always better to acknowledge your child's feelings, as described in the next item.

2. Acknowledge your child's feelings.

In *10 Days to a Less Defiant Child,* I wrote that understanding your child is just as important as loving her. The same holds true for parenting distractible children. So, to acknowledge your child, you might simply say, "I'm glad to know that," or "I understand." Trust me, your acknowledgment means so much to your child, and often is all she needs to hear. Also, given her tendency to distraction, reflecting her feelings can help keep her focused.

3. Take a moment before you say "no."

Parents of distracted children are usually very stressed out. This stress often leads them to react hastily with their children. Even if your final answer will still be "no," try saying, "Let me think about what you're saying for a minute and get back to you." I know your distracted child wants an answer from you *now,* but slowing down forces you to not make a snap judgment, regardless of your child's request. Pausing makes your child feel heard, because you have stopped to consider her opinion. It also diminishes the chances of a power struggle between the two of you. The added benefit of this approach is that you are modeling this wonderful skill of slowing down to your child. The more your distractible child sees you pause to gather your thoughts, the more likely she is to adopt this way of relating for herself.

4. Share your thinking out loud.

Your child will appreciate being included in your thought process as you work out your answers to her questions. Donna, a parent in my practice, used this tactic with her eleven-year-old son, Jacob. When Jacob asked for a sleepover, she said, "I know you want a sleepover, but your grandmother may want to see you this weekend when she visits. Let me please first talk to her." This kept Donna from bottling up a feeling of pressure, which parents often feel in response to the urges of a distractible child. Donna did let Jacob have his sleepover, but she also effectively planted the seed that he would need to spend time with his grandmother that Sunday evening at dinner.

5. Avoid attacking your child's character.

If your distractible child acts out verbally, instead of saying, "You're a spoiled brat. How dare you speak to me that way!" try saying something like, "That kind of language is not okay." This approach helps ensure that you are separating the behavior from the child. As I stated before, distractible children have significant self-esteem issues. Given this concern, you want to avoid expressing any implication that your child is intrinsically bad, or making her ashamed of her feelings.

6. Tell your child how her behavior impacts you.

I encourage all parents to share, rather than hide, their feelings. In fact, calmly expressing your feelings may be the best form of discipline. Honest comments allow your child to know where you are coming from, when you are concerned about her behavior. Examples of such comments are "I am very disappointed in what you did" or "I feel sad that you deliberately misled me." Remember, you're sharing your feelings to get them out there, not to attack your child or elicit a reaction from her. It doesn't matter whether or not your child acknowledges you.

7. Tell your child how you feel.

By sharing how you feel about yourself, you let your child know that you have feelings, and help her learn how to express her own. This provides effective modeling of emotion, or as relationship expert John Gottman terms it, "emotion coaching." You might say, for example, "I had a bad day at work today, I'm feeling sad" or "I'm sorry I made a mistake." Be aware, however, that if you spend too much time talking about how you feel, your child may feel overwhelmed (or bored) by your level of emotion. On the other hand, if you never articulate your feelings, your child may not feel comfortable articulating her own.

8. Selective use of fantasy can help.

Playful fantasy can sometimes be a tool to help you understand your distractible child. If your child badly wants something that she can't have, encourage her to imagine what she wants and talk about it. You could say, "What would you do if we could stop the car right now?" or "I bet you wish your mother was not away this week on that business trip. What would she do to help you feel less overwhelmed?"

9. Ask your child what she wants to change.

If your distractible child complains about something specific, you might ask her to suggest some improvements. For example, if she says, "I hate music class because Mr. Smith is so mean," you might first ask, "What's the meanest thing Mr. Smith did?" Then, you can follow up with, "What do you wish your teacher had done instead?" The bottom line is that you will understand how to help your distractible child much better if you use dialogue to find solutions. By first letting your child vent negative feelings, and then asking her to imagine a different scenario, you are encouraging her not only to discuss the problem, but also to become part of the solution.

10. Use humor—but not at your child's expense.

I know that parenting your distractible child is a serious concern. But not every conflict needs to be resolved through serious discussion. Sometimes humor is the best road to understanding where your child is coming from. If your child shouts at you, you could say, "Ouch, that hurts!" instead of "Don't talk to me that way, young lady!" Rather than "Clean your room right now!" you could say, "This place is like a big chemistry experiment! I don't see mold yet, but it'll start growing soon!"

In the spirit of keeping things light, you could even suggest your child watch a scene from a favorite comedy movie before starting his homework. Lightening things up can reduce tensions and increase your ability to understand your child.

11. Tell a funny story about yourself as a child.

Most kids love to hear stories about their parents growing up. You might tackle a tough topic by describing what happened to you in a similar situation when you were a kid. You could tell her a story about how you got in trouble with your own parents when you procrastinated on a project. If your child sees that you are also human and that you can identify with her struggles, she will feel safer opening up to you about them. Just be sure not to turn all conversations into stories about you. Constantly saying, "I know how you feel, let me tell you what happened to me" will eventually annoy more than amuse.

12. Focus on the positives before bringing up the negative.

Distractible children have heard more than their fair share of criticism. In your effort to be an understanding, supportive parent, it's important for you to balance negative feedback with positive comments, whenever possible. For example, if your child pulls a practical joke that makes a mess, you might say, "Clever and brilliant! Now I would like you to please clean it up." Or if your child brings home a test with mistakes, first comment on what she got right before discussing what she got wrong.

13. Admit your mistakes.

My best friend likes to say, "The only perfect people are in the cemetery." As long as we are alive, we have things we can work on to improve ourselves. Distractible children in particular love to hear their parents admit they were wrong. The more you can "own" your mistakes, the more you are modeling accountability for mistakes for your child. It also creates an empathetic bond, making you more approachable in the eyes of your child. When you and your child are wrestling with a problem, you might say to her, "Is there a better way I can be doing this? Should we try to figure it out a different way?"

14. Keep it simple.

Distractible children feel better understood when communication is kept brief. A one-sentence answer may be much more effective than a long explanation. Children are often satisfied with a simple, direct answer that addresses their main concern. A lengthy explanation may confuse or bore your child.

Another option is to leave her a brief note. Sometimes older kids respond better to a written note than to a verbal nag. You might post a note saying: "Please write down here what time you will be home" or "Today I would like you to please clean your room." As long as the atmosphere is cooperative, some kids enjoy writing lists and charts themselves, as a way of solving problems with their parents.

15. *Be mindful of your tone as much as your words.*

At times, it's not what you say, but the way you say it that makes an impact. Even though your child has problems with her attention, don't underestimate how closely she notices how you approach and relate to her. Distractible kids can be quite tuned in to what their parents are feeling. Often, your child is not listening to your words so much as looking at your face and reacting to the tone of your voice.

16. *Listen to yourself from your child's perspective.*

If you feel a conflict brewing, ask yourself, "Would I like to be spoken to this way?" If you don't like the way you sound, ask yourself, "Am I mad about something without realizing it?" In my first book, *Why Can't You Read My Mind?*, I discussed the concept of mindfulness as it applies to couples. I wrote of the importance of partners in intimate relationships being aware of what they say to one another. Vigilance in choosing your words with precision applies to parenting distractible kids, as well. Be aware of your words as you are speaking them, because if you are, they will more likely be words that your child can hear.

17. *Avoid leading questions.*

Leading questions, or questions that include an answer—such as, "Do you just not care about doing your homework at all?" or "Don't you want to change your clothes before we leave?" or "Can't you understand how taking forever to get ready messes up my schedule, too?"—are really statements of blame, not questions. This way of communicating to your child is condescending. These questions are likely to provoke a sullen response, or a plain old "no." Instead, ask valid questions. Questions like "What do you like (or not like) most about school right now?" will produce real answers. A real question about schoolwork may be, "You seem upset about math homework lately. Can you please tell me what's going on?" In comparison, a leading question on the same topic would be, "Aren't you going to fail English if you keep avoiding your work?"

18. Avoid general questions.

Whether you have a preschooler or a preteen, well-meaning but general questions such as "How was school?" often produce only one-word answers, such as "good," "bad," or "okay." General questions usually lead to dead-end conversations.

Instead, ask specific questions to inspire productive conversations. Refer to something that happened recently, for example. Questions such as "Is Spanish class getting any easier?" work because they draw on your distractible child's unique experience, which sticks out more in her mind and therefore elicits specific responses.

19. Take a break and listen to your child.

Using specific actions to actively engage your child—like making eye contact, kneeling down to your child's level, and even tilting your head—shows your child you are listening. These strategies also help *you* stop and really listen. If you can't talk at that moment, you can say, "Let's talk in a few minutes. Right now I'm in the middle of something." Just make sure that you don't become distracted yourself and forget to make yourself available to listen after you've finished what you were doing.

20. Be tuned in, and repeat what you hear.

It's often useful to restate what you hear and put your child's feelings into words. To show your child that you are invested in understanding her, you might say, "You wanted me to take you to Jessie's house as soon as you finish your schoolwork, didn't you?" or "You seem sad about going to school today." These reflective statements acknowledge and give words to your child's feelings.

21. Ask specific questions to gather more information.

If your child fails to hand in her homework, your job is to understand what got in the way. While being calm and establishing a climate of trust, you could say, "Can you please tell me exactly what happened?" Or if it makes sense to talk some more, you might ask, "What upset you the most about your teacher's response?" Follow-up questions both acknowledge your child's feelings and get her talking about them. And they help you gather more information, so you can better understand what actually happened and how your distractible child is thinking about the situation. Remember, the key is to be calm, firm, and noncontrolling.

22. Silence can say a lot, too.

Much of today focused on how you can best verbally engage your child to help her feel understood. Please keep in mind that distracted children need time and space in order to collect their thoughts and express themselves. There will also be times when the best way to help your child feel understood is to say nothing. Just a smile or reassuring pat on the shoulder can be very comforting. If you remain silent yet supportive when your child has a hard time talking, she is more apt to open up to you when she's ready to talk.

DAY 2: SUMMING IT UP

Today you have made giant steps forward in understanding the emotional concerns and demands your distractible child faces. Your understanding will set the stage for applying the myriad of strategies that you'll find in the remainder of this ten-day program. Keep the following points in mind as you continue on this important journey:

- Understanding how you think about and relate to your distracted child is crucial to being able to understand her.
- Understanding your child creates emotional safety for her to trust you.
- Your distractible child feels disempowered, and your understanding helps her feel reempowered.
- Distractible children are frequently misunderstood, and your commitment to understanding your child is a wonderful gift.
- The more you understand your distractible child, the more open she will be to letting you help her.

Avoiding the "Demanding Attention" Trap

Cathy glared at me with rising frustration. "Dr. Jeff, I understand that you are saying Brian did not choose to have his distraction problem, but you don't get it!"

I could feel my stomach sinking. Doing my best not to get defensive, I encouraged this parent to explain what I did not understand.

She said, "I feel like I'm going crazy because I can't stop demanding that he pay attention to things, and my emotions always end up boiling over!"

I assured Cathy that this was common for parents of distractible children, and thanked her for being honest about her difficulty controlling her frustrations and reactions. Then I said, "So Cathy, I think what you're telling me is that it feels almost impossible for you to not overreact to Brian's distractibility?"

Cathy let out a heavy sigh and said, "Yup, now you got it."

So I said, "Then you understand what it is like to feel out of control. It sounds like you and Brian feel the same way. Brian has a real hard time controlling his distractibility, and you have a tough time managing your reactions to it."

Cathy looked at me sheepishly and said, "OK, I think I'm the one finally getting it now." She added, "Jeff, please

help me. I really need some tools to help me stop overreact-
ing with Brian. It's like I can't control myself."

Cathy and so many other parents have seen firsthand that there
is a paradox in trying to help: *The demands involved with meeting*
the needs of a distractible child influence parents to be demanding of
their child, leading to more distracted behavior. I have worked with
well over a thousand parents and children over twenty years, and
I can tell you that falling into the trap of overreacting and imposing unrealistic demands on your child is extremely common. For
example, when it seems like your child is not listening to you, it's
natural to raise your voice to try to get the message across. But
it will only worsen his distractibility. Since controlling your own
reactions to your child is such an important concern, the topic is
our focus on Day 3.

Let's go back to Cathy for a minute. What she "got" was the
reality that it's very hard to not let your own frustrations boil over.
After possibly years of notes from school warning that your child is
in academic hot water, and dealing with crisis after crisis at school
and at home, who can blame you? You've probably spent a lot of
time feeling angry, burnt out, sad, and inadequate as a parent.
You may even have worried about how your child will ever make
it in this world. You are not alone. This roller coaster of concern
and stress takes a toll on even the most patient of parents.

The good news is that you no longer have to feel so out of
control while trying to stay on top of it all. Today I am going to
give you the tools to effectively manage the negative emotions
influenced by your distractible child. This is a huge and crucial
step for you because it will free up your energy, allowing you to
truly help your child. The more positively you handle your parenting stresses, the more positively your child will respond to you.
Alternatively, if you are prone to overreacting in self-defeating
ways, your child will follow your example in this case as well.

Today you will learn to work smarter instead of harder to manage your child's needs.

Distractibility Triggers Overreaction

Parenting a distractible child is a harrowing experience. You never know when the next demand or obstacle is going to pop up. Let me help get you in touch with all the "stuff" that goes on in your world. Take a look at the list below of "distractibility triggers" that may lead you to overreact to your child. As you're reading, consider how each example impacts you. This list is not exhaustive, but it's representative of the major issues faced by parents of distractible children.

- Repeating for the fifth time how to do the math problems, while your child is more interested in fiddling with his pencil
- Receiving a negative note from your child's teacher
- Observing your child playing a video game, surfing the Internet, or watching TV, for hours at a time
- Hearing your child tell you that he has no homework when you know this is not true
- Hearing your child complain when something isn't done for him that he could have done for himself
- Being told by your child when driving him to school (he missed the bus) that he forgot that he has a big project due today
- Having your child tell you that his teacher does not answer his questions, when you've heard at a conference that your child never asks for help
- Seeing your child doing homework halfheartedly (e.g., feet on the couch, backside on the floor, and writing illegibly)
- Being assured by your child that he is prepared for a test, and then he gets an F on it

- Realizing your child did not follow through on chores or requested tasks
- Discovering that your child "forgot" to turn in his homework
- Discovering that your child never wrote down what his homework was in the first place
- Finding D's and F's on your child's report card
- Getting a call from a neighbor because your child got in a fight with her son
- Finding marijuana in your teen's pants when you do the laundry—and he denies that it is his

The Overreaction to Distractibility Checklist

Now that you know your triggers, let's look at the ways in which you may overreact to them. The following are the overreactions common to parents of distractible children. Having one or more of these reactions does not mean you are a bad parent. My concern is that these reactions get in the way of your being the best parent you can be. You may already have realized that these overreactions are counterproductive to your efforts to guide your child to better places. Check off the items below that apply to you:

_____ Yelling at him
_____ Shaking your head
_____ Throwing up your hands
_____ Imposing sudden and harsh consequences
_____ Shaming him with negative comments
_____ Mocking him through words or actions
_____ Ignoring your child
_____ Making unfavorable comparisons to other children
_____ Using negative labels (e.g., spoiled brat)
_____ Giving your child the cold shoulder

_____ Nagging your child

_____ Lecturing your child to do better

_____ Threatening to send your child away to boarding school

_____ Predicting out loud that he will ruin his life because he does not apply himself in school

Why Overreacting Is a Serious Problem

When you *over*react, you are helping your child to *under*achieve. This is because your overreactions emotionally overwhelm your child, causing him to have less motivation. I want to be clear that I am not telling you that occasionally overreacting makes you a bad parent. Nor am I telling you that *you* are the *cause* of your child's distractibility. What I am saying, however, is that if you frequently overreact, not only will this prevent you from effectively using the strategies in this ten-day program to reduce your child's distractibility, it can actually worsen the problem.

Alex's Story

Years ago, I worked with Burt and Cynthia, who described their ten-year-old son, Alex, as "lazy, conveniently clueless, and manipulative." They were seething with anger because of Alex's resistant attitude toward school and his failure to do his homework. It also did not help that Alex did not follow through on chores at home. Alex could not understand why his parents thought chores were such a big deal. Burt had called me to tell me that washing Alex's mouth out with soap did not seem to help. I was grateful that Burt was open to seeing what did not work.

Yet, when they first saw me, Burt and Cynthia rigidly insisted that Alex "could get things done if he wanted to." Their frustration was quite evident in their first meeting with me, when they said, "We have had it, Dr. Jeff. We keep hitting a brick wall. To encourage Alex to try harder, we have taken away many privileges like watching TV and playing video games, and we stand over him to get him to do his work. But none of this works, the problem seems to be getting worse, and our relationship with him is terrible."

I reviewed Alex's developmental and school history. Based on his longstanding pattern of erratic grades and overall underachievement, I strongly suggested to his parents that they have his school conduct an assessment of his learning strengths and weaknesses. A few months later, the results of Alex's testing clearly indicated learning concerns that had not been previously identified, especially in his focusing, organizational, and language skills. Now that Burt and Cynthia knew that there was "something going on," they changed their mind-set. They worked closely with the school to support an educational plan with more realistic expectations for Alex.

Alex, now feeling more understood and less defensive with his parents and teachers, became more open about his academic struggles. His negative attitude, at home and at school, dramatically decreased. Now there were steps in place that could be taken to address his learning difficulties.

Alex had initially shared with me in a counseling session that he was "very dumb and stupid and that school was a waste of time for him because he would never learn." Thankfully, after he learned about the results of his testing, Alex understood that distraction-related learning challenges did not make him stupid. In fact, the evaluator shared Alex's many strengths with him, and this helped Alex develop a sense of responsibility, enhanced self-esteem, and optimism going forward in his life.

The example of Alex illustrates what a positive difference parents can make when they control their reactions and focus on helping their children. If Burt and Cynthia had continued to overreact instead of acting wisely, Alex would have continued to drift further away from them, as a result of feeling distraught and alienated. Frequent yelling and carrying on by parents does nothing but make the distractibility problem even worse. It also causes four other problems, as described below.

It makes your child feel hopeless.

When you overreact, you overwhelm your child's efforts to collect his thoughts and work through his feelings. Distractible children do not do well under the pressure of their parents' intense scrutiny and reactivity. Your child will begin to feel hopeless in the face of your overreactions. When children feel hopeless, their motivation to improve goes out the window. Many distractible children often describe their hopelessness with alternative words, such as "tired," "bored," or "angry." Often, though, once I probe further and these kids lower their guards, they acknowledge that they actually feel hopeless in response to their parents' strong overreactions.

It makes your child feel unloved.

Your overreactions can also make your child feel as if you no longer believe in him. All children (and adults) share a deep need to feel valued. In the words of Victor Hugo, "The supreme happiness in life is the conviction that we are loved." It's hard for distractible children to feel loved when they feel that they are letting their parents down.

Sarah, age fourteen, told me, "My parents care more about me getting my work done than they do about me." How sad that Sarah saw things this way. Her parents did love her—very much so. But it was not until they stopped overreacting to Sarah's academic and homework problems that Sarah could more readily feel her parents' love. When your child hears you overreacting, it's like hearing static when you listen to the radio. The caring words get lost. Ironically, it is your deep concern and love that drive you to react strongly. However, if you don't properly manage your reactions, your child cannot really hear you.

I am grateful for a positive relationship with my own three children. But I also remember how some of my past overreactions left me playing "emotional catch-up" with them after I "emotionally lost it."

It makes your child learn to react negatively.

Yelling or getting overly upset also gives your child a front-row seat to lessons in hypocrisy. You are modeling that adults aren't capable of emotional containment. Unfortunately, to your child, overreactions erode your validity as a safe person to talk to.

I encourage you to hold yourself accountable by literally observing yourself as you relate to your child. As you interact, think about how confident you would be having your reactions to your child broadcast on national television. By the same token, please give yourself credit for the times you react in a positive manner.

It makes your child feel misunderstood.

I asked several of the distractible children I work with to describe what it's like to feel misunderstood by their parents. Twelve-year-old Lorraine told me, "When my parents don't get me, even though I try to explain things, I feel like I want to scream and yell and go ballistic." Robert, age fifteen, said, "When they don't understand me, I feel anger and a lot of other things." Thirteen-year-old Charlotte profoundly said, "I feel sadness, because when people misunderstand me, I really don't get to be who I want to be or what I want to be."

In speaking with these children, I was taken with the intensity of their feelings on the topic. Clearly, the most poignant response was the final one. When a child feels misunderstood, he feels like he can't be himself. No wonder our children sulk, scream, throw tantrums, and cry at these moments. When our children think we're not listening to them, they experience powerfully negative emotions that threaten the very core of their being.

Getting Upset Is Not Your Only Option

As the parent of a distractible child, you may have fallen into the trap of believing "the only time he listens to me is when I let him know that I am upset." Nothing could be further from the truth. Take twelve-year-old Ian, for instance. Ian did not say much during our first session together. Near the end of the session, I thanked him for coming in and told him that I really hoped I could help him. All of a sudden, his eyes started to tear and he began to sob.

Ian shared that he hated school, homework, and himself. Ian's father, Dirk, like many parents, had a "hot button" issue: his son's lax attitude toward completing homework (see "Day 5" for strategies to help you conquer homework madness). Like so many parents, Dirk felt that reacting strongly to the homework problem was his only option. Fortunately, I was able to help Dirk learn to understand Ian, which enabled him to slow down and stop overreacting. Ian deeply appreciated this, and needed it in order to feel better about himself. The following are a number of ideas to help you control your emotions and stop overreacting.

Twenty-Eight Anti-Overreaction Power Tools

For the reasons I have shared today, and more you will learn about over the course of this ten-day program, most parents feel that managing their distractible child at school and at home is like having a second job. I certainly appreciate that controlling your emotions is not easy. The truth is that it can feel very overwhelming. There are many ways to help distracted children listen, learn, focus, and behave, but all the strategies in the world won't work unless you can stay in control of your reactions during the process. Here are twenty-eight strategies to help you avoid demanding attention from your child.

1. Avoid labeling your child as a liar.

When you feel repeatedly misled, it's easy to view your child as a liar. In my book for couples, *Why Can't You Read My Mind?*, I discuss how toxic thoughts such as labeling (e.g., "You are a selfish husband.") erodes intimacy between partners. Toxic thoughts can also occur in parenting. You hear, "I thought I turned the homework in," and you think, "Why are you lying to me? You had no intention of turning it in." There is no doubt that being deceived by your child is very upsetting. But misunderstanding the reasons for your child's evasiveness is a big problem, and consequently labeling your child as a liar will only make matters worse. Remember the age-old adage: "Give someone a label and they will live up to it."

In the words of Jimmy, a thirteen-year-old client of mine, "I lie because I don't want to tell my parents the truth because they'll get mad. I also tell lies because it will make them happy with me. But then later they find out the truth and it hurts them, but it also hurts me."

Try not to overreact or label your child a liar. Don't argue the evidence—this will just turn into a power struggle. Remember, your goal is not to prove your case, but to open and maintain a dialogue with your child. Don't focus on the lying. Instead, focus on solving the problem. Say something like, "Well, okay, maybe you turned in your assignment, but let's still talk about less stressful ideas for getting your work turned in."

2. Realize that your child feels vulnerable and scared when he makes excuses.

Based on the way they make excuses, distractible children can give parents the impression that nothing really bothers them.

I chuckled to myself when I heard Jamie, a third grader, tell his mother, Rose, "If the teacher was nicer, I'd listen better and I would sit in my seat." Trust me, based on all the emotional outbursts and tears that I have seen in my office, I can tell you that your child is much more concerned than he lets on to you. More often than not, distractible children feel vulnerable, hopeless, and scared—this is what leads them to make excuses.

3. Don't drown in the drama.

Try not to get upset by your distractible child's emotional meltdowns. But also don't fall into the trap of believing that your child is simply being melodramatic and making a fuss over nothing. While some distractible children may have a flair for drama, that does not diminish the intensity of their emotions.

If you are angry, upset, or out of control as a result of your child's drama, you cannot provide the type of emotional support and discipline necessary to resolve the problem. Distracted by negativity, your mind is driven from one thought or activity to the next. Remember that these children often struggle with feelings of low self-esteem and a loss of hope for future success. They tend to rely on counterproductive or self-defeating coping behaviors to deal with these feelings of failure, hopelessness, and humiliation.

Keep in mind that some distractible children seem to experience emotions more intensely than children who do not struggle with distractibility. The problem for distractible children is their tendency to act out negative emotions with defiant behavior, instead of talking about them.

4. Get off the fishhook.

Being a parent of a distractible child is often like being a fish in a bucket. When your child drops a hook, you get snagged. I actually have had several parents share with me that this fishhook metaphor is helpful for them. Whether it is a missed assignment, a missed chore, or sassy backtalk that's irritating you, envision a fishhook gently brushing by you. If you don't open your mouth wide with an overreaction, the hook will just float away—at least for the moment. Of course, the less you bite, the fewer hooks will come your way.

So don't let your child's denial, weak excuses, or even provocative statements get the best of you. Try not to scream or freak out, because harsh responses are ultimately ineffective. Unfortunately, your screaming won't solve the distractibility problem and change the behavior "once and for all." More importantly, when you lose it and get into an emotional tug of war with your child, you foster guilt and shame. You end up squelching your child's emotions and preventing him from expressing himself. In short, you end up destroying the sense of emotional safety your child needs in order to explore his concerns with you. This emotional safety is not only necessary to allow your child to address issues related to the distractibility, but to life in general.

5. Be clear and specific.

The clearer you are with your child, the less you will doubt yourself. The less you doubt yourself, the more calm you will be. Your distractible child also needs specific expectations to follow. So instead of saying, "Please clean up your room," say "Please make your bed and pick your clothes up off the floor." Try saying, "Please be home by 6:00" instead of "Don't be late." Or, instead of saying, "It's bedtime," say, "It's 9:00 PM; please go upstairs to take your shower before bed."

Also important, especially with strong-willed children, is to tell your child what you expect in a positive, nonthreatening manner. A positive way of setting a boundary could sound something like "If you want to ride your bike, I would like you to please use your helmet at all times." Again, the more clearly and precisely you express yourself, the more your child will be able to meet your expectations, and the less prone you will be to overreacting.

6. Take a serenity break.

Distracted kids can create serious parent burnout, so give yourself respite where you can. Everyone needs a break from being a parent once in a while. Take turns with your partner overseeing the schoolwork while the other one gets away. Take turns sleeping late on the weekends. If you're a single parent, ask friends and relatives to help by running some errands for you. Maybe they could watch your child while you go out. I also find the serenity prayer helpful: "God grant me the serenity to accept the things I cannot change, courage to change the things I can, and wisdom to know the difference."

7. Instead of shaming the child, focus on the behavior.

As distractible as your child is, don't let yourself get distracted when trying to manage him. Try to avoid letting the fact that your child forgot to take out the trash (after the fifth reminder) influence you to label him as irresponsible. Making a comment such as "When are you going to learn to be responsible?" will not only shame your child, it will also make it hard for him to connect to the real issue at hand. So instead, say, "I am asking you to take out the trash so we can both feel good about you watching your TV show."

8. Be calm, firm, and noncontrolling.

As I mentioned earlier, in 10 *Days to a Less Defiant Child,* I advised parents to be calm, firm, and noncontrolling in response to challenges from their defiant children. This approach works wonders with distractible children as well. Distractible children are very sensitive to their environment. The more emotional you are during encounters with your child, the more difficult it will be for him to stay focused.

My calm, firm, noncontrolling approach helps reduce chaos

while offering parents the opportunity to be clear about their expectations and values. In short, this approach allows you to avoid overreacting, clearly state your expectations, and avoid getting sucked into the abyss of power struggles.

9. Follow the golden rule and be nice.

Given the toils of parenting, you have likely been quite stressed out at times. And when you're stressed, you may end up having an edge to your demeanor. Your child will pick up on this. It amazes me how just remembering to say please and thank you can help foster cooperation from children.

One way to help yourself be pleasant is to give yourself an imaginary videotape reality check. Every so often, as you are interacting with your child, ask yourself, "If I saw this current interaction on videotape, would I feel good about it?" A father I worked with named Bruno found this tool for emotional accountability quite effective with his fourteen-year-old son, Andre. He told me, "Jeff, it's amazing how once I really looked at how I was interacting, I realized that I had to change my demeanor with Andre. Once I became more positive and pleasant with him, Andre, who usually does not comment much on things, even noticed how I changed for the better."

10. Don't confuse losing your temper with being a bad parent.

Don't overreact to your overreactions. This happens to so many parents. It's similar to getting more anxious because you realize that you are anxious. If you lose it and become overdemanding and overreactive in a situation, don't beat yourself up. Just imagine having an imaginary mop and bucket, clean up the mess, and move on.

The reality is that most parents yell and lose their temper with their children. It's okay to feel angry, but it's not okay to take it out on your child. When you're really angry, take a break. Go for a walk or call a friend to come help you. If you feel angry with your child almost every day, or have trouble controlling your temper, get some professional help. A qualified mental health professional can help you sort out and manage the problematic thoughts that are driving your anger.

11. Be an ally instead of an adversary.

Let your child know, through words and actions, that the two of you are on the same team. The walls of avoidance and resistance to doing schoolwork place many parents in an adversarial position with their distracted child. When their emotions are peaking, distractible children may perceive you as rushing to negative judgments. But every interaction you have when your child is emotionally charged is an opportunity for him to see you as an ally, not a judgmental adversary. Start conversations with comments such as "Let me hear what you think," or "You look like you need to talk. Let's find a private place."

Look at issues through your children's eyes. When your child complains that his teacher is not fair, for example, you can acknowledge his concerns without having to agree with him. Also keep in mind that using a nurturing tone of voice and showing an open mind send the message that you want to listen to your child's point of view, even if you see the situation differently.

12. Listen before leaping into action.

As a parent of a distractible child having challenges and problems, you may panic and impulsively try to intervene. Remind yourself not to by saying, "Slow down. I do not have enough information to come to any conclusions yet." You can also tell your child something like "I understand your feelings better now; let's try to figure out what we can learn from this situation. Maybe there's a lesson here for both of us—a way for you to understand yourself better and a way for me to understand you better."

13. Share the responsibility to share.

Don't be afraid to talk about your own contributions to an upsetting situation. Meryl shared with me that she was appalled when she found out that Liz, her sixteen-year-old daughter, had tried marijuana. Meryl felt she "had done everything for this kid," referring to years of working around Liz's attention and behavior problems. I counseled Meryl not to initiate another conversation with Liz yet, and spent a few sessions working with her to help her contain her initially strong reactions. Next, I met with Meryl and Liz together. While clearly not condoning her drug use, Meryl told Liz that she was proud of her for not denying it. Meryl was also smart in not pressuring Liz to talk. Sure enough, Liz opened up, and Meryl was open and supportive. With a renewed sense of mutual trust, Meryl and Liz discussed how their strained relationship, combined with increased peer pressure, left Liz more vulnerable to trying marijuana. This open, trusting dialogue helped knock down the roadblock that had built up between this mother and daughter over the years.

14. Share your story.

Use examples from your past as well as others' to show that all people have struggles. One fourteen-year-old boy I worked with made a bad decision when he shoplifted from a local music store. His mother and father kept asking him why he did it, and the boy just repeatedly shrugged and said, "I don't know." Things shifted, however, in a follow-up counseling session when the father shared how he had been caught drinking and driving as a teenager. This disclosure led the boy to open up about the frustrations that prompted the shoplifting incident.

Another strategy is to discuss examples of famous people who have had to overcome bad decisions, adversity, or both. You will likely find that once you generalize the discussion in this way, your child will tend to be more open and honest about his mistake.

15. Be good to yourself.

Throw in a distractible child, the extra time required to parent him, the extra financial strain, perhaps a challenging school district, and the additional stress within your family, and you have a formula for full-blown stress. Do not forget to take care of yourself. You can't adequately care for your child if you're mentally and physically exhausted. Do something special for yourself from time to time. Eat healthy foods and get enough rest. Join a support group, take a new class, pet your cat, go to a CHADD (Children and Adults with Attention Deficit/Hyperactivity Disorder) meeting, go see a movie, go shopping, or see a counselor.

16. Trust your instincts.

No one knows your child better than you. Our instincts are what urge us to respond. They are a powerful motivation or impulse. Learn to listen for your inner voice. Trust your heart, and when you speak to your child, speak from your heart. Pay attention to what you are feeling as well as what you are thinking. The first steps toward trusting your heart are acknowledging and appreciating your distracted child's inner struggles.

One mother I worked with was petrified to tell her seventeen-year-old son about a rejection he received from a college he'd hoped to attend. After she and I met to discuss how she would speak to her son, she decided to be herself and share the news. While her son was disappointed, he thanked his mother for sticking by him throughout the years of academic challenges. Two weeks later the boy was accepted at another school. This time his mother was able to share the joy in her heart.

17. Don't let guilt get you.

It's not unusual for parents to feel guilty about the disproportion-ately greater amount of time they have to spend parenting their distractible child, compared to the time they spend on other family members. This is the nature of parenting a distracted child, and you're not doing anyone any good by unfairly pressuring yourself to spend more time on others. Just do the best you can, and be prepared for backlash from other family members who may feel neglected. Remember that all parents get frustrated trying to keep this challenging balance. Make a list of all the things you do for your partner and other children, to reassure yourself that you are doing all you can.

18. Look within yourself to find patience.

Don't be upset if you have to keep working at being patient. Patience may be a virtue, but having to scramble to find it does not make you a poor parent. You will get a certain satisfaction when you slow down, take a few deep breaths, and remind yourself that all will be okay. Give yourself a pat on the back for every time you remember to be patient. Keep a journal or log, and note how you calm yourself down in different situations. Feel good about the wonderful example you are setting for your child by learning how to soothe yourself in a healthy way.

19. Understand and accept your child's distractibility.

I have encountered some parents of distractible children who have had a difficult time because they are mourning the loss of the child they thought they had or wanted to have. When you believe that your child's difficulties are going to interfere with your own hopes and dreams for him, it's natural to feel a sense of loss. But unless you acknowledge that loss and move on, you cannot begin to value your child for who he is.

I had one overreactive father named George who felt that he should have been able to protect his son, Will, from some painful struggles during his childhood. Will barely scraped through high school, and life had not been easy for him. George and I explored how he felt guilty because he'd had problems similar to Will's when he was a child, but couldn't save Will from them. I was pleased to hear good news from this family, however, at the time of writing this chapter. As it turns out, Will went on to complete a two-year degree at a local community college and then made plans to transfer to a four-year college.

20. Pass out advisor stickers.

I am making this recommendation while being somewhat facetious. Many people you will meet think they know a lot about your child, but they are actually far from being experts on the topic. Some people may doubt that your child is distractible, insisting that he is "just lazy." I have even heard about relatives saying, "It's just bad parenting. I could straighten him out in a week." Nothing is further from the truth.

Don't get mired down by other family members and friends constantly telling you what you "should" be doing. If your efforts to educate others fall on deaf ears, make up advisor stickers and affix one to everyone offering you unsolicited advice. Or, to avoid losing some well-intentioned yet tact-deficient friends, I have a better idea: just fantasize about the stickers—but be careful not to smirk when you hear their words of wisdom.

21. Have fun.

Parenting a distractible child can present serious challenges. Yet, there needs to be fun on even the most serious of journeys. I often think about an eight-year-old boy with attention problems who could correctly sense that his mother was disappointed and angry with him. I empathized with this mother's frustration, and we discussed ways in which to help her son begin to feel special in his mother's eyes. This mother scheduled a "private time" once a week, which involved going to a local donut shop for breakfast before school. The boy proudly told me about this private time with his mom. This special time helped improve their relationship and helped the child feel loved and accepted. This type of effort leaves a huge deposit in the self-esteem savings bank.

22. Remember that the frustration is mutual.

It is helpful to keep in mind that when you are frustrated with your child's behavior, your child is also feeling the same level of frustration. Many parents lose sight of this fact. One distractible teen I worked with told me how much he hated feeling that he was a disappointment to his parents. Fortunately, this teen's parents were able to convince him that, while they were disappointed in some of his decisions, they were never disappointed in him as a son.

When your child is distracted, he may seem momentarily frozen in time, like a deer caught in headlights. His natural desire to please and conform is overshadowed by his emotional state. With each demand you make for him to "snap out of it," each time you dismiss the pain in his eyes, the "headlights" get brighter. Stay mindful that your child is feeling just as frustrated about his distractibility as you are.

I encourage you to stop this downward spiral by focusing on your child's positive behaviors (they are there, if you look for them), and either ignoring or calmly dealing with the negative behaviors. This approach creates a major shift in the way your child will see himself and the world. Training yourself not to overreact to your child's distractible, impulsive, or inappropriate behavior requires an understanding of what your child can and can't control.

23. Stay connected to your child's strengths.

Robert Brooks, author of *Raising Resilient Children*, explains that every child has "islands of competence," or areas of strength, upon which you can build. Parents must identify and reinforce these islands, so a sense of hope and optimism may replace feelings of despair. I encourage you to help your child find his strengths. Use concrete examples, but avoid false praise. For instance, you might tell a child who seems to make friends quickly, "You're a real people person."

Similarly, I encourage you to really connect the help you offer with your children's interests. If your child enjoys drawing pictures, coach her to draw pictures of math problems she is struggling with.

I also suggest that you identify books, videos, Web sites, or places in the community that can help your child build on strengths and interests. One distractible teenage girl I worked with loved interacting with younger children. Her parents affectionately referred to her as the "Pied Piper of the 'hood." Her sense of responsibility increased greatly when she was asked to watch two neighborhood siblings one afternoon a week. A thirteen-year-old boy with attention difficulties volunteered one afternoon a week at a local nursing home, playing chess or checkers with the residents. This activity nurtured his confidence. I have also seen many distractible teens experience a boost to their self-esteem through holding a part-time job. If you continue to reinforce positive movements toward success, that is how your child will begin to define himself—as a success.

24. Demystify the distractibility.

I have been amazed at how many children have come into my office who have never had their attention problems explained to them. They have no clue that they have distractibility, or what the implications are for learning. The more your child understands himself, the easier it will be for you to show that you understand him, and the less you will overreact to his distractibility-related escapades.

Sadly, in many cases, distracted children mistakenly refer to themselves as lazy. I much prefer the term *motivationally blocked* to *lazy*. Once children can identify that they have certain academic weaknesses (or personal ones) related to their attention problems, they will feel more willing to explore ways to improve. And contrary to the fears of many parents, having children become clearly aware of their weaknesses does not promote excuse making or shirking of responsibilities.

25. Operate with optimism.

You can also control your proneness to overreaction by being realistic, but optimistic. Help your child realize that he can improve. For example, encourage your child to realize that his weaknesses may not disappear, but that at the same time, he can improve them. Point out future possibilities for success given your child's current strengths. For example, one child I worked with did a wonderful job of discovering a poetry Web site and submitting his poems. The child's parents praised his healthy desire for self-promotion and talked about how this ability to reach out for goals will help him attain them. Even though this child rolled his eyes, I could tell he loved hearing this.

26. Expect some ups and downs.

It's not unusual for your distractible child to do well one day, and not so well the next. If you think your child can perform well in school today because he did so yesterday, you are setting yourself up for excess frustration. Children struggling with distractibility often take two steps forward and then one or two backward. As long as you and your child hang in there, the ups will eventually exceed the downs.

27. Remember that mistakes can be gifts.

All children are concerned about making mistakes and looking foolish. However, children with problematic levels of distractibility and learning problems typically experience more failure situations than their peers who do not have these problems. Therefore, they are even more vulnerable and fearful about failing. How your child makes sense of this reality is very important.

An important concept found in psychology textbooks is the *attribution theory,* which suggests that children with high self-esteem view mistakes as experiences from which to learn, while children with low self-esteem perceive mistakes as things they cannot change—often prompting them to avoid or retreat from tasks. To help your distractible child tackle problems and stay out of life's ruts, it's essential to help him develop a more positive attitude toward making mistakes.

I recall one child I worked with, thirteen-year-old Josh, who had a history of really getting down on himself in the face of setbacks. Josh used to say things to me like, "I am stupid and I'll always fail." Josh and I worked hard in counseling to help him stop falling victim to this type of negative self-talk. It was gratifying for me to see Josh learn to say things like, "I know I can do better next time, if I don't leave the studying to the last minute." He internalized positive coping statements and did do better—something that would not have happened had he believed he was stupid.

Provide your child with effective ways of coping with mistakes and developing positive views about setbacks. Focus on making things better, rather than dwelling on mistakes. This promotes feelings of emotional safety in children, so they can explore what to do differently next time.

Unfortunately, many parents overreact to mistakes by screaming, cursing, or giving up and saying, "I quit." Out of frustration, some parents have said to their distractible kids, "I told you it wouldn't work!" or "You don't try hard enough!" or "Why don't you use your brain!" When children make mistakes, they need our support, and we should use a problem-solving approach. They should hear us say, "That's okay. Let's figure out how we can succeed next time." Prepare your child for the possibility of mistakes by saying in advance, "If this doesn't work, there are other things we can try."

28. Focus on your family, too.

As frustration and stress levels rise while managing your distractible child, you may find that the rest of your family is quite stressed out, too. Sometimes, I see parents begin to find fault not only with the distractible child, but also with siblings and with each other. This can set up negative triangles within the family, built on blame. Punishment then becomes the norm in dealing with the children. Instead, follow the strategies I've offered that work for you. Apply them to all family members.

Five Empowering Statements to Help You Keep Your Cool

I have provided you with many strategies to control your reactions in the face of the challenges and demands common to distractible children. Please feel good about yourself for investing the time and energy to learn what you have so far. Below are five phrases you can say to yourself, to help you when you feel depleted and discouraged.

- *It's okay for me to feel discouraged at times because I always get through the challenges.*
- *As long as I try my best to support my child, I cannot ask anything else of myself.*
- *I am proud of myself for all I do to help my child.*
- *Today's challenges will not necessarily be the same as tomorrow's.*
- *I am grateful for so much, and reminding myself of this feels so good.*

DAY 3: SUMMING IT UP

Today you learned why being overdemanding and overreactive is so problematic when parenting your distractible child. Managing your emotions will put you in a much more favorable position to guide and support your distractible child through his challenges. Keep in mind the following main points about overreacting when it comes to distractible children:

- Overreactions take a terrible toll on your distractible child's already damaged self-esteem.
- It's important for you to understand and be mindful of the circumstances that trigger your patterns of overreaction.
- Overreacting is counterproductive with distractible children, as it tends to increase their internal sense of confusion and frustration.
- Your child is just as frustrated about his problems as you are—even if he does not admit this to you.
- There are many hands-on, easy-to-use strategies to effectively manage your emotions and avoid overreacting.

Overcoming Distractibility at School

We've all had fantasies of our children eagerly going to school and loving it. Or at least tolerating school and not having any big problems. But the reality of having a distracted child often means having to drastically readjust your hopes and dream for your child's educational experience. This can be painful to do, and being caught up in this funk is not easy for you or your child.

I ask most children that I work with to fill out a self-esteem questionnaire. This gives me the opportunity to see how they feel about various areas of their lives. I have found most children are very open and honest in completing this questionnaire. I'm sure it will come as no surprise to you how distractible children respond to the question about whether they hate school. You guessed it—a resounding "Yes!"

As you will see today, hating school is a big part of a distractible child's life. Your child likely wishes that someone could wave a magic wand and make school go away. School is terribly difficult for your child as she tries in vain to contend with a myriad of school demands. I still recall, as a distractible child myself, nights when I incessantly called the weather service during a snowstorm, hoping and praying that school would be canceled the next day. Wishful thinking at its best!

Today you will learn how to encourage and influence your child's success at school. I realize that this may seem like a daunting task, given how much distractible children struggle in this challenging realm of their lives. But this chapter will arm you with strategies to maximize your child's success at school, improve learning, and head off issues before they become problems.

A Closer Look at Distraction at School

Despite their intelligence, distractible children generally have intensely negative feelings about school because they associate it with tremendous emotional pain. Much like an adult trapped in a job that he can't stand, your distractible child has the same feeling of persecution, and often also a profound sense of hopelessness, about school.

As I was writing this chapter, I asked some of my clients to share with me their perceptions of what it is like to struggle with distraction at school. Here are some of the responses they gave me:

Gene, a seven-year-old boy with ADHD, stated, "I get confused and Mrs. Berke gets upset with me. I get in trouble a lot for talking and not listening, and then my parents get mad at me, too."

Elisa, age ten, said, "School is hard and it is hard to keep up with my work. I really try to pay attention, but I just keep seeing my friends doing things."

In the words of a twelve-year-old gifted client of mine, named Michael, "When I get distracted at school it is like déjà vu because I have already learned it, and it is so familiar to me. So I just end up bored and I just don't listen."

Fifteen-year-old Samantha, who struggled with anxiety that caused her distractibility, said, "It's like I can't shut my mind off. I'm so often worrying about things like if my friends are mad at me or if I will do well enough that I completely lose track of what the teacher is saying. I end up going home and trying to teach myself what I missed in class, but sometimes that does not work."

Seventeen-year-old Leslie, a junior struggling with depression, said, "When I get sad, I can't think straight. Even though I don't think they are really out to get me, the last thing I can deal with are my teachers riding my butt about me not turning in work."

Each of these children struggles with distractibility at school. The underlying causes may vary, but the sense of deep frustration and demoralization is similar among distractible children.

Many distractible children have expressed their troubled thoughts to me about school. Other examples of the negative school-related thoughts of distractible children include:

- *School is dumb and my teachers are stupid.*
- *I always seem to fail. I'm dumb. So why keep trying?*
- *Kids don't want to play with me at recess. No one likes me.*
- *This is so dumb because I can't understand it and all those other kids can. I wish I was smart.*
- *I'm doing really bad in my classes, I hate my teachers because they are bugging me, and it is such a waste of my time.*
- *I hate doing bad. My parents keep telling me I don't care, but this is not true.*
- *I'll never be good at school like my brother is.*
- *If my teacher is cool and nice to me, I'll try, but if I hate my teacher, then I don't care.*
- *I want to do better, but I can't pay attention so why should I try? I'm just stupid!*

These internalized negative messages seriously impact your child's will and ability to get through school. Worse, they also make an indelible mark of self-doubt in her mind about being able to succeed as an adult. Thoughts such as *learning new things never came easy to me,* and *I've never really been that smart* can hinder adults with distraction issues.

Today is about empowering you to work effectively with your child's educators to help reduce her distractibility at school.

Obviously, you can't go into the school and write your own educational plan for your child. You are not the teacher's supervisor, and you can't dictate teaching strategies and school policies. However, what you can do is position yourself as a concerned parent with helpful suggestions. By being polite and cooperative when working with the school, you will also avoid being perceived as an intrusive parent.

I am here to encourage you to be the best advocate you can be for your child's education. Teaming up with your child's school will improve her chances of success. The vast majority of the school personnel I have worked with are very open to collaborating with parents to meet the needs of their students.

I can also tell you that teachers respond most positively to parents who aren't looking to blame them for their children's struggles. Meeting in person with teachers and being courteous and responsive with your phone calls and e-mails will set the tone for cooperation. At the same time, I have seen far too many parents become overemotional and turn off teachers by being overly suspicious and critical. You've probably heard the expression "the squeaky wheel gets the grease." Make sure that you are heard and your child's needs are attended to, but try not to be too "squeaky" about it.

Know Your Distracted Child's Legal Rights

The goal of this chapter is to provide you with an empowering mind-set for working with your child's school. I also offer specific strategies to help ensure that educators use tools to lessen, or compensate for, your child's distractibility at school.

Below, I provide a brief overview of how education laws can support your efforts. Even if your child is not deemed formally eligible for special education efforts, hopefully you can still encourage the school to use the educational interventions that are presented in this chapter to help your distracted child.

To begin with, your child has the right to a free and appropriate public school education. Many parents are not aware that they have a right to be a part of everyday decision making regarding their child's education. Finding out if your child needs special services is part of this everyday decision making.

NOTE TO READERS

Today's discussion provides an overview of education laws, but laws change over time. I encourage you to check with the U.S. Department of Education at www.ed.gov/index .jhtml as well as your state's department of education, to get the latest information on education laws that may apply to your child's educational needs. The Web sites for these organizations also provide examples of educational programs and interventions that are consistent with the latest approved regulations. Finding an advocate familiar with these regulations may be helpful to you.

An Overview of Federal Education Laws

Your distractible child may have important legal rights to receive assistance at school, under federal and state law. Whether your child qualifies for assistance depends on the nature of your child's disability and the kind of assistance she needs. Because state laws differ from state to state, they are not discussed here. But federal law protects every eligible child. There are two key federal laws that you should know about: the Individuals with Disabilities Education Improvement Act and Section 504 of the (federal) Rehabilitation Act of 1973.

The Individuals with Disabilities Education
Improvement Act (IDEA)

The Individuals with Disabilities Education Improvement Act protects children who are eligible for "special education." (Please note that IDEA is also referred to as IDEIA, but I use the more often cited IDEA throughout this book.) To qualify, your child must have a disability that is covered by the law *and* need "specialized instruction." Covered disabilities include learning disabilities, mental retardation, and many others. The category of disability that applies to many distractible children under this law is "Other Health Impairment." This category includes children with "limited alertness" to the "educational environment" due to chronic or acute health problems. ADHD with and without distractibility is specified in the law as a condition that may result in "limited alertness." The law recognizes ADHD's distractibility may interfere with a child's ability to focus in class, complete her homework, and perform at an appropriate level.

To qualify for the protection of IDEA, your distractible child must also need "specialized instruction," also known as an individualized education plan (IEP), which is instruction that is specifically adapted to the needs of your child by changing *what* your child is taught or *how* it is taught to her, to help her succeed. For instance, a child with a learning disability may need the general curriculum to be adapted to allow for one-on-one reading instruction with a reading specialist each day, using specially adapted reading materials. A child with a severe attention problem may require both an adaptation of the classroom materials and one-to-one teaching assistance in order to achieve at an appropriate level. This is what the "special" means in "special education." It also can include "related services," such as the assignment of an aide to help a child control the behavior that is interfering with her participation in classroom activities.

Section 504 of the Rehabilitation Act of 1973

If your distractible child does not qualify for special education under IDEA, she may still qualify for assistance under Section 504 of the Rehabilitation Act of 1973. This law, which covers both children and adults, is designed to eliminate discrimination based on a person's disability. It applies to schools and provides for services to any child with a physical or mental impairment that substantially limits one or more major life activities, such as walking, speaking, and learning. So your child may qualify for protection and assistance under Section 504 if her distractibility substantially interferes with her learning at school.

If your distractible child is protected by Section 504, she is legally entitled to accommodations to provide her with the opportunity to gain the same benefits and achieve the same results at school as her nonhandicapped peers. In the case of a child with ADHD, for example, typical accommodations might include extended time on tests, an extra set of textbooks for home use, a behavior intervention plan, and preferred seat assignments. As you can see, these "accommodations" are different from the "specialized instruction" described earlier that special education students require. Although Section 504 offers some legal protection to your distractible child that can help her achieve meaningful results, it is not as broad as the protection and legal rights provided by IDEA to special education students.

Tips for Advocating for Your Child at School

Keep the following suggestions in mind as you investigate your child's eligibility for supportive educational services at school.

- **Talk to your child.** Using your best calm, firm, and noncontrolling voice, talk to your child about school. Find out what she likes and dislikes and what kind of frustrations she is experiencing. Understanding what your child is going through at school is an essential part of being her advocate. Remember the old expression that it's difficult to listen when your mouth is open. The more you tell your child what to do, the less she may tell you what she wants you to do.

■ **Keep all paperwork.** Keep copies of all reports and paperwork regarding your child. Also, keep a record of all the school personnel, including dates when you spoke to them. Try to learn as much as possible about IDEA and other laws that could help your child. Talk to knowledgeable parents or school professionals you may know. The Resources section at the end of this book also provides some ways to find more information.

■ **Don't be afraid to question things.** School laws are not easy to interpret, and there is no such thing as a dumb question. Your main objective is to work together with the school to plan your child's education. Take your time and look over any paperwork carefully. Don't sign off on anything unless you understand it. Don't be afraid to say, "Please let me think about this." Remember that it's okay to ask for clarification, request further testing, or challenge the school's decision regarding services.

■ **Stay levelheaded.** I have seen far too many parents wearing "I don't trust you" signs on their foreheads when meeting with school personnel. Being involved in a process where lots of people are talking about your child can be very emotional, but this does not give you license to be disrespectful. Remember that the teachers and other educational staff want to help your child, even if you disagree with how they are going about it. Your child will benefit the most if you hear everyone out and express yourself in a calm, firm, and noncontrolling manner.

■ **Talk to an attorney.** If you are still unclear as to whether or not your child is covered by IDEA or Section 504, you may wish to consult an educational law attorney. Be aware that pursuing this avenue may be a costly option. However, educational attorneys are qualified to guide you through the process of determining how your school is meeting your child's educational needs, based on the types and level of distractibility-related problems she has. For many parents, the return on investment is the peace of mind of knowing all their concerns have been carefully considered.

Thoughts That Interfere with Advocating for Your Child

It's crucial that you have the right mind-set when advocating for your child at school, and the right mind-set begins and ends with how you view yourself. Your input really does count, and, if constructively presented, it will make a difference. The key to offering helpful input is to not allow these destructive thoughts to get in the way:

- *I feel I should be doing a better job at home.*
- *She needs to fail, and then she will respect her teachers.*
- *I don't know how much help to ask for.*
- *The school won't really help.*
- *This is all only going to get worse.*
- *I am embarrassed to ask the school to help.*

Thoughts That Promote Advocating for Your Child

To create an empowered, success-geared attitude for advocating for your child at school, try thinking in the ways shown below.

- *Being involved shows teachers and educators that I take my child's education seriously.*
- *The more I get to know my child's teachers, the less room there is for misunderstandings.*
- *I am helping my distractible child by helping her teachers understand her.*
- *The fact that my child's problems have not gone away overnight does not mean my efforts are not productive. I must remember that the problems were not created overnight.*
- *The more I work at constructively helping my child, the more my child will learn to help herself.*
- *I will never question myself for giving my child my best effort, if I keep doing the best I can.*

How to Approach the School

The more involved you are with your child's school, the more you can help her. I have worked with many parents over the years who have had difficulty understanding what appropriate advocacy means. I suggest you approach the school with what I call the three C's of advocating: Courteous, Cooperative, and Constructive. You should also bear in mind that there are many types of solutions for your child's issues. Your child's teacher, school psychologist, guidance counselor, and principal will all likely be knowledgeable about the range of services that may be accessible for your child, so don't be shy about asking them. It's also important to avoid rushing things and trying to find an immediate solution. I have seen some parents determinedly push for an IEP before they have adequately considered all of the possibilities. Staying invested yet flexible is best for your child, since other solutions may be much less restrictive and more appropriate. This section offers more advice for advocating for your child at school.

Assess How Your Child Does in the Classroom

If you have a younger child, you can spend time in your child's classroom. Perhaps you can volunteer as an aide for a day or two to see what's going on. Be mindful of the classroom dynamics with your child. Note whether your child feels comfortable and relaxed with her teacher. The more she feels liked and accepted by her teacher, the better she will learn. This being said, also note if your child somehow pushes the teacher's buttons in a way that makes it difficult for the teacher to like her. If your child does not seem to feel comfortable, then consider whether there a mismatch in the teacher-child relationship causing your child to feel misunderstood or angry. These are just a few of the types of observations that you can make as a classroom observer. You should also try to observe (or find out) how your child interacts on the playground at recess. Is she being teased or frightened and then acting out in an attempt to get someone to notice she's in trouble? ("Day 6" provides an in-depth look at distracted children and their peer relationships.)

The bottom line is that you want to ensure that your child has a positive classroom experience. If there is a conflict between your child and her teacher, try to work through it with the two of them. If this does not work, then explore the issues with the principal. Perhaps your child can be moved to another class. If an adult who connects well with your child (such as a teacher's aide) can be added to the classroom, sometimes this is enough to smooth out troublesome behavior. The reality, however, is that a student who does not have an IEP will likely not get such an accommodation.

If you don't have the ability to go to the school, or if your child is in middle school or high school, arrange to have a child therapist, school psychologist, or learning specialist evaluate your child in the classroom. Obviously, it's also valuable to get the input of your child's classroom teacher, who has observed her behaviors firsthand.

Establish a Working Relationship with Your Child's Teacher/Team of Teachers

Ask for a conference with your child's teacher (or team of teachers) before school begins. Explain why you are coming in for the appointment. Bring with you to the conference a list of your academic and behavioral concerns, as well as your child's strengths and what you consider to be her weak points. Let the school know if your child has been officially diagnosed with any psychological concerns, health concerns, learning disabilities, or ADHD, and whether she is on any medications. Unfortunately, this information is sometimes not shared, leaving the teacher(s) unaware of the child's challenges. If there are two parents involved, then it's better if both parents can be at this meeting. If that's not possible, then try to take another support person with you.

Try to establish a win-win atmosphere during this meeting. Remember, teachers are often overworked, have many individual student concerns, and may be reluctant to deal with additional problems. Indicate your willingness to work together to make this team effort as easy as possible for both of you and prevent future problems. You're standing up for the rights of your child, but you also need to be at least somewhat flexible in the process. It's very important to understand that you may need to compromise.

Share What Is Working

Whenever I work with children and families, I look for their strengths and for ways to make them work in other areas. Marshalling one's strengths to compensate for weaknesses is a big part of a growing positive psychology movement in mental health circles today.

More often than not, there are past parent practices or other areas of your child's life where things were working well, and these may now be overlooked. Perhaps you used to use positive reinforcement in the form of stickers to reward your young child or granting more time for your teen to spend with friends, and this can be adapted for use today with more age-appropriate rewards (I discuss reward strategies in more detail in "Day 8"). For an older child, perhaps praise alone will motivate her. Share with her teacher what is working. Does encouragement, praise, or classroom recognition help? Share what you do, and discuss how it might work in the classroom. Convey your child's unique strengths and show her teacher that not only do you want her to succeed, she wants to succeed as well.

Be Prepared to Ask Questions

Whenever you meet with the teacher, write down your main points ahead of time and even practice speaking them. As a lawyer acquaintance of mine says, "The best antidote to anxiety is preparation." Preparing will help you come across more confidently and assertively while clarifying the points you want to make.

Completing class work and homework is a source of intense frustration for distractible children. I coach parents I work with to consult with the teacher about her expectations in each area. I talk further about homework in "Day 5."

It may also be helpful to review the following guiding questions with your child's teacher or team of teachers:

- Instead of a typed report, would a visual presentation be acceptable from time to time?
- Will my child's efforts be recognized, even though she struggles? Will her grades suffer as a result?
- Will the classroom rules be clearly explained at the beginning, and reinforced throughout the school year? (Remember to convey how much your distracted child needs reminders.)
- Explain that your distractible child functions best with structure and clear expectations. Ask if your child has difficulty with transitions, especially from an unstructured activity such as

gym or recess to a structured one that requires self-restraint and independent work. Give suggestions for improving this. A few minutes of quiet time to readjust may help, as may a very definite routine.

Use Your Ears and Listen

Remember that it isn't enough to ask questions and speak confidently—you must also listen carefully. Take notes and ask for clarification when in doubt. Set future conference dates to discuss progress or to problem-solve. Hopefully, any future complaints about your child will first be directed to you, before the teacher goes to her supervisors. Indicate your willingness to resolve problems, and discuss when it would be best to hold telephone conferences when necessary. Establishing early communication and a consistent link to your child's teacher and the school helps resolve situations before they lead to a crisis.

Follow Up by Using an E-mail Loop

As long as you don't abuse and overly burden teachers with it, you can stay easily connected to your child's school performance via e-mail. From what I have seen, keeping in touch via e-mail has helped many parents and teachers stay on top of the daily functioning and progress of distracted students.

Say Thank You

Many beleaguered teachers have shared with me how much they appreciate being appreciated. So send a thank you note to your child's teacher after the conference. Thank her for meeting with you and for her willingness to work with you. Teachers often hear only complaints. They are much more willing to work with someone who praises as well as complains.

Go on Record

Keep a simple file folder to record your child's progress. Put in it communications, conference notes, and home/school procedures that have been set up. Record improvements and what you believe is working, along with continuing problems. Share this with your child's teacher during the year. This shows that you take your child's education very seriously and that you are working hard with the school to bring about success. Share this progress with your child as well. Let her know that you and the school are working together to help her succeed. This is especially important because you want your child to believe that you are involved because you care about her, not because she is a problem.

Points to Keep in Mind about Special Education Measures

In the event that your child receives special education services, stay aware of the following points:

- If your child does receive special education services, you and your child have the right to participate in the development of the IEP. You will work with your child's teachers and a representative from the school administration who is qualified to recommend and supervise special programs and services, as well as representatives from other agencies that may be involved in your child's transition services (if your child is age sixteen or older). You can also request an advocate to help you better understand your rights and responsibilities as a parent, and request that this person be present during the development of the IEP. Your local Children and Adults with Attention Deficit/Hyperactivity Disorder (CHADD) chapter or local organizations that support parents of children with learning disabilities will likely have names of advocates you can contact.

- Always remember that your child has a right to the least restrictive environment possible. Be on the lookout for terms like "inclusion" and "mainstreaming," which mean that your child will likely remain in her regular classroom for part or much of the day, as opposed to being pulled out often or placed in self-contained settings. Unless members of the IEP team can justify removal from the general education classroom, your child should receive instruction and support with classmates who do not have disabilities. Also be sure that special education services or supports are available to help your child participate in extracurricular activities such as clubs or sports.

- During an IEP meeting, the IEP team will develop goals for any related services, such as occupational or speech therapy, that could help your child. Be sure the team specifies how often and for how long these services will be provided, as well as in what setting the services will be provided. This team will also identify behavioral strategies to support your child's learning in school and at home.

- You have the right to challenge the school's decisions concerning your child. If you disagree with a decision that has been made, discuss it with the school and see if an agreement can be reached. If all efforts fail, IDEA provides other means of protection for parents and children under the law. These other ways of settling your dispute allow parents and school personnel to resolve disagreements. Options include mediation with an impartial third person, a due process hearing, or a formal hearing in a court of law.

- IEP meetings must be held once a year, and comprehensive reevaluation must be done every three years, unless you and the school agree it is unnecessary. However, you may request an IEP meeting (or consideration of reevaluation) at any time.

- Parents have fewer rights under Section 504. The school does not have to invite the parent to the meeting when the 504 plan is developed, but must notify the parent that a 504 plan has been developed. In short, Section 504 has fewer procedural safeguards to protect you and your child.

Good Teachers Motivate, Poor Teachers Aggravate

I want to be very clear that I'm not blaming teachers for the problems distracted children have in school. However, every distractible child I have worked with has acknowledged that the quality of her relationships with her teachers has a huge impact on her motivation level. Unfortunately, teaching strategies alone are not enough to help distractible students to succeed. Distractible children need teachers who encourage success by praising and encouraging them for effort, avoid negative comments and sarcasm, offer extra help whenever needed, and take an interest in their lives. I have seen over and over how this type of dedication from teachers and informal interactions with students can help distractible students feel as though they can succeed, much like a pat on the back.

In addition, knowing a child's outside motivation, interests, and strengths can help teachers more effectively encourage her learning inside the classroom. The better a teacher knows a child, the easier it is for her to understand her difficulties and needs. One of my young fifth-grade clients arrived at a session recently beaming from ear to ear because her teacher was planning to stop by her upcoming gymnastics meet. Obviously, teachers have busy lives and their time outside of class is understandably limited, but when possible, participating in or seeing students in their extracurricular activities can help teachers learn about their different sides. If the teacher can't attend extracurricular events, looking at pictures and asking about an event are the next best thing. Students appreciate this extra effort and interest, and teachers can use their new insights to help the student succeed academically.

Motivating students to learn often means directly involving them in the learning process. Students need to have input into the types of instructional material used, teaching methods, and scheduling. Active and participatory learning activities, such as games, simulations, media-based activities, computer-based learning, and group work can also motivate students.

Tests and grades can help motivate students as well as discourage them. They are only motivation when the topic or difficulty level allows that particular student a high rate of success. When students repeatedly do poorly, especially when they are trying their hardest, they quickly become demotivated and shut down. When students cannot rise to the challenges being presented to them, most will become frustrated and stop trying.

I have generally found teachers to be conscientious and willing to give their all to help distractible students. It has been a pleasure for me to collaborate with so many outstanding teachers. At the same time, teachers who negatively perceive distractibility can be very upsetting to you and your child. They may seem to give up on your child or rigidly see her in a negative light.

Some of your child's teachers may view her off-task behavior as "only trying when she wants to" or being an underachiever. This type of teacher also likely perceives distractible students as lazy. This is unfortunate because distractible children have a problem that renders them motivationally blocked—they don't have a character flaw. Below are strategies that teachers can use to spur success in distractible children. You may wish to use them as a basis for discussions with your child's teacher about ways to help her in the classroom.

Thirty-Six Strategies for Teaching Distractible Children

There is no one magic solution for managing distractibility in the classroom or at home, but there are dozens that can work. The effectiveness of any strategy at school depends upon the persistence and follow-through of individual teachers, the educational team, and supportive parent(s). Many of the strategies below are equal opportunity strategies. By this I mean that you may find them just as helpful at home as the teacher does at school.

The following classroom suggestions are intended for teachers of children of all ages. Some suggestions will obviously be more appropriate for younger children, others for older children, but the overall themes of structure, proactive measures, education, and encouragement are the same throughout. These tips represent a combination of several sources of information, which are included in the Resources section at the end of this book. There are also references for more in-depth information. While your child's teacher may already practice some of these strategies, it never hurts to revisit them or apply them in a unique way. Reviewing and implementing these strategies will help your child move through barriers.

1. Break down large tasks into small tasks.

If a distractible child is overwhelmed at school, she tends to react with an emotional "I'll-NEVER-be-able-to-do-THAT" kind of response. When tasks are broken down into smaller chunks, your child can avoid feeling overwhelmed. Dividing up a task to make it more manageable is one of the most crucial of all teaching techniques for children with distraction problems. When teachers break a task down, each component looks small enough to do. My guess is that you have personally seen how breaking tasks down can make things seem less overwhelming (e.g., sorting out a bill pile, separating a laundry pile, or strategically looking at a list of errands to accomplish).

Bearing this in mind, I have coached many parents on how large tasks quickly overwhelm distractible children. For example, a high-school sophomore told to write an essay on the causes of tornadoes may find this project daunting. To make this assignment seem more doable for the student, the teacher could provide her with a series of steps, such as: 1.) find relevant research materials, 2.) read and summarize the materials, 3.) write a brief outline, 4.) expand the outline with more details, 5.) write a rough draft, 6.) edit the rough draft. The teacher could evaluate the work at each stage and provide immediate feedback. This type of approach helps children with some of the requirements for organization and self-regulation.

Justin, a twelve-year-old client of mine, told me that his social studies and English teachers would break down essay writing into outlines, which helped him stay more focused. Besides doing better in these subjects, Justin also found them more enjoyable. With small children, task breakdown and management can be extremely helpful in avoiding tantrums resulting from anticipatory frustration. It can help older children avoid the defeatist or defiant attitude that so often results when they feel helpless and want to lash out.

2. Think "front and attention."

When it comes to where your child should sit in class, she does not have to follow the military code and sit front and center. However, when your child sits close up front, this allows the teacher to easily make eye contact with her. Even better, there won't be twenty-five children in front of your child, providing all sorts of distraction.

Teachers should be aware that if they move a child from a back seat to the front, it should not be done in a shaming, embarrassing way. One of my young clients, ten-year-old Terry, told me about a time when his teacher moved him to the front of the class after a month in fourth grade. This teacher was "mean" in Terry's eyes because of the way this change was made, and it had a negative impact on Terry. However, research confirms that, when it is done in a caring, low-key way, moving distracted children to sit closer to the teacher helps them sustain their attention.

3. Distinguish inability from noncompliance.

Review with your child's teachers her behaviors of concern. Politely remind the teacher that if your child can't control her distract- ible behavior, it is not noncompliance, and she therefore can't be labeled as an underachiever. Also, continue to find and point out your child's areas of strength.

4. Keep the encouragement flowing.

Distractible children are often in trouble or falling short of expec- tations. It's very important for your child to be encouraged and praised for successful behaviors at school. Children may not let on that they enjoy the supportive comments, but they really do. Eli, age eleven, told me that he often just thinks, "Yeah, whatever" when he receives a compliment from a teacher. But when I pressed him further about this, he said, "Most of the time I like it because it tells me I am doing better."

5. Pursue extra time for exams and projects.

Permitting additional time for exams and projects can compensate for the difficulties with attention common to many distracted stu- dents. Sami, age fourteen, shared with me that when her teacher gave her the option to take more time for a test during her free period, it helped her feel less pressured. This accommodation is often given to children who qualify for special education services. At the same time, your teacher may be able to afford this option even if your child does not meet the formal criteria of IDEA or Section 504, discussed earlier.

6. Determine if your child can share notes.

Many distractible students can't concentrate on the lecture while writing. Being able to fill in the gaps with notes from a peer may be helpful. One of my clients, fifteen-year-old Rose, told me, "When I have a friend share notes during class it helps me get all the stuff I need in my notes, and then I do better on my tests."

7. Be aware of the support available to the teacher.

Teaching in a classroom where there are two or three kids with distractibility can be exhausting. Try to determine the extent to which your child's teacher has the support of the school. Make sure there is a knowledgeable person that your child's teacher can consult with, when he has a problem with your child, such as a learning specialist, behavior specialist, child psychologist, social worker, school psychologist, or pediatrician.

8. Know the teacher's limits.

Encourage your child's teacher to ask you for help. Let the teacher know that you do not expect her to be an expert on distractible children. Most importantly, keep the lines of communication open. Always bear in mind that it's best not to be overbearing.

9. Encourage the teacher to ask your child what will help.

Your child may be more intuitive than you or her teacher knows. She may be able to guide the teacher in what will help her compensate for her distractibility in class. One of my twelve-year-old clients, Sophia, told a teacher that she liked to learn by making up songs to remember vocabulary words for math class. Your child is by far the best expert on how she learns, if she can articulate it.

In addition, make sure your child understands her own distractibility. This will prevent her from unfairly blaming herself for finding school challenging.

10. Promote structure.

Distractible children need their environment to structure externally what they can't structure internally on their own. Encourage your child's teacher to have her make lists. Children with distractibility benefit greatly from having a chart or list to refer back to when they get lost in what they're doing. Also convey that your child benefits from reminders and whatever additional direction and structure can be given.

11. Emphasize the emotional part of learning.

Teachers are only human, and some may lose sight of the emotional pain that distracted students have inside them. Remind the teachers how your child struggles to gain a sense of mastery instead of failure and frustration, and excitement instead of boredom or fear. It's essential for teachers to pay attention to the emotions involved in the learning process. Earlier in this chapter, I shared some negative, problematic thoughts of distracted children. Tom, age fifteen, told me that his math teacher yelled at him for asking another kid for help. Yes, classroom boundaries are important. But when Tom was sent down to the office, this left him feeling embarrassed and subsequently disconnected from the teacher. As seen by this troubling example, creating emotional safety in the classroom is crucial.

12. Ask for directions to be repeated.

Ensure that the teacher writes down directions for your child and clearly expresses and repeats them. In the words of fourteen-year-old Ari, "I never listen the first time because either people are talking or I just forget what was said. So hearing it again helps."

Reinforce that your distractible child needs to hear things more than once.

13. Use eye contact.

Ask the teacher if she uses eye contact (in a nonshaming way) to "bring back" your distractible child in class. The teacher should not do this in a punitive manner, or the child may feel that he is not trusted to pay attention. But a caring and engaging glance can bring a child back from a daydream.

14. Encourage limits and boundaries.

Monitor if the teacher consistently, predictably, promptly, and clearly sets boundaries for your child when necessary. It's crucial that the teacher not get into complicated, lawyer-like discussions about fairness. Please note that 10 Days to a Less Defiant Child has both a chapter and an appendix of advice for teachers, to help them manage problem behaviors of students at school.

15. Determine if there is a predictable schedule.

Transitions and unannounced changes are very difficult for distracted children. They become discombobulated by them. Kevin, age eleven, shared that the color of the sheet on the bulletin board in his classroom would cue him to the activities for the day. Teachers can post a schedule on the blackboard or the child's desk. Ensure that it is referred to often. If the teacher is going to vary it, as most interesting teachers do, your child should be given a lot of warning and preparation. Announcing what is going to happen and giving repeat warnings as the time approaches will help ensure success.

16. Use schedules to avoid procrastination.

Your child's teachers may find it helpful to work with your child to make a schedule for a project. They can support your child by being directly involved in coming up with a feasible time line to complete the work but allow her to determine the specifics of the project on her own. This can help to avoid one of the hallmarks of distractible children: procrastination. Roberto, age seventeen, found that his senior project involving volunteer work and a paper was much more doable when his teacher helped him to develop a workable time schedule to follow.

17. Allow for escape-valve outlets.

You have likely heard the expression that an ounce of prevention is worth a pound of cure. If it can be built into the rules of the classroom, an escape-valve outlet—such as allowing your child to leave the room rather than "lose it"—can really help her save face. Your child will also begin to learn important tools of self-observation and self-modulation. Steve, a nine-year-old client of mine, had a guidance counselor who arranged that if he lost his patience he could walk out without getting in trouble. This helped Steve feel less trapped, and he was consequently calmer in his mind and in class.

18. Encourage the teacher to consider quality rather than quantity of homework.

Children with distractibility often need a reduced workload. As long as they are learning the concepts, they should be allowed this. Talk to the teacher and explain that your child will put in the same amount of study time, but won't get buried under more than she can handle. "Day 5" offers more on tackling the homework hassles of distracted children.

19. Monitor and celebrate progress often.

Children with distractibility benefit greatly from frequent feedback. If the teacher gives you and your child ongoing feedback, it helps keep your child on track, lets her know what is expected next, and can be very encouraging. Along these lines, if possible, weekly report cards can also be helpful. To make things easier, they can be communicated via backpack express or e-mail.

20. Seek out and underscore success as much as possible.

Encourage the teacher to remember that your child lives with a lot of failure. This point cannot be overemphasized: Distractible children need and benefit from praise, especially from teachers, who hold so much perceived power over them. They love encouragement. Often the most devastating aspect of being distracted is not the distractibility itself, but the secondary damage done to self-esteem.

21. Remember the memory issues.

Remind the teacher that your child may benefit from little tricks like mnemonics or flashcards to help her memory. Distracted kids often have problems with memorizing information because their minds are pulled in so many directions. Any little tricks you can devise—cues, rhymes, code, and the like—can help a great deal to enhance memory, especially if they are done with a fun, innovative spirit. In the words of fifteen-year-old Dan, "My teacher is cool. We play Jeopardy to go over key stuff in class, and this stops me from getting bored and I learn it better."

22. Toe the line on outlines.

Encourage the teaching of outlining. I tell kids that making an outline is like building a skeleton. Afterward, the flesh can be put on top. (You may want to get rid of the skeleton and choose a more lively metaphor.) However you want to look at it, outlines help a great deal because they structure and shape what is being learned as it is being learned. This helps your child feel more in control when learning new concepts or studying known ones for tests.

23. Get an extra set of textbooks for home.

So often with distracted kids, the books don't make it home. Arranging with the teacher to have an extra set of textbooks at home is handy and helpful. Jordan, an eighth grader, shared that this helps her because "I always forget my books, even though I try not to."

24. Try to simplify.

See if your child's teacher is willing to simplify instructions and simplify scheduling for your child. The simpler the verbiage, the more likely that your child will understand it.

25. Promote real self-awareness.

Children with distractibility are often clueless about how they come across or how they have been behaving. Suggest that the teacher ask your child questions that promote self-observation, like, "Do you know what you just did?" or "How do you think you might have said that differently?" or "Why do you think that other girl looked sad when you said what you said?" The teacher can hopefully be patient and supportive while trying to encourage your child's self-awareness. I have met many distracted children who are aware of how they feel, but not aware of how to talk about how they feel.

26. Test out the test-taking skills.

Ask your child's teacher to review some of her suggested strategies for test preparation and test taking. While teachers may vary in their suggestions, some common and helpful test-taking strategies include:

■ Eat before a test. Having food in your stomach will give you energy and help you focus, but avoid heavy foods that can make you groggy.

- Go over any material from practice tests, homework, sample problems, review material, the textbook, and class notes.
- Don't cram, and do try to get a good night's sleep before the test. (Surprisingly, I have had sixth and seventh graders stay up till two in the morning cramming for tests, unbeknownst to their parents.)
- Keep a positive attitude throughout the whole test, and try to stay relaxed. If you start to feel nervous, take a few deep breaths to relax.
- Keep your eyes on your own paper. You don't want to appear to be cheating and cause unnecessary trouble for yourself.
- When you first receive your test, do a quick survey of the entire test so that you know how to efficiently budget your time.
- Do the easiest problems first; don't linger over a problem that you are stuck on, especially when time is a factor. Maybe on another part of the test there'll be something that will help you out with that question.
- Do the problems that have the greatest point values first.
- Don't rush, pace yourself. Read the entire question and look for keywords.
- Ask the teacher for clarification if you don't understand what she is asking for on the test.
- Write legibly. If the teacher can't read what you wrote, she'll most likely mark it wrong.
- Always read the whole question carefully. Don't make assumptions about what the question might be.
- Put the main ideas/information/formulas onto a sheet that can be reviewed.
- If you aren't satisfied with your grade, go to your instructor and see if there's a make-up exam or any extra credit work that you can do.
- Save the test to study for future cumulative tests.

27. Point out the point value, especially if your child is young.

A point system can be part of a behavioral modification or reward system for younger children. Children with distractibility respond well to rewards and incentives.

28. Emphasize the value of "connectedness."

Support the teacher's awareness that your child needs to feel engaged and connected. As long as she is engaged, she will feel motivated and be less likely to tune out.

29. Encourage and enforce a home-to-school-to-home notebook.

Logs that keep teachers and parents connected are very helpful. E-mail is equally effective. This can really help with daily parent-teacher communication and avoid crisis meetings. It also helps with the frequent feedback these kids need.

30. Encourage a structure for self-monitoring.

There's a wonderful adage that I love: "Give a man a fish, and he'll have dinner. Teach him how to fish, and he'll never go hungry." In this vein, ask your child's teacher to encourage your child to monitor herself. One child I worked with would subtly make marks on a tic sheet whenever she daydreamed in class. She would review the tic sheets with the teacher at the end of the week to monitor her own attention and get support to improve her concentration.

31. Prepare for unstructured time.

Distractible kids need to know in advance what is going to happen, so they can prepare for it internally. Spontaneous unstructured time can be overstimulating. Teachers can stay on top of this by being proactive in preparing the child for free time and reminding her of the rules.

32. Have older kids write reminders for any questions they have.

By writing herself a reminder whenever she has a question, your child will be taking notes not only on what is being said to her, but on what she is thinking as well. This will help her listen better. One "cool teacher" I worked with handed out sticky notes for students to put their thoughts (the ones they were willing to expose) on their foreheads.

33. Explore alternatives to handwriting.

Handwriting is difficult for many distracted children. Speak to the teacher to see if she will consider developing alternatives to handwriting for your child, if necessary. Alternatives include having the child learn to use a keyboard or letting her take tests orally.

34. Broadcast that signals can work.

Encourage your child's teacher to work with her to develop a signal to get the child's attention before beginning a lesson. A signal could be a certain type of look, a subtle hand gesture, or even a movement to a certain spot on the floor.

35. Ask about a study friend.

Determine if the teacher is willing to arrange for your child to have a "study friend" in each subject, and get their phone numbers. This may not work in all cases, but I have seen it be very successful when the child is on board with the strategy.

36. Meet with the teacher often.

You certainly don't want to wear out your welcome in the teacher's classroom. At the same time, most teachers have more problems with uninvolved parents than with strongly involved ones. So stay a familiar, friendly face and avoid the pattern of just meeting around problems.

DAY 4: SUMMING IT UP

School is meant to be a place of learning, but for many distracted children it becomes a place of agony. Advocating for your child at school is a very important part of helping her compensate for her distractibility. Please keep the following points in mind:

- Distracted children not only struggle in school, but have negative thoughts and feelings about being there.
- Depending on your child's situation, education laws may help provide her with additional supports.
- Whether or not your child's distractibility is addressed by laws, you can make a big positive difference by effectively advocating for your distracted child at school.
- The emotions experienced by you, your child, and her teachers will greatly impact her motivation, for better or worse.
- There are many strategies described here that you can share with your child's teacher to help your distracted child perform better in the classroom.

Heading Off Homework Wars

Doris and Mark sat in front of me looking intently at Adam, their twelve-year-old son. Doris, frustrated and at her wits' end, complained, "Every night it's the same ridiculous battle, and I am getting so sick of it."

Tearing up, Adam looked blindly ahead.

Mark added, "We can't get him to get his homework done, and when he finally does do it, he forgets to turn it in."

Doris sighed and again looked at Adam. She then said, "We don't know what to do. It's just a losing battle."

If this scenario sounds familiar, you're not alone. Most distractible children can't stand doing homework. Distracted children repeatedly share with me how upset they get about having to do homework, and how much they hate it or think it's stupid. They also justifiably feel that homework is ten times harder for them because they often forget how to do it.

As human beings, we seek to move toward pleasure and avoid pain. For distractible children, homework is painful. Many distractible kids do not see the value in completing all of their homework every day, and some deliberately leave books, worksheets, and folders at school so that they will not have to deal with them that evening at home. In most cases, however, missing homework assignments will lower your child's grades, and his failure to do homework will leave him less prepared for tests. Today you will learn how to get the homework headaches under control.

Why Distracted Children Resist Homework

Most children resist doing their homework at times. However, motivating a distracted child to start and complete homework assignments can feel like an insurmountable task. Distractibility really zaps homework motivation. Homework helps kids practice what they have learned in class, prepare for future class work, and do well on tests, but distracted children, more than other children, fail to see that homework can be helpful.

There are many reasons why distractible kids avoid doing homework. The most common are listed below. Check off any that seem to apply to your child:

_____ He finds it too easy, too boring, or too difficult. He may also view it as punishment.

_____ He finds it too difficult, but is unwilling to ask for help.

_____ He has difficulty focusing his attention for a long period of time and needs to do the work in small segments.

_____ He does not understand what he has to do.

_____ He finds the work uninteresting.

_____ He dislikes repetition and rote learning.

_____ He has difficulty reading.

_____ He does not understand the need for the homework.

_____ He complains that he is tired and/or hungry.

_____ He says that the place where he does his work is uncomfortable.

Managing the Emotional Impact of Homework

In "Day 3," you learned how to avoid overreacting to your distracted child. Now that you have the skills for controlling your emotional reactions, I encourage you to reach out to your distracted child to help him with his homework. You may groan and say, "Why do *I* have to reach out? Shouldn't he do his homework on his own? Isn't it my child's responsibility, and not mine?" I understand your frustrations. But please keep in mind that your child did not choose to develop a distraction problem, and without your help, he likely won't overcome it. Besides, your goal is to help your child do his homework, not do the homework for him.

Today I provide you with the tools that have worked for so many families in my practice. You will also learn how to manage your distracted child's negative emotions about homework, which will enable these tools and strategies to work most effectively.

The bottom line with homework is that you can arm yourself and your child with the best tools in the world, but unless you can help your child react to homework with less angst and negativity, he will be always be resistant to doing it. If you learn how to manage your child's homework resistance, he will accept the ideas and strategies that can truly make a positive difference. Helping your child with his homework is about a lot more than just getting through math problems or nailing down challenging spelling words. You must also be able to cope with his denial, fragile emotions, and—most specifically—the fear of failure in these tasks.

These emotions have a powerful influence on your distracted child's ability to learn. When your child is interested and excited about something, it is much easier for him to learn. However, if he finds the subject matter frustrating, boring, or upsetting, learning becomes almost impossible. Negative emotions not only further distract your already distracted child from the task at hand, they also use up the attention that he needs for learning. With distracted children in particular, attention is an extremely limited mental resource. There is just not enough to go around.

In *10 Days to a Less Defiant Child,* I talked about the critical importance of avoiding power struggles to help reduce defiant behavior. In short, I encouraged parents to be calm, firm, and noncontrolling to avoid getting sucked into counterproductive emotional tugs of war. As you will see below, the calm, firm, and noncontrolling approach is ideal for tackling the thorny demands of homework. It will help you better convey your positive intentions, which will support your new interventions.

The following is an overview of two different problematic approaches I have seen parents use to influence their distracted kids to do homework. I call them the passive approach and the sledgehammer approach. The italicized text represents an example of the approach, and the text that follows it provides a brief explanation.

Problem: The Passive Approach

"I think it would be good if you sat down and maybe finished your homework." Nine-year-old Jeremy's parents had a hard time expressing appropriate limits and boundaries about his homework. Jeremy ran the show at home, and this left him empowered to avoid his homework. Eventually, after we worked together in counseling, Jeremy's parents became more assertive, and they felt empowered to guide Jeremy out of his homework-shirking strategies.

Problem: The Sledgehammer Approach

"You're lazy and stubborn. If you don't do your homework, then I'm sending you away to reform school." These were the words thirteen-year-old Kirstin heard from her exasperated parents. Kirstin's parents actually made this threat, and at the time they felt justified in doing it. They soon realized, however, that as their emotions continued to rise, Kirstin's homework production continued to decline. Fortunately, I was able to help Kirstin's parents realize that threats were not good—either for them or for Kirstin.

Time to Stop the Insanity

The definition of insanity is doing the same thing over and over and expecting a different result each time. So now I'm encouraging you to stop the homework insanity. The passive approach will not work because your child will see you as weak and will ignore you. The sledgehammer approach will likely lead to a destructive power struggle—and a one-way ticket on the express train to drama city. If you have been either too passive or too threatening, don't beat yourself up. As parents, none of us are perfect. It's time, however, to stop being too passive and to put down your homework sledgehammers. There is a better way. You just need to be calm, firm, and noncontrolling.

Solution: The Calm, Firm, Noncontrolling Approach

I worked with a sixth grader named Jon who was by no means a homework lover. Jon's mother, Sylvia, had also worked with me for a few months. She had cycles of being too passive and then becoming too explosive in response to Jon's resistance to doing homework. This pattern, by the way, is common for many frustrated parents who feel helpless.

I coached Sylvia to use the calm, firm, noncontrolling approach. Sylvia later reported to me, "I calmed myself down and really let Jon know that I realized how hard it is for him to get his homework started and how overwhelmed he feels by it. But I also told him to please sit down and give it his best. I reminded him that I could not force this, but that I knew deep down he really wants to succeed." Sylvia told me, "Your calm, firm, noncontrolling approach really helped us. Jon did not feel that I was pressuring him too much. We made so much progress getting the homework done and the senseless power struggles disappeared."

As I was writing this chapter, a client of mine named Lynn

shared an amusing story. Lynn is the mother of a sixth grader named Jack. She told me that for the past few months, much to her growing dismay, every afternoon went the same way. Lynn would repeatedly check to see if Jack had started his homework. Jack, meanwhile, would just be unproductively staring at his notebook without accomplishing anything. Lynn would "pick a fight" and fruitlessly argue with her son. Much drama would ensue, but not much homework would get done.

One day Lynn had a huge epiphany. She realized that the homework power struggle was just not working. She walked up to Jack, smiled warmly, threw open her arms, and hugged him. She playfully said, "Honey, what am I going to do with you?" Half an hour later, Jack completed his homework. Go figure.

Charles, a father from my practice, recently shared another example of success with the calm, firm, and noncontrolling approach. One night his son was "doing homework" and talking with his girlfriend on the phone. Charles said, "I went up to him and calmly asked him to hang up the phone. Charlie then went on and on about how he can 'multitask.' At this point, I knew it was going to get ugly, so I firmly said, 'Charlie, if this is a very important phone call, then I just ask that you please finish your conversation and go back to doing your homework.' Jeff, I guess so much of how things go is dictated by my delivery. Because Charlie then turned his back to me, apologized to his girlfriend, and told her he would call her back later. How about that?"

I can't give you a 100 percent guarantee that keeping your emotions in check will turn your child into a homework lover. But for many of the children that I have seen in my office, when parents back off the homework demands, kids step up to meet them. I have even seen it confirmed at school team meetings—being calm, firm, and noncontrolling has a strong positive effect on homework compliance.

Further Fostering Homework Compliance

To really be calm, firm, and noncontrolling, you must share with your child that you understand his frustration and resistance to doing homework. In "Day 2," in the section called "Common Symptoms" I discussed the challenges faced by distracted children. They have short attention spans, poor organizational skills, difficulty managing time, problems with procrastination, and problems following directions. These struggles are roadblocks to homework success. Please try to stay mindful of how difficult it is for your child to deal with these distraction-related problems. Stay connected to his challenges so you can help him continue to accommodate his distractibility.

It's All in Your Approach

Children (and people in general) do not like to feel controlled or forced to do things. It makes no sense to try to force your distractible child to do anything, especially homework. If you use my suggested approach of being calm, firm, and noncontrolling, you will avoid major power struggles with homework. Remember, a power struggle just fuels your child to avoid rather than approach homework tasks.

The field of psychology talks about the "approach/avoidance conflict," which I believe has strong relevance to your child's motivation toward homework. The approach/avoidance conflict occurs when an individual moves closer (physically or psychologically) to a seemingly desirable object, only to have the potentially negative consequences of contacting that object push back against the approaching behavior.

So let's apply this to your child and his homework. The approach part of the conflict would suggest that your child desires homework. Okay, I certainly get that your distractible child may not ever see homework as desirable. But on some level he likely knows that doing his homework could help him stay out of academic trouble, and this is desirable. However, your distracted child's angst in struggling through the toils of homework turns him off (avoidance). So, based on this theory, homework becomes a civil war in your child's mind. On one hand, he may realize that doing homework could end the hassles of suffering grades, embarrassment with teachers, and conflict with you. On the other hand, he avoids the immediate pain of trying to do homework, which is boring and not pleasurable. As a parent, your challenge is to encourage your child to do his homework without tripping off the possible explosions that can result from his own inner turmoil about doing it.

Bearing in mind your child's homework resistances, it's essential that your communications spur motivation instead of more avoidance. Below are more homework-encouraging statements that employ the skills of being calm, firm, and noncontrolling. I provide a comparison to the passive and sledgehammer approaches, to highlight the differences.

	PASSIVE	SLEDGEHAMMER	CALM, FIRM, NONCONTROLLING
Example 1 Child blames teacher to avoid doing homework.	"Okay, I know you are upset. The teacher must not be preparing you. I'll call the teacher tomorrow. You can go to your friend's house, just be back by 7:30."	"Either you get your homework done now or you are grounded for a month."	"I understand your frustration. You think your teacher is stupid for giving you this assignment. But you still need to do it. I'm ready to help, and I'm asking you to please give it a try."

	PASSIVE	SLEDGEHAMMER	CALM, FIRM, NONCONTROLLING
Example 2 Child procrastinated on a homework assignment	"Maybe I can write a note and get the teacher to extend the deadline."	"You had all week to get this done, and you wasted your time. You just don't care about anything, do you?"	"I know the deadline came up quicker than you expected. Let's break this down and do all we can to get it done."

More Ways to Get Homework to Happen

The following section provides more suggestions on how to motivate your child to do homework. Realize that this is still part of the all-important attitudinal/motivational realm, which sets the stage for the actual homework strategies to be successfully implemented. I can't emphasize enough that the emotional atmosphere needs to be free of major turbulence and storms before any strategies and plans can be successful. Keeping these points in mind will help ensure that the strategies in the following sections will be effective.

Stop nagging and start listening to your child's frustration. As Sylvia and Lynn discovered in the examples earlier, you need to stop nagging your child to get the homework done. Nagging tends to be a very big problem for some parents—especially when it comes to homework. Perhaps this is why I have not yet seen any self-help books with titles such as *How to Nag Your Child to a Successful Life*. Instead of nagging, start listening to your child's concerns and frustrations. In the words of one high-school sophomore I worked with, "Dude, my parents are all over me to get my homework done. They just don't get how that makes me nuts and want to not even deal with it at all." Fortunately, this young man's parents listened to me and used the calm, firm, noncontrolling approach to be supportive while backing down from nagging.

While this did not bring forth homework miracles, it did spur more homework manageability.

Be a connected parent.
I recently did a talk at a local school about increasing self-esteem in children with learning-related challenges. A woman in the audience shared that she found it helpful to "just keep talking." This wise mother of a nine-year-old girl further shared that the more she kept her daughter engaged—about anything—the more she could discuss her difficulties with homework. Remember that listening leads to connection.

To connect with your child by listening, you need to come up with some phrases that encourage further talking, such as "Tell me more," "Go on. . . . ," "How do you feel about that?" and "I know what you mean," or "Then what?" Instead of butting in with your advice or opinion, listen for and name the feelings you think you hear, based on what your child is telling you. "Sounds like that made you pretty mad, didn't it?" or "You seem really happy about that!" These are reflective, connected responses to draw out your child's feelings. Also, use problem-solving phrases when needed. "What do you wish you could do?" or "What do you want to happen?" or "What do you think will happen if you do that?" Most importantly, by staying connected you will avoid denying, discounting, or distracting your child from the feelings he is expressing.

I have also seen repeatedly that distracted children are more motivated to do classwork and homework for those teachers they feel similarly connected to. The more positive rapport your child has with his teachers, the more likely it is that he will be willing to meet in-class and out-of-class requirements.

Try to empathize.
Really put yourself into your child's shoes. Empathizing with your distractible child may take imagination and patience, but try to focus on underlying feelings that he may be having difficulty

expressing. Empathizing helps parents and children avoid that toxic power struggle cycle. Instead of arguing, listen. Show your understanding while maintaining your position.

At the same time, there is no bigger homework communication squasher than "Why didn't you just ask for help?" Most children, especially distractible ones, don't always know all the reasons behind their actions and feelings. You can bet that your child's negative thoughts about homework play a role in his avoidance. Unless you empathize with his negative thoughts, your child will likely not feel emotionally safe sharing his frustrations and fears. Remember, by empathizing you are not agreeing with or condoning homework avoidance. Rather, you are removing communication barriers that block the ability to discuss the avoidance.

Manage your expectations.

Is it realistic to hope that this book will help you turn your kid into a homework lover? Probably not. Homework resistance in your distracted child may never completely disappear. In fact, you may have to continue to be vigilant to help guide your child to it and through it, until the end of his school days. At the same time, your child's homework hassles will be much more manageable if you apply the principles of this book in earnest. Try to stay patient and realize that progress usually comes for those parents and children who stick with it.

Remember that Rome wasn't built in a day. I have seen many distracted children end up doing well after graduating from high school. Many go on to college and excel. Others find trade jobs and work their way to being very responsible and successful at what they do. I have even seen kids who drop out of high school later pull it together, go back to school, and then soar through college. In many cases, distracted children eventually get ahead. Try to be patient.

Getting Past the "I Can't Do Its"

Despite your best empathy, supportive responses, and truckloads of patience, suppose your child says, "I can't do it" about his homework? Then you wonder *So, now what, Dr. Jeff?* I suggest that you still use your best calm, firm, and noncontrolling voice.

Next, you should act "as if." That is, try to encourage your child to act *as if* he can do it. Tell him to pretend that he knows, and see what happens. Then leave the immediate area and let him see if he can handle it from there. If he keeps telling you he doesn't know how to get his homework done, and you decide to offer help, concentrate on asking more than on telling. The following supportive probes may also help you get past the "I can't do its."

> *"What parts of the instructions do you understand?"*
> *"Can you give me an example of where and how you are getting stuck?"*
> *"Tell me what you think the answer is."*
> *"How could you find out?"*

Twenty-Four Tips to Help Get Homework Done

Here are twenty-four tips to help your distracted child complete his homework. We are now talking logistics rather than emotion management. Some of these strategies may fit with your style or your child's abilities more than others. Use the strategies that work now, and tuck away the others, as they may be helpful in the future.

1. Strive for a satisfactory study area.

A study area should have lots of light, have supplies close by, and be fairly quiet. In most cases, your child will do best if he studies in the same place every night. Importantly, let your child help choose the space. It doesn't have to be a bedroom; for many kids, the kitchen table or a corner of the living room works just fine, but it should be a quiet place with few distractions. If your young child wants to do his work with you nearby, too, you'll be better able to monitor his progress and encourage good study habits.

Your child may enjoy decorating a special study corner. Have fun with it. The better the homework experience feels, the more approach and the less avoidance. A brightly colored container to hold pencils, and some favorite artwork taped to the walls can make study time more pleasant. For older kids, CD jackets showing favorite bands can induce relaxation.

If you live in a small or noisy household, try having all family members take part in a quiet activity during homework time. You may need to take a noisy toddler outside or into another room to play. If distractions can't be avoided, your child may want to complete assignments in a nearby library.

Please realize that some children do better with some activity in the background. In some cases, music or some activity in the background may feel soothing or comforting to certain children. Try to be open to this possibility, as it may help.

2. Establish a schedule.
Deciding when to sit down and do homework may be overwhelming for your distracted child. However, you will all benefit from knowing that a certain time every day is reserved for studying and doing homework. I have found that with distracted kids, the best time is usually not right after school. Most children, and especially distracted children, need time to decompress and unwind. Many parents I have worked with have found that it's best to include their child when choosing a time for homework. Even if he doesn't have homework (which is rare these days), the reserved time should be used to review the day's lessons, read for pleasure, or work on an upcoming project.

Over and over again, I have seen how establishing a homework schedule makes a huge positive difference. The predictability of a schedule keeps distracted kids in a routine. Joan and her thirteen-year-old son, Seth, met with me a few times to discuss various schedule options (e.g., starting homework right after school or waiting an hour). An ever wise (and calm, firm, noncontrolling) Joan encouraged Seth to add input about a time schedule that could be adhered to as realistically as possible. Joan's measured, supportive, and collaborative demeanor helped Seth embrace the schedule plan, and it worked out successfully. Joan no longer had to "hunt down" or "corral" Seth to do homework. They also were able to agree that phone calls, TV, and everything else could wait until the work was completed.

I also realize that many children have outside activities, such as sports or music lessons, which may mean that you need a flexible schedule. Your child may study after school on some days and in the evening on others. If there isn't enough time to finish homework, your child may need to drop some outside activity. Homework must be a high priority.

You may need to work more with your elementary-school child to develop a schedule. An older student can probably make up a schedule independently, although you'll want to make sure it's realistic. It may help to write out the schedule and post it in a place where you'll see it often, such as the refrigerator door.

3. Assign yourself to your child's assignment book.
Think of yourself as your child's auxiliary organizational brain, and coach him in keeping his life together. Make sure he writes his required assignments in his assignment book. I bet you would not be shocked if I told you how many distracted kids forget about their assignment books! If your child's assignment book keeps getting abducted by aliens, you will need to arrange with the school to have someone help out. Your goal is to ensure

that your child leaves the school with his homework assignments properly recorded. These days, more and more teachers are listing the current day's homework on their classroom Web site. This provides you and your child with a way to cross-check what is written (or not written) in the assignment book with the actual course requirement.

4. Know how your child learns best.

If you understand your child's learning style, it will be easier for you to help him. For example, does your child tend to be a visual learner? Does he learn things best when he can see them? If so, drawing a picture or a chart may help with some assignments. For example, Tracy, a parent I worked with, found that her seventh-grade son, after reading his science book, did not remember the difference between the nucleus and nucleolus in a cell. But by repeatedly drawing a picture and labeling the cell structures, he could remember them easily.

Does your child learn things best when he can hear them? In this case, he may need to listen to a story or have directions read to him. Too much written material or too many pictures or charts may confuse him. Does your child understand some things best when he can handle or move them? For example, an apple cut four or six or eight ways can help a younger child see spatial relationships. Personally, the pizza as a pie-chart visual works best for me.

5. Find out the teacher's/school's homework policy.

At the start of the school year (or now, if you are reading this later in the school year—better late than never), ask the teacher:

- How long is my child expected to take to complete assignments?

- How should I be involved when my child hits homework impasses?
- What do you suggest I do if my child does not grasp a concept?

As you probably know, teachers' expectations vary. Recently, I was at one school conference where two teachers admitted that they don't check homework as much for accuracy as for seeing that it has been completed.

So, ask your child's teacher what you should do. Should you just check to make sure the assignment is done, or should you do something more? Some teachers want parents to go over the homework and point out errors, while others ask parents to simply check to make sure the assignment is completed. It's also a good idea to ask the teacher to call you if any problems with homework come up.

6. Make prioritizing a priority.

For many distracted children, deciding what to do first during homework is a major source of tension. Darlene, a fifth grader I worked with, had a tendency to dwell over this choice for a long time. I helped Darlene's father coach her on picking out the most challenging work to knock off first.

Encourage your child to number assignments in the order in which they should be done, before beginning his homework session. He should start with one that's not too long or difficult, but avoid saving the longest or hardest assignments for last. Most children will do best if the more challenging work is tackled early on. Please note, however, that for some children, finishing an easier assignment first will get them into the groove to work on the harder challenges. Be open to what works best for your child.

7. "Catch" the correct problems first.

Parents sometimes have a habit of zeroing in on the incorrect answers. Vince told me how changing his modus operandi in this regard made a tremendous difference when working with his eight-year-old daughter, Loretta, who was in second grade. Vince initially came in upset because going over spelling homework left him frustrated and Loretta in tantrums. Once Vince began emphasizing Loretta's "mini victories" in spelling instead of highlighting her mistakes, both of their patience levels surged. Tina, another parent, found the same lesson valuable in helping her fifth-grade son with math problems.

Next time your child brings you schoolwork to look over, focus first on how well he did on the correct problems, spelling words, and so on. For the answers that are incorrect, try saying something like, "I bet if you go back and check these over, you may get a different answer." As Vince and Tina discovered, establishing a positive feeling by focusing on what is done right (along with your encouragement) will help your child when the work gets more challenging. This may also prove useful in getting through the "I can't do its," which I discussed earlier (see page 116).

8. Talk about the assignments.

Too often, homework becomes a taboo topic between parents and their children. Don't let this happen to you. Ask your child questions about his homework in a calm, firm, and noncontrolling manner. As long as you keep up the positive rapport with your child, guiding, supportive questions can help him think through an assignment and break it down into small, workable parts. Here are some sample questions:

- **Do you know what you're supposed to do?** A friend once told me that he was going to cook a meal, when he asked his son, who was brimming with enthusiasm, to get him a wok. The son smiled and said "Okay, Dad." Five minutes later, the boy sheepishly returned and asked his dad, "What's a wok look like?" Hopefully, you see my point here. When it comes to homework, first let your child read the instructions, and then have him tell you in his own words what the assignment is about. I recall one fifth grader who needed help subtracting fractions before she could do her assignment. Another elementary-school child needed to be clear when to use capital and lowercase letters. A high-school junior I worked with had a hard time differentiating sonnets from ballads. If you understand the subject yourself, you may want to work through some examples with your child. But let him do the assignment himself. (If your child can't read yet, the teacher may have sent home instructions that you can read to him.) If your child doesn't understand the instructions, read them with him and talk about the assignment. Make sure that there are no words that he doesn't understand. If there are, help him find out what they mean. If neither you nor your child understands an assignment, call a classmate or contact the teacher.

■ **Do you have everything you need to do the assignment?** Distracted kids often have disorganized book bags and desks. Sometimes your child may need special supplies, such as colored pencils, metric rulers, maps, or reference books. Distracted kids often forget what they have or where they have it. Make sure that your child has all the necessary supplies, and that they are kept in one place for easy access. If you can't provide necessary supplies, check with the teacher, school guidance counselor, or principal for possible sources of assistance. Also, check with the local public library or school library for books and other information resources.

■ **What's the best way to get this done?** Many distracted kids find it soothing to talk through the steps that are required to complete an assignment. Sometimes a written list can help lower anxiety. While he may give you the evil glare, it can help to encourage your child to review his notes (or reread a chapter in his textbook) before he does the assignment.

- **Have you seen problems like these before?** New material is often scary to distracted kids. Obviously, there is no avoiding learning new concepts. Whenever possible, try to anchor your child in a successful mind-set by pointing out times when he has tackled similar problems to those he is facing now.

- **Does your answer make sense to you?** Distracted kids tend to rush through their homework without thinking about it. Teaching your child to stop and think about his responses to homework is important. Coach him to consider if his response to a math problem seems logical. In a similar vein, encourage him to question his own writing. It helps to remind your child that most kids need to check over the math problems or revise paragraphs before they turn them in.

- **Where did you get stuck?** We all hit walls from time to time. But when distracted kids hit them, they often get plastered. Often a child is almost "right there" in terms of getting an assignment done, but then will face an obstacle and get discouraged. Be mindful of this and coach your child to persevere when he can. There is nothing wrong with judiciously helping your child get past a few sticking points. This is far different from enabling his distractibility by doing the assignment for him.

9. Use time, instead of letting time use you and your child.

Many distracted students are no further along after one or two hours than after ten minutes into an assignment. The only thing achieved by allowing a child to linger on, hour after hour, with very little performance is increased feelings of inadequacy. Distracted children feel inadequate enough without adding that to the mix.

Rachel was a parent at her wits' end because most nights her fifteen-year-old son, Phil, dragged out his homework for several hours. Phil was actually quite invested in trying to get his homework done, but he kept getting distracted and lost in the process. I helped Phil feel less threatened when his mother coached him to stop the homework activity when he was not being productive.

Effective clock management can help in many cases. With clock management, you are using the perception of time to motivate rather than demotivate your child to get his homework started and completed. For example, if your sixth grader knows he's expected to spend half an hour doing part of his homework, he may be less likely to rush through assignments so that he can watch television. If you check over his assignment before he watches his show, you can ensure that the work was not done in a slipshod manner and still give him a goal to strive for. A required amount of time to do homework may also discourage your child from "forgetting" to bring home assignments and help him adjust to a routine.

Alternatively, your child may find homework easier to approach if you guide him toward working in fifteen-minute or twenty-minute bursts with breaks in between. Don't be rigid with the time allocated for homework. Do what seems to work best on a given day. Varying time increments may need to be "road tested" in order to determine how best to get moving (and keep moving) down the homework highway.

10. *Monitor, but avoid finishing, assignments for your child.*

I mentioned earlier that you don't want to enable your child's homework avoidance by doing homework for him. I have seen many parents agonize over letting their children work through problems alone and learn from their mistakes. This can lead some parents to complete an entire assignment for their children.

It's not always easy to know where to draw the line between supporting your child's homework effort and enabling his homework avoidance behavior. The last thing you want to teach your child is to shirk responsibility. Doing too much to help your child to finish a difficult assignment may feel good to him, but it's not good for him. In fact, the end result may be very destructive, as enabling your child in this way will only foster increased dependency and feelings of helplessness in your child.

Elementary-school students often like to have someone in the same room when working on assignments, in case they have questions. If your child is cared for by someone else after school, talk to that person about what you expect regarding homework. In my experience, baby-sitters who promote pro-homework vibes are usually helpful in supporting children to complete their assignments. In fact, sometimes taking the parent out of the homework supervisor role can be a very welcome change in family dynamics.

It's usually a good idea to check to see that an elementary-school child has finished his assignments. If a junior high school student has trouble finishing assignments, check his, too. If you're not there when an assignment is finished, look it over when you get home. After the teacher returns completed homework, read the comments to see if your child has done the assignments satisfactorily.

Bearing all of the above in mind, if your child cannot complete assignments, and he has honestly tried, write the teacher a note explaining the circumstances, such as:

- The instructions were unclear.
- You can't seem to help your child get organized to finish the assignments.
- You can't provide the necessary supplies or materials.

- Neither you nor your child can understand the purpose of the assignments.
- The assignments are often too hard or too easy.
- The homework is assigned in uneven amounts—for instance, no homework is given on Monday, Tuesday, or Wednesday, but on Thursday four of your child's teachers all give big assignments that are due the next day.
- Your child has missed school and needs to make up assignments.

Most teachers will understand the situation. If your distracted child has severe learning problems or a high tension level, he may be faced with tremendous frustration, anger, and disappointment. Additional academic support services may be needed. If this seems to be the case, please go back to Day 4 to review the options for more specialized education plans.

11. Use checklists.

Help your child get into the habit of keeping a to-do list. It's very reinforcing to be able to cross tasks off a list. Joe, a ninth grader I worked with, was the epitome of a distracted teen, who made it clear that he didn't "give a crap about homework." We worked together for a while. After I encouraged Joe to get a part-time job as a cashier at a grocery store, Joe soon realized that success in school meant he would not be working at the same store as a cashier in thirty years.

Empowered by his new insights and realizing that there were no pending federal laws to get rid of homework requirements, Joe tried something he had not attempted in the past. He used checklists and realized that crossing off completed items from the list really gave him a sense of accomplishment. Coach your child to use checklists to post assignments, household chores, and reminders about what needs to get done. If the assignment book does not work for your child, he will likely benefit by keeping a small pad or notebook dedicated to listing homework assignments.

12. Keep organized notebooks.

I don't know about you, but when I have a stack of papers or bills, I get pretty overwhelmed. Trust me, your distracted child gets mega-overwhelmed when his backpack or desktop is overflowing. Help your child keep track of papers by helping him sort them out in his binder or notebook. This will help him review the material for each day's classes and organize the material later to prepare for tests and quizzes. Use dividers or color-coded notebooks to separate class notes. Separate "to-do" and "done" folders help organize worksheets, notices, and items to be signed by parents, and provide a central place to store completed assignments.

I encourage you to work with your child to sort through book bags and notebooks on a weekly basis. Old tests and papers should be organized and kept in a separate file at home. I recommend that you keep separate boxes at home for dated assignments, class notes, and tests. One mom I know literally had lockers installed in her kids' rooms for more dated materials.

Whatever the storage method, the contents inside the storage area should be arranged by subject and in chronological order, in case your child has to reference them at some future time. I suggest to kids that they keep them in roughly chronological order, but not to sweat too much about keeping them exactly chronological, since that's too onerous and therefore they won't do it. A pile with older stuff on the bottom is usually good enough. As the child gets older, he can make adjustments to this system. This is a wonderful way for your child to keep his binder organized and current, and not loaded with dated material. The less weighed down his backpack is, the less weighed down your child will feel. It may be helpful to have a teacher oversee the cleaning out of your child's school locker as well.

13. Activities are best when done in moderation and within a routine.

Kids often get scheduled in a bunch of after-school activities (karate, soccer, religious training, and scouts are just a few examples). Also, in this chaotic world, we have electronic communication (TV, phones, and a myriad of other communication devices) impinging on the routines and predictability of home life. To the greatest degree possible, try to establish and stick to a regular dinnertime and a regular bedtime. Routines can be quite soothing. This will help your child fall into a pattern at home. Children with a regular bedtime go to school well rested. Try to limit television watching and computer play to specific periods of time during the day.

14. Keep a master calendar.

Diane, the mother of three children with ADHD and wife of an ADHD husband (what a lucky lady), found tremendous value in keeping a large, wall-sized calendar for the household, listing the family's commitments, schedules for extracurricular activities, days off from school, and major events at home and at school. You can use this method to note dates when your child has big exams or due dates for projects. This will help you keep track of each other's activities and avoid scheduling conflicts. You may find that this helps you keep your sanity, as well.

15. Prepare your child for the day ahead.

Before your child goes to bed, encourage him (in your best calm, firm, and noncontrolling voice) to pack schoolwork and books in his book bag. It also helps if the next day's clothes are laid out with shoes, socks, and accessories. I doubt your sixteen-year-old will go for this, but you get the general idea. Any proactive organizational strategies to manage life will cut down on morning madness and confusion, and allow your child to better prepare for the day ahead.

16. Use a tutor.

If you have the resources to hire a tutor whom your child gets along with, this can be a very helpful aid in the homework process. Certainly, most tutors are used for helping children learn concepts that they can't easily learn at school. At the same time, tutors can also serve to coach your child to power through assignments. Using a tutor also helps mix things up in a positive way by giving your child a break from you as the overseer—and you get a break as well. Some community libraries offer tutoring for free. It may be possible to get free tutoring for your child from the school, as well.

17. Obtain an extra set of textbooks.

As mentioned in "Day 4", having a spare set of textbooks at home can improve your child's homework and studies. Your child's school may be cooperative about this, or they may not. It will depend on your child's school and whether or not they have lots of extra copies and a cooperative attitude. Start by finding out who's responsible for providing the spares. Then contact this individual with a good reason and something to back it up. Allison was a thirteen-year-old seventh grader I worked with, who had a propensity for forgetting books at school. When her father, Marty, requested and obtained an extra set of books, the homework hassles largely ended. What also ended was Marty driving Allison to the school at night and pleading with the janitor on duty to let her in to get to her locker.

ADVICE FOR SECURING AN EXTRA SET OF TEXTBOOKS

As I mentioned in tip 17, every school administration is different and there is no guarantee that your child's school will agree to provide him with a spare set of textbooks. However, there are steps you can take to tip the odds in your favor:

- If your child qualifies for an Individualized Education Plan (IEP) or 504 Plan, request that it be written into his plan that he will receive an extra set of textbooks. This way the school is required by law to provide this accommodation (see "Day 4" for more information on these educational plans).

- If your child is seeing a psychiatrist, psychologist, neurologist, or learning specialist who believes his forgetfulness is a result of his distractibility or a related disability, ask that health-care professional to write a note to the school explaining that your child needs an extra set of textbooks for this reason. Many administrations will agree to hand over extra books in response to a doctor's note.

- If your child has an orthopedic or other health condition that renders a backpack too difficult to carry, ask his doctor to write a note to the school explaining the situation and requesting the extra set of textbooks. Similarly, if your child is frequently absent from school due to medical issues, a note from his doctor can help justify a spare set.

- Lastly, you can try appealing to the school's common sense by explaining that a spare set of textbooks at home will help your child better comply with school assignments or that your child needs them to work with a tutor. For further information on this topic, visit the following Web site: http://specialchildren.about.com/od/schoolstrategies/tp/sparetextbooks.htm

18. Set a good example.

Children are more likely to study if they see you reading, writing, and doing things that require thought and effort. Perhaps you can sit close by and pay your bills or read a book during homework time.

Another way of creating a good example is to talk with your child (when he is not doing his homework) about ways that you successfully manage your own life. It also can help to share your past organizational challenges and difficulties and what you learned from them. The more you share your own foibles and vulnerabilities, the more your child will feel you truly understand where he is coming from and connect with you.

19. Show an interest.

Make time to take your child to the library to check out materials needed for homework (and for fun, too), and read with your child as often as you can. Talk about school and learning activities in family conversations. Ask your child what was discussed in class that day. If he doesn't have much to say, try another approach. For example, ask your child to read aloud a story he wrote or discuss the results of a science experiment.

Another good way to show your interest is to attend school activities, such as parent-teacher meetings, shows, and sports events. If you can, volunteer to help in the classroom or at special events. Getting to know some classmates and other parents not only shows you're interested, it helps build a network of support for you and your child. Encourage activities that support learning—for example, educational games, library visits, walks in the neighborhood, trips to the zoo or museums, and chores that teach a sense of responsibility.

20. Stay on top of long-term assignments.

Remind your child that an elephant far in the distance looks pretty small—but when he's right in front of you, he's a giant. Your child needs to have the same perspective on long-term school assignments.

Teachers generally give students tips on how to prepare for long-term assignments, but it takes time and practice to develop good habits. You can reinforce these habits at home. One way to go about this is to help your child structure time in order to complete assignments. Suppose, for example, that your eighth grader has a book report due in three weeks. You can discuss all the steps he needs to take to complete it on time, including:

- Selecting a topic
- Doing the research by looking up books and other needed resources
- Having the necessary materials on the topic and taking notes
- Figuring out what questions to discuss
- Drafting an outline
- Writing a rough draft
- Revising and completing the final draft

21. Help your child learn to study.

When I got into college, I did not know how to study. At the time, I saw a lot of other students hanging out in their dorm rooms or lounges with highlighters in hand. I'm not sure how much those highlighters helped them, but they did not help me much. I would end up coloring my whole textbook!

It is pretty clear that no one is born knowing how to study. I consider studying being able to actively engage in class material and really digest it and understand it. It is a process that does not have to be learned in one fell swoop. The following pages offer some basic study tips to help you get your child started.

BE A QUICK STUDY ON
GOOD STUDY HABITS

Here is a primer on study skills that should be helpful to pass on to your child. Remember to be calm, firm, and noncontrolling when sharing these with your child. Tailor them as needed to fit your comfort zone and your child's, as well.

MANAGE YOUR CHILD'S TIME

Nothing creates more stress than last-minute cramming for tests. Gloria, a mother of twin eleven-year-old boys with ADHD, found the value in helping her fifth-grade sons study for their social studies tests well before they were given. She coached her sons on how to work out a schedule of what they needed to do. They made up practice tests and wrote down answers to the questions they made up. Here are more ways to help manage your child's time and inspire him to do so as well:

- Use a calendar to keep track of projects, assignments, meetings, exams, and events. Abe found that by using a calendar, he could help Carl, his thirteen-year-old son, look ahead to avoid overwhelming workloads. In fact, their slogan became "Look Ahead to Look Out." As this father and son learned, the key is to spread out the work and avoid crunch time.
- If your schedule permits, use Sunday evenings as a planning time. Work with your child to look at what's

coming in the next week and plan his schedule so he has time to do everything he needs to do.

■ Help your child keep a to-do list with everything ranked in order of importance. Aubrey coached her son, Ethan, to cross off completed work, and each time he did, she and her son did a cathartic high five. So the lesson again here is: don't put off the difficult or important things. If a task looks overwhelming, break it down into smaller pieces and prioritize those, too.

TACKLING TEXTBOOKS AND READING ASSIGNMENTS

Reading assignments can be very intimidating to distracted children. Coaching your child to use the strategies below can help take the sting out of them.

■ Have your child initially scan the title of the chapter and think about what he already knows about the subject.

■ Coach your child to read the introductory paragraph and note what the main idea of the chapter is.

■ Emphasize the value of paying special attention to subheads, anything in bold or italic print, any illustrations and their captions, and the summary and/or conclusions. These will alert him to main themes and important concepts.

■ Another useful strategy is to have your child read any questions at the end of the chapter before he reads the chapter itself. These will tip him off to the major points of the chapter.

- As your child reads through the chapter, have him take notes either in a separate notebook or by using a highlighter and writing notes in the margin. Taking notes will help him focus on the material—this can really level the playing field for distracted children.
- Work with your child to make up practice tests and have him take them. Help your third grader prepare for a spelling test by saying the words while he writes them down. Then have him correct his own test.

Several books and pamphlets listed in the Resources section of this book give more tips on how your child can get organized and develop good study habits.

22. Give encouragement and praise.

People of all ages respond to encouragement and praise. Children need encouragement from the people whose opinions they value most—their parents. No child of any age has ever complained to me that her parents give her too much encouragement and praise. Remember that encouragement reinforces the effort, and praise recognizes the outcome. Both are important.

Here are some samples of encouraging statements:

- "You really tried hard on that math even though you couldn't finish it. I'm proud of you."
- "I know you don't like reading the book you were assigned, but I like how you are trying to tough your way through it."
- "Even though you received a C, you worked your backside off on that project, and I am impressed with all your effort."

Here are some samples of praising statements:

- "Good first draft of your book report!"
- "You did a great job and got your first A this year, fantastic!"
- "You are doing so much better than last year—wonderful!"

Remember that encouragement and praise can go a long way toward motivating your child to complete assignments. Distracted children need your support—big time. Make criticism constructive. Instead of asking your third grader, "You aren't going to hand in that mess, are you?" try saying, "The teacher will understand your ideas better if you use your best handwriting." Then give praise when a neat version is completed.

23. Ensure that the homework gets turned in.

Many distracted children do not turn in their homework—even when it is completed! This makes most parents understandably want to pull their hair out. To keep your sanity, I encourage you to stay in communication with your child's teachers, either through phone calls or e-mails. Communication between teachers and parents is very important to staying on top of and solving homework problems. In some cases, the school guidance counselor may be helpful in resolving such problems.

At one school I worked with, a child was made to stay after school each time he did not get his homework done. This gave the child a choice about where he would do his homework in the future. You guessed it—he chose to start doing it at home. The bottom line is that the more often your child turns in his homework, the better his grades will be. Whether the added accountability comes from you, the school, or both, time and energy put into getting homework turned in are well spent.

24. Request to meet the teacher about continued homework problems.

Tell your child's teacher briefly why you want to meet. It may not be your first meeting at this point, and that's okay. You might say, "Robbie is having trouble with his math homework. I've been trying my best to help him, but I'm worried about why he can't finish the problems and what we might do to help him." Don't go straight to the principal without giving the teacher a chance to work out the problem with you and your child.

Approach the teacher in a cooperative spirit. Believe that the teacher wants to help you and your child, even if you disagree about something. It's hard to solve problems if teachers and parents view each other as enemies. If you have a complaint, try not to put the teacher on the defensive. For example, avoid saying that you think the assignments are terrible, even if you think so. You might say, "I'm glad Calvin is learning to add and subtract in the first grade, but he doesn't want to do his math worksheets. Can we find another way for him to learn the same material?" This might encourage the teacher to let Calvin (and the rest of his classmates) try another approach. Perhaps he can learn addition and subtraction by moving around buttons or shells.

Many times homework can be structured so that a wide range of children will find assignments interesting. For example:

- Different approaches to the same topic or lesson can be offered to students.
- Extra assignments can be given to students who desire more challenge.
- Specialized assignments can be given to students having trouble in a particular area.

While meeting with the teacher, explain what you think is going on. Also tell the teacher if you don't know what the problem is. Sometimes a distracted child's version of what's going on isn't the same as the teacher's version. Be aware that your child, wittingly or unwittingly, may be spinning the facts. For example, your child may tell you that the teacher never explains assignments so he can understand them. But the teacher may tell you that your child isn't paying attention when assignments are given.

Also make sure that communication is clear. Listen to the teacher, and don't leave until you're sure you understand what's been said. Make sure, too, that the teacher understands what you have said. If, after the meeting, you realize you don't understand something, call the teacher to double-check. It may help to summarize what you've agreed to do, at the end of the meeting, as in the following example: *OK, so to keep track of Ken's assignments, I'll check his assignment book each night and write my initials by new assignments. Each day, you'll check to make sure he's written down all new assignments in his book. That way, we'll be certain that I know that his assignments are completed. Am I correct about all this?*

Follow up to make sure that the approach you agreed to is working. If the teacher told you, for example, that your child needs to spend more time practicing writing skills or division, check back in a month to talk about your child's progress.

DAY 5: SUMMING IT UP

Homework is very hard for distracted children to start, stay focused on, and complete. Helping your child with homework is an opportunity to improve your child's chances of doing well in school and in life. By helping your child with homework, you can help him learn important lessons about discipline and responsibility. The younger your child is when you start to do the kinds of activities suggested here, the better. However, it's never too late to get homework under control and make a huge difference in your child's education and life. Please keep the following points about homework in mind:

- Pay attention to the powerful negative emotions (your child's and yours) that can interfere with homework production.
- Be calm, firm, and noncontrolling to reduce homework power struggles.
- Work with your child to encourage and support his homework efforts.
- Stay connected and involved with the school to ensure that homework is a success for your child.
- Whether you succeed in doing all of the activities suggested here is not what's most important. What's most important is that you are willing to take the time and make the effort to be involved in your child's education and help manage his distractibility.

Overcoming Perils with Peers

Anita, **mother of** ten-year-old Eddie, half-jokingly told me that she longed for a return to the play dates of Eddie's toddler years. "They were so much easier and less upsetting," she sighed. Eddie was in fifth grade when I worked with him, and he was having a miserable year. Thanks to his uncontrolled distractibility, impulsiveness, and anger problems, Eddie had alienated himself from all of his peers.

During that first session, Anita shared with me some heartwrenching stories of Eddie's experiences with peers during his elementary-school years. Eventually, through his enrollment in a social skills group and my work with him, Eddie became much more successful in negotiating peer relationships.

While the challenges of making and keeping friends are not easy for any child, distracted children in particular have problems forming and maintaining peer relationships. Distracted children differ from other children in the higher number of misjudgments and inappropriate behaviors they exhibit in social relations. They are also often scattered during conversations and cannot maintain them, leaving peers confused about what they are trying to say. Distracted children who are also hyperactive tend to engage in more teasing and physical jostling of peers. All of these out-of-sync behaviors and social blunders can lead to peer rejection.

Today I focus on helping you understand your child's peer challenges and difficulties. You will learn powerful ideas and strategies to help steer your child toward healthier peer relationships.

Survival of the Socially Fittest

The harsh reality is that peer problems can lead to major difficulties in the life of your distracted child. For example, children with peer problems tend to also be at a higher risk for anxiety, behavioral and mood disorders, substance abuse, and conduct issues as teenagers. The good news, though, is that through modeling helpful skills, being understanding, and acting with compassion, you can help guide your child out of perilous peer relationships and into healthier ones. The following are some representative stories from distracted children I have worked with who have overcome problems with peers.

Brett's Story

Brett is a twenty-one-year-old diagnosed with ADHD, whom I had counseled, along with his family, a few years ago. He came in to see me for a "check in" during a break from college. The young man who sat before me had changed remarkably from when I saw him years ago. In those days, Brett had a serious problem with peer rejection. His poor eye contact, tangential comments and clumsy conversational skills, and his supercharged, enthusiastic way of relating to others made him few friends. But on this day, Brett triumphantly shared with me that he was doing well in college, currently had a girlfriend, and was considering a career in accounting.

Clearly, Brett is quite a success story. However, as we spoke, he reflected on his past, which was very difficult for him. Brett's struggles were largely due to his distractibility, which made getting through school a nightmare. This, in turn, had adversely impacted his peer relationships. Brett told me, "Back then, when I had tests in school, I'd say, 'I don't care about how I do on this,' because I'd thought it would be easier to be seen as 'bad and cool' than stupid. I never realized how this also made me actually look like a loser to so many other kids."

While Brett's experience is common, I have also seen that the converse can be true: children and adolescents with problematic social functioning may find that it affects their academic performance. In these cases, distracted children can become so demoralized about their peer problems that they lose motivation to meet their responsibilities, especially regarding school.

Brett further reflected on his past: "Dr. Jeff, back then I was failing everything. I just did not give a crap about anything—I was lost and down. The kids that also got into trouble were the ones I hung out with because the popular kids didn't accept me. So I got in with the losers, the bad crowd, where I was accepted. I am just glad I got my act together because at one point I thought I might end up in jail." Brett was referring to the time he was caught shoplifting. Fortunately, Brett had very patient and supportive parents, who helped spur his eventual academic and social turnaround. They refused to give up on Brett, and he refused to give up on himself.

Darryl's Story

Darryl, age eleven, had also seen me for counseling. At the time, he was on a community league basketball team. Most distressing for Darryl were his problems focusing on where the ball was—actually, Darryl had a knack for being where the ball wasn't. Suffice it to say, things did not go well on the basketball court, and this spilled over onto Darryl's relationships with his peers on the team. Consequently, Darryl's self-esteem plummeted like a boulder rolling down a mountain. So did his appeal in the eyes of his teammates. Darryl suffered a lot of that painful harassment that eleven-year-olds are so good at dishing out.

Still trying to stick out basketball, one year later Darryl was diagnosed with Tourette's syndrome, an affliction that is characterized by nervous tics (I discuss Tourette's and other coexisting conditions further in "Day 7"). As I probed further into Darryl's peer situation, he said with teary eyes, "The kids on my team suck. I hate them."

During the course of our counseling sessions and with the support of his father, the main custodial parent, things did get better. Darryl also switched his energies from sports to scouting, which seemed to be a better fit. It has been my experience that civic organizations, such as the Scouts, tend to be more accommodating to children with special needs, including distractibility. When Daryl made these attitudinal and logistical shifts in his life, things started to change for the better.

Chelsea's Story

Girls with distraction don't have it any easier than boys. Fourteen-year-old Chelsea struggled with social anxiety during her freshman year in high school. This often left her feeling distracted and at a big social disadvantage. Sitting down to lunch with a table full of girls and not knowing what to say typically escalated her anxiety.

Chelsea shared with me one particularly sad story about eating lunch with her friends in the school cafeteria. She had been feeling unsure of herself socially, yet it seemed that Allison, a girl Chelsea thought she had finally befriended, was being nice to her. On this one day, however, when Allison got up to get a drink, Desiree, a friend of Allison's, sarcastically remarked to Chelsea, "The only reason she's nice to you is because she feels sorry for you." Years ago there was a hit song entitled "Girls Just Want to Have Fun." To that song, based on many similar stories I have heard over the years, I would add the line, "But watch out when the fun is over and they get nasty."

Crushed by this negative experience, Chelsea began skipping lunch by either walking the halls or going to the school library.

This caused her to be written up for disciplinary measures by a rigid assistant principal, which just added insult to injury.

Things started to improve for Chelsea when her parents, her guidance counselor, and I worked together to improve the situation. Chelsea, springboarding from this support and encouragement, took a healthy risk and joined a church social group. With renewed confidence, she toughed it out for the rest of her freshman year at school. While she never fully clicked with the girls at the lunch table, she ended up feeling better about her overall peer situation. Chelsea also learned not to take the snipes, manipulations, and melodrama of her fourteen-year-old peers so seriously.

Austin's Story

I also worked with a thirteen-year-old named Austin, when his parents decided to divorce. Austin began to worry and feel very confused in response to the escalating discord between his parents. These stressful circumstances caused Austin to become distracted and less engaged with his peers. Over the next few months, with the help of counseling, Austin began to accept his parents' dissolving marriage and was able to reconnect with peers.

These stories represent common social ups and downs faced by children plagued by different types of distractions. As soon as you are aware of your child's peer problems and conflicts, it's best to get involved to help support her. Just keep in mind, however, that it's never too late to lend your support to your child at any age. Remember, to survive and thrive in her current world and beyond, it's crucial for your child to learn how to connect well with others.

Signs That Your Distracted Child Has Peer Problems

Listed below are some typical observations and situations common to distracted children with peer concerns. Please read through the list and check off those that apply to your distracted child:

_____ She complains that she has no friends.

_____ She is not invited to birthday parties and social gatherings with classmates and neighborhood children.

_____ She is withdrawn and spends a lot of time by herself (and would prefer to be with peers).

_____ She has difficulty participating in team sports or community group activities.

_____ She has difficulty sustaining silence and composure in movies and events.

_____ She has social difficulties relating to peers in the classroom (as reported by the teacher) or in the neighborhood.

_____ She complains that peers exclude her from recess activities, bully her, or ignore her.

_____ She resents or won't listen to your suggestions (this often occurs when children begin to feel more independent, usually at age nine, ten, or older).

_____ She rarely has friends over.

_____ She's mean to her siblings.

_____ She gets no phone calls.

_____ She begins to dress atypically for her age and group setting.

_____ Her free-time activities seem different from those of her peers.

A Closer Look at Why Distracted Children Have Peer Problems

There are different explanations as to why distracted children tend to have problems with peers. The most obvious and simple explanation, supported by research, is that distracted children have difficulty reading social cues and knowing how to respond to them, because their attention is scattered in many different directions. Occasionally, this happens to everyone. But it repeatedly happens to children who are distracted. Chronically distracted children also tend not to pick up on the social interactions that their parents and peers model, because they aren't paying attention.

For most children, social skills are learned by "osmosis"— through watching how others deal with everyday situations. But with distracted children, who have so many crossed thought signals in their heads, distractibility interferes with the absorption of modeled social skills and/or the ability to apply them. The limited ability distracted children have to "read" their peers renders them less emotionally intelligent.

Distracted Children Often Lack Emotional Intelligence

Research on distracted children shows that they tend to lack something called emotional intelligence. A lack of emotional intelligence is basically a lack of emotional maturity. Psychologist Daniel Goleman popularized the concept of emotional intelligence, which involves our ability to understand, use, regulate, and manage our emotions as key determinants of our life success and happiness.

Emotional intelligence appears to be a key predictor of children's abilities to establish suitable peer relationships, develop well-balanced outlooks on life, and reach their academic potentials at school. The term encompasses the following five characteristics and abilities:

1. **Self-awareness:** Knowing your emotions, recognizing feelings as they occur, and discriminating between them.
2. **Mood management:** Handling feelings so they're relevant to the current situation and you react appropriately.
3. **Self-motivation:** "Gathering up" your feelings and directing yourself toward a goal, despite self-doubt, inertia, and impulsiveness.
4. **Empathy:** Recognizing feelings in others and tuning in to their verbal and nonverbal cues.
5. **Managing relationships:** Handling interpersonal interaction, conflict resolution, and negotiations.

Chances are your distracted child has lower than normal levels of emotional intelligence, which is a big reason that getting along with peers is so difficult for her. Try not to let this discourage or scare you. Just be aware that many of the behaviors you perceive your child "choosing" not to do with peers (e.g., being more self-aware, controlling impulses) may actually be things she is struggling to do. The more your child can learn to work around her emotional immaturities and limitations, the better her chances of forming healthy friendships and keeping them.

Missed Cues Mess Up Relationships

As I mentioned above, because they are often internally preoccupied, distracted children have trouble accurately processing the behaviors and actions of their peers. This leaves them feeling socially disconnected, further rejected, and often dejected. Based on my observations and conversations with over a thousand distracted children and their parents, in my practice, workshops, and seminars, I have some further thoughts on what contributes to the chaotic peer relations of distracted children.

In my first book, *Why Can't You Read My Mind?*, I discussed the way toxic thoughts (e.g., "You always have to be right" or "You're just a selfish husband") create tremendous strain in intimate adult relationships. Toxic thoughts in couples lead to what I term the Three-D Effect: Distraction, Distance, and Disconnect.

The Three-D Effect also seems to contribute to the peer problems of distracted children. Specifically, their distractibility leads them to inaccurately perceive and respond to their peers' words and actions. These misunderstandings lead distracted children to form toxic thoughts about their peers. As you saw in "Day 4" and "Day 5," distracted children tend to make negative and exaggerated associations toward school and homework, as well. While all children have toxic thoughts toward peers to some degree, I have observed that many distracted children frequently view their peer problems in an all-or-nothing, toxic manner (e.g., "I hate her"). This can be a big problem in making and keeping friends.

While all children are in the process of learning how to make and keep friends, and may have some occasional toxic thoughts, the toxic thoughts of distracted children toward their peers can create an unfair disadvantage for them. Distracted children, with their limited ability to focus, have a short fuse and lack the ability and patience to go through the daily ups and downs with friends. So if a distracted child faces a disappointment with a peer—feels that she is not being directly listened to, is being ignored, or is being teased—she is prone to dwelling on or exaggerating this negative event. Examples of the toxic thoughts that distracted children have toward their peers include:

> *"He always has to butt in."*
> *"He is always a jerk to me."*

> *"She is stupid."*
> *"He always gets me in trouble."*
> *"Nobody cares what I think."*

This is a problematic cycle that just continues to get more self-defeating. When distracted children are besieged with toxic thoughts, it further adds to their distractibility. By this I mean that it promotes more confusion and prevents them from making sense of what is happening in their interactions with peers. Let's take a closer look at each "D" in the Three-D Effect.

Distraction

It takes a certain amount of attention for children to think before they talk and act. Attention is also necessary for children to control their expression of emotions. Jody, age ten, was a distracted child who tended to be exuberantly impulsive. She would come on like a freight train, hauling tons of enthusiasm and crashing into her peers, who were never quite ready for her. Jody would blurt out all kinds of emotional reactions when around her peers, some of which were genuinely comical. Yet some of Jody's outpourings caused her to be perceived as weird among her fledgling friendships. When this happened, Jody, prone to having a short fuse like many distracted children, would go toxic and convince herself to "hate" her friends.

Your child may get distracted by toxic thoughts about peers, if one or more of the following statements apply to what happens in her peer conflicts:

_____ She ends up arguing about something other than the original problem or issue.

_____ She cannot accurately remember why arguments started.

_____ She unfairly labels the peer negatively (e.g., "He is a jerk").

_____ She feels like a victim and fails to see her role in the conflict.

_____ She says things she later regrets.

_____ She uses phrases like "you always/never/should."

_____ She exaggerates or accuses peers of exaggerating the situation or problem.

_____ She ends up using bad argument behavior, such as screaming, blaming, name-calling, or cursing.

_____ She has a short fuse and blows up quickly with peers.

_____ She is unable to simply discuss problems—it always turns into an argument.

These problematic peer interactions can lead to poor adjustment. Take the case of nine-year-old Timmy. On the playground, he would often misread the cues of other children and yell at them. Consequently, Timmy thought he was being teased—all the time. One loyal friend did not initially reject Timmy, but after repeated negative interactions, he too refused to play with him. Timmy was brought to me because he did not understand why this child, and others, refused to play with him. My first priority was to supportively challenge Timmy's view that he was teased twenty-four hours a day, seven days a week. Through role-plays and coaching with me, and a school-based social skills group that provided support, Timmy was able to understand how he unwittingly sabotaged his friendships. He also learned to channel his frustrations to me, his family, his school guidance counselor, and his supportive teacher, rather than acting them out on the playground.

Interactions with peers are very complex and require many different abilities. Your child needs support in developing the ability to correctly observe others. She needs guidance to best interact with the varying styles of other kids. She will also benefit from gaining tolerance to frustration and the maturity to compromise and share.

Consider another example of a distracted child I worked with who had social challenges. Ted, age fifteen, impulsively and wrongfully accused his friends of stealing his money. As exemplified by this situation, he found that his limited ability to control his anxiety and reactions was a detriment to his peer relationships. He turned his best friends into his enemies, which resulted in his being ostracized. Bewildered, Ted sat in my office complaining that his friends "all suck and are stupid." Falling prey to these distorted, toxic thoughts, Ted became distracted by this line of thinking and lost his ability to appreciate the good times with his friends.

The above examples show how both Jody and Ted, locked in their own separate toxic-thought-laden peer struggles, let their distorted perceptions lead them to have inaccurate, unfavorable emotional reactions to their peers. When I worked with these children individually and managed to get through their hurts and defensiveness, I was not surprised to hear them say things like "Nothing I do is right" and "I can't get anyone to like me." When distracted children get mixed up in their thinking about peers and become frustrated, it drives them to become increasingly distant from their peers as well.

Distance

When distracted children start to feel that they are not clicking well with peers, they tend to distance themselves. Most of us know what it is like to feel socially disconnected and rejected. It really stinks. It is natural to try to avoid further rejection and hurt. So it makes sense that when distracted children associate their peers with pain, they start to avoid them. While the distance may feel safer to the distracted child, it will put her at even more of a social disadvantage because she is missing opportunities for more positive interactions.

Let's briefly go back to the approach/avoidance model that I discussed in "Day 5" regarding homework resistance. If you recall, the approach/avoidance model accounts for rivaling positive and negative pulls on a child's motivation to do certain things. With regard to peer involvement, if your child begins to suffer rejection, then she will begin to believe that the pleasure of peer interaction (approach) is outweighed by the unpleasantness (avoidance). Simply put, in the minds of many distracted children, it is easier (and safer) to avoid peers than to engage with them.

Unfortunately, distracted children who distance themselves socially tend not to be missed by their peers. This is because their peers tend to welcome the break from what has been for them a difficult relationship.

Kenny, age twelve, began distancing himself from peers. His escape was video games, which he became more and more involved with as a result of his difficulties connecting face-to-face with friends. Kenny's father urged him to go out and play football with the neighborhood kids each day after school. Unfortunately, the more that Kenny's father pushed him, the more Kenny soothed himself by playing video games. I had a counseling session with Kenny and his father separately, and then I saw them together in a follow-up session. Kenny's father's expectations became more realistic and Kenny became more successful at making friends. For example, Kenny found that he did better when inviting a friend over to shoot baskets, instead of joining the frenzy of a pickup neighborhood football game.

Disconnect

If enough distance occurs in a distracted child's peer relationships, she runs the risk of becoming altogether disconnected. Fourteen-year-old Briana was quite emotionally wounded and depressed by her social failures. Diagnosed with writing-related learning disabilities and ADHD, Briana also had poor academic achievement. During our first session, Briana showed up with her parents, and her eyes were glued to the floor. Dressed in black, with black eyeliner and black nail polish, Briana both appeared and seemed trapped in darkness.

As Briana got to know me, she began to loosen up a bit. When she discussed some of her problems with friends, she seemed to feel a sense of relief that I did not cast judgment on what she shared with me. Unbeknownst to her parents, Briana had been starting to smoke marijuana shortly before she was brought in to see me. To her credit, she soon stopped doing this once she began to trust me. Her peer struggles did not make a miraculous turnaround, but they did get better.

Remember that all children struggle socially. Distracted kids may find social situations even more challenging due to their limited abilities to accurately process their interactions with others as they occur. Misreading others, lower emotional intelligence, and toxic thoughts toward peers don't have to spell social gloom and doom for your distracted child. The good news is that these issues can be compensated for and overcome, and I am excited to show you how.

What You Can Do to Help

I know that a lot falls on your shoulders as the parent of a distracted child. You have been managing the stress of trying to keep your cool with your child, preserving (or trying to establish) family harmony, and helping your distracted child with school issues and homework.

Now that I am asking that you consider coaching her social life and creating strategies for this arduous endeavor, your first reaction may be to want to toss this book in the fireplace. But before you do that, understand that your child can't break her peer rejection cycle unless she learns some new ways to relate to others and conduct herself. If you use the ideas and strategies presented in this chapter, it will help your child take a huge step forward in her social functioning.

As I emphasized in "Day 2" and throughout this ten-day program, it's very important to understand your distracted child. Truly understanding your child is a wonderful way to build her self-esteem. As you seek to help your child have more success with peers, it's crucial for her to feel good and confident about herself. The more she likes herself, the more secure she will feel with others and the less self-destructively attention-seeking she will be.

Building Your Child's Self-Esteem

As I have been saying throughout this ten-day program, it's easy for distracted kids to feel that they're always in trouble and that no one—not even Mom or Dad—likes them. Let your child know that—in addition to loving her—you like her and are always there to understand her. This may make it easier for her to share her positive qualities with others. Check out the following pointers to learn powerful ways to build your child's self-esteem:

Love your child unconditionally.

Accepting your distracted child regardless of her strengths and weaknesses is crucial for expressing unconditional love to her. As I have said before, no child or even adult has ever complained to me about being overvalued or overloved. While your child's distractibility may have led you to find some of her choices and behaviors disappointing, make it clear that you are never disappointed in her as a person. It's important that your negative reactions to your child's experiences do not convey negative feelings about her as a total person.

I recall working with Russell, a high-school junior, who erroneously felt that his parents thought he was a "loser, failure, and not worth anything" because he had failed Spanish that year. Counseling sessions helped Russell realize that, while his parents were concerned that he failed Spanish, he was still loved and respected as their son.

Foster success by setting your child up to succeed.

Too often, children with distraction problems have a sense of failure—at home, at school, and with peers. Tragically, their many competencies and talents can go unrecognized and undervalued, as a result.

Allow your child to accept herself by showing that you accept who she is, including her strengths and weaknesses. Explore your child's interests and successes in academics, and her athletic, artistic, and musical abilities. One eleven-year-old girl with whom I worked had problems connecting with peers at school, but she was talented in the junior orchestra. Her mother wisely used this opportunity to host some orchestra-related get-togethers at their home, and the girl began to make some new friends.

Create emotional safety to empower your child.

Keep the message consistent and strong to your child that she does not have to worry about losing the security of your understanding and acceptance. I know I've said it before, but I cannot emphasize enough that being understanding toward your child is one of the most precious gifts you can give her. This will encourage her to pursue new activities and opportunities for self-development.

While you should not push too hard, you can certainly provide new opportunities and encourage positive exploration of new subject areas and activities that interest your child. Many children have expressed to me how grateful they are for their parents being open and accepting of their needs. One example from my practice is Aaron , whose father was a retired professional athlete. Aaron's dad did a fantastic job of supporting Aaron's zestful foray into theater programs and celebrated this with pride. Aaron's artistic talents took his father into a world other than the one he knew, but to his immeasurable credit, Aaron's father understood that it would not be wise or supportive to impose his preexisting ideas of what his son *should* do. Always keep in mind that what you may find stimulating and exciting may not be viewed the same way by your child.

Be mindful of how you speak.

Words really are quite powerful. As adults, we can attest to the power of the words of our parents—for better or worse. Try to keep in mind that using caring words is crucial to your child's self-esteem.

Children love to hear phrases that build self-esteem, such as "Thank you for helping" or "That was an excellent idea." I have found that with my own three children, expressing these common courtesies creates a true sense of cooperation and mutual respect. At the same time, monitor your parental frustrations so you don't use negative phrases that decrease self-esteem, such as "How many times have I told you . . . ?" or "Why did you do such a stupid thing?" These ways of relating are far from self-esteem boosters. In fact, they leave a toxic, indelible mark on your child's self-perceptions.

Encourage exploration to increase concentration.

Encourage your child to be creative by exploring interests that are fun and engaging. The more your child learns to explore the world around her, the less trapped or frustrated she will feel by her distractibility. Offer avenues for her to explore her interests, such as sports for her often boundless energy. Visit ice rinks or fun amusement parks, or go on field trips to libraries, museums, or bookstores. You can enhance concentration and promote turn-taking through new small-group activities like card games, board games, tennis, or golf.

Promote discipline and focus by pursuing other activities that kids of your child's age do, like karate or dance classes. Also, while many distracted kids tend not to be fans of required school reading, many do like pleasure reading. Whatever the interest area, talk with your child and take part in her excitement about what she is doing, reading, and thinking.

Have realistic expectations and goals for your child.

When you repeatedly expect more than your distracted child can do, she will repeatedly feel disappointed—and she'll perceive that you feel the same way. Sadly, she will eventually internalize the image of herself as a disappointment. Keep your expectations of your child realistic. This goes a long way toward encouraging her to set realistic goals for herself. The more your child can develop realistic goals and achieve them, the more she will start to believe in herself, and up goes her sense of self-worth.

Sixteen-year-old Leo worked with me because he idolized both his mother and father, and yet he felt very inadequate in their eyes. His father was a highly successful architect, and his mother headed up a large organization. Leo had a very difficult time keeping up with his classes at school. Despite his best efforts, C's and a few scant B's were usually what he achieved. Leo's father could not relate to this lower level of achievement. His mother was a bit more understanding, although Leo's flagging grades also created high levels of tension in her.

As it turned out, Leo took a part-time job at a restaurant and decided that he really liked working with the chef. The chef took an instant liking to Leo and saw him as his new apprentice. Once Leo identified this interest, he changed his high-school curriculum to prepare for cooking as a career. Leo's father had a hard time initially accepting that "my son will never be a doctor or a lawyer." However, in time, his parents' acceptance grew—and so did Leo's self-esteem.

Be a positive role model yourself.

Let your child know that you feel good about yourself and that you can make mistakes and learn from them. At the top of your "doing the right thing" list can be showing your child how to do the right thing. Liberally provide her with opportunities to demonstrate basic judgment and moral values (respect, kindness, sharing).

One teenager I worked with was impressed that his mother accidentally broke a mirror and told the truth when she returned it to the department store. Interestingly, this young man had a friend whose mother, only a few months earlier, had lied to the clerk when returning an item that she had damaged. So look for opportunities to model appropriate behavior when engaging others, and demonstrate how to constructively solve problems when they arise.

Be involved, to show your child that she is important.

Let your child know that what she does is important to you. Talk with your child daily about her day's activities, interests, and schoolwork. This really makes a wonderful contribution to her self-esteem. Do the best you can to attend your child's athletic events, parents' day at school, musical concerts, and award ceremonies. Be available to support her and her chosen activities. Even if your child just grunts, gives you an eye roll, or does not wave back at you, rest assured that she values your being there.

I recall a situation where a father made a more determined effort to become involved in the activities of his children. Though it took a while for her to admit it to him, this man's ten-year-old daughter told me how much she valued her father's attendance at her gymnastics meets. No adults I know have ever complained about having parents who were too interested and involved in their lives while they were growing up.

Twenty-Two More Ways to Help Your Child Get Along Better with Peers

Here are twenty-two easy-to-apply strategies for promoting success in your child's peer relationships. These tips come from the trenches—from distracted children and their parents with whom I have worked over the past twenty years. Don't worry about getting immediate results. The less you focus on changing your child and the more you focus on giving her your best supportive efforts, the sooner true changes will occur.

1. Model and encourage good listening.
So much of good social connection comes from good listening. Listening is a skill that will be invaluable to your child in her peer relationships. A fifteen-year-old girl I worked with named Becky learned firsthand the power of listening. After hearing her victim-laden war stories about why girls her age were rotten, I encouraged her to do one simple strategy as consistently as possible, going forward. This was to talk less and listen more when she was with peers. Becky was shocked to see how harnessing the power of listening helped her develop closer and more dependable relationships. It also helped her avoid getting sucked into the ever-shifting and volatile cliques that adolescent girls tend to form. Make listening worthwhile in your child's eyes by reinforcing its benefits: having more friends, and being more aware of things going on around her.

2. Teach your child what interferes with good listening.

Below are some of the key obstacles to listening that are common to distractible children. Review these and share them in conversations with your child.

- **Interrupting others:** Explain how interrupting can leave others feeling dismissed and resentful of not being heard.
- **Dominating conversations:** Share with your child that talking about herself too much is a huge turnoff. Remind your child to ask her peers questions about themselves. One creative parent I worked with coached his son to talk less by using a stopwatch to give a concrete lesson on how "less is more."
- **Talking too loudly or shouting:** Discuss how talking too loudly can leave peers feeling uncomfortable. Another innovative parent I knew crafted a paper plate with a volume dial, to playfully remind her child to "practice turning down her volume." This parent wisely gained permission from her daughter to coach her in this way.
- **Going overboard with too many negative comments or put-downs:** Help your child understand that if she can't think of something positive to say to a friend, it's best not to say anything at all. Stress the value of complimenting others. Middle-school years are particularly fraught with kids teasing each other. Distracted kids often have a difficult time knowing when enough is truly enough. Discuss this important issue with your child in a calm, firm, and noncontrolling manner.
- **Getting mad when others won't do things her way:** Talk to your child about the importance of slowing down and taking a deep breath if something occurs that disappoints her. Teach her to use words to express her feelings about what's happening, instead of lashing out physically or running away. Remind her of the importance of listening to and trying out peers' ideas. Most

importantly, share the all-important insight that your child is in charge of how she feels—no one *makes* her feel any particular way. In "Day 7," I discuss the cognitive therapy techniques I use with children to drive home this important point.

3. Reinforce respect.

Remind your child about the importance of being respectful to others, and demonstrate this behavior yourself. One of the ways children learn to show respect for others is by observing their parents. Be willing to look at how you handle disagreements. How do you address people? Do you talk negatively behind the backs of others? Do you unfairly blame others for your difficulties?

Remember that children learn what they live. Even if their peers show less than acceptable levels of respect, never discount how deeply your actions and values will penetrate to your child's core. Having heard many adults reflect back on their childhoods, I can assure you that your values are the ones that will stick in your child's mind in the long run.

4. Promote accountability.

Children need to learn to be accountable for their actions, especially if they have distraction issues. Acknowledge your child when she recognizes actions and words that are inappropriate. If she does not recognize her inappropriate behaviors, ask her some guiding questions to help her figure things out. For example, you could say, "Do you think that yelling at your friend when you were disappointed in the soccer game was the best way to handle your frustration?"

Don't get emotionally hooked if your child is initially defensive as you help guide her. Just supportively explain why a certain tactic is unlikely to get a good result. Empathize that friendships are not easy. Keep it human and share some of your past social challenges and victories—and stress how you learned from mistakes you owned up to. It may also be helpful to constructively use examples of well-known third parties—for example, athletes, musicians, politicians, and adults in your community who show accountability and a commitment to improve themselves.

5. Model to your child how to apologize.

Too often, distracted children, who may repeatedly make the same mistake because of their learning challenges, get defensive and refuse to apologize. Remind your child that she does not have to be perfect and that appropriate apologies are the right thing to do. Start by encouraging her to apologize when appropriate. Then rehearse how to deliver the apology sincerely and effectively. Praise her for progress, and point out how she can continue to improve.

6. Remember that less is more.

Your distracted child will likely have more success with peers if her contact with them is brief. Distractible kids whose social skills are lacking often don't pay attention to how others are reacting. Therefore, distractible kids tend to do better with fewer peers to focus on at once. Sometimes social activities with only one or two peers are most successful.

I recall a ten-year-old boy I worked with who tended to have social difficulties when he spent extended periods of time with peers. His parents gradually steered him toward more afternoon get-togethers than sleepovers. Follow the same gradual progression with your own child. Once things improve, expand very gradually to a larger group of peers and longer durations, in order to build on her success.

7. Role-play and/or discuss difficult situations.

Younger children (under age ten) tend to do better with role-plays than older kids. I have seen that for children over ten years old, open discussion usually works well.

One issue that is important to address with your child is rejection by others—this, of course, is inevitable for all of us. Distracted children, however, may encounter it on a more frequent basis. Coach your child about the challenging social settings she might face, and help her come up with ideas about what to do about them. For example, if your child finds herself sitting off to the side while kids are playing, help her practice asking, "Can I play, too?" in a low-key manner. Even though it may feel uncomfortable, role-playing these scenes will help your child start to feel more confident in social settings. Also, talk with your child about how to handle positive and negative outcomes. It's not easy to prepare your child to respond to rejection, but learning to cope when things don't go her way is an important social skill.

You should also keep in mind that popular wisdom suggests that it's most helpful to problem-solve, role-play, and discuss concerns right after a difficult situation has occurred. You know, strike while the iron is hot. But I encourage you to be cautious and go slow. Your child is likely rife with negative emotions. Wait until your child is calm and in control. Talk things over and break down the social interaction into smaller parts. Try to focus on one behavior at a time, to maximize success. When you try to help your child problem-solve social situations that have gone awry, keep these guidelines in mind:

Be as clear and concrete as possible. Go over what happened and why it was problematic. If possible, do this not just for your child, but also for the other children or adults who were involved. Don't promote playing the blame game. It's important not to blame anyone for botched social interactions, including your child.

Brainstorm and role-play with your child other ways that she could behave. This helps your child learn to be proactive if such a situation comes up again. Practice saying and doing things with different tones of voice and with appropriate body language. Throw in a few unexpected things that other children might do or say, to see if she can come up with socially acceptable responses. Discuss the pros and cons of solutions she comes up with. For example, one brawny thirteen-year-old I worked with soon realized that if he physically intimidated peers, it did not end his being harassed—it just invited more kids to gang up on him. He also found that it caused the kids to be more passive-aggressive, trashing him behind his back. To this young man's credit, he decided that a more effective response to obnoxious peers was simply to consistently say "whatever," in a minimally reactive tone.

Keep practicing. A one-time effort is not likely to stick. I encourage all children I work with to keep being proactive. This means to keep talking about social ups and downs and to repeat role-plays, for those kids who are willing. This gives distracted children something specific to focus on and helps them to stop feeling like a victim in the face of judgmental, manipulative peers.

8. Stay connected and informed by networking with other parents.

The more you ask and stay mindful of what is going on in your child's social world, the more apprised you'll be of how she is doing. Parents of other children may have valuable, constructive input about your child, but they may be reluctant to volunteer it, for fear of offending you. Unfortunately, I have seen many hypervigilant parents be too easily threatened and overreactive to the well-meaning feedback of other parents.

Too often, I have seen this result in strained relationships between parents who end up ignoring one another (not exactly the best modeling of working through conflict). The less defensiveness, and the more grace and dignity you convey in support of your child, the more other adults will rally to support her. Communicate with other parents, sports coaches, and other involved adults about any progress or problems that may develop with your child.

9. Facilitate flexible social connections.

As you use your positive connections with other parents, try to find out how peers perceive your child. If your child had a group of friends whom she no longer "hangs with," try to find out what went wrong. To make things easier all the way around, don't encourage your child to dress or act in the extreme. Try to keep your child involved in social activities that kids pursue, like bowling, movies, board-game playing, ice skating, or other sports. Engaging your child in any of these types of activities will enhance her confidence, abilities, and composure.

You should supervise your child's activities with other kids, at least tangentially. Try to find ways of structuring get-togethers with kids you feel positive about. Minimize contact with kids you feel are negative influences on your child. Look for activities with kids with solid social skills. Help your child see the negative repercussions of being with children with aggressive behaviors or poor social skills. Your distractible child may have a proclivity toward relationships with peers who have a negative influence, so stay aware of what is going on in your child's world. The less forceful and the more calm, firm, and noncontrolling you are, the better able you will be to lead your child away from unrewarding, destructive relationships.

10. Be mindful of other adult influences.

Stay tuned in to how teachers, school counselors, after-school activity leaders, health-care providers, and religious leaders relate to your child. Discreetly inform them, in a proactive manner, of your child's social challenges. When possible, ask them to help your child improve her peer relationships. For example, one Boy

Scout leader I knew unwittingly made some jokes about a distracted child in front of his peers. The peers then started teasing this child. The lesson here is that if the adult in charge belittles the child (wittingly or unwittingly), the other children will think it's okay for them to belittle the child as well.

11. Teach your child to delay gratification.

There is no doubt we live in a "I want it yesterday" world. As I have mentioned earlier, soothing oneself in a healthy way is an important skill, especially in this increasingly fast and demanding time. Distracted children, regardless of outside influences, tend to be impatient. To the best degree you can, coach your child about the value of earning rewards over time. This will serve her well in life. Explain to your child the importance of working toward and completing a specific task or goal, and the feeling of accomplishment this will give her.

12. Involve your child in activities with her peers that work best for her.

Many distractible children do well with structure in their daily routines, so look for a class or program that interests your child and meets consistently. Find an activity your child really likes and support her efforts. Stay mindful that distraction-prone children tend to do better in small groups of people than in large groups. For example, an art class of eight students that meets every Wednesday at 3:00 PM may suit a child with ADHD better than a soccer team of twenty kids that practices on Tuesday at 6:00 PM and Friday at 3:00 PM, and holds games on random weekends.

13. Look for a social skills group geared toward your child.

There is a saying that "Birds of a feather flock together." I have seen many children with similar types of problems caused by distractibility learn crucial social skills in well-facilitated groups. These group experiences can provide a hands-on forum for your child to practice connecting with other children. Over recent years, I have seen social skills groups being offered in more and more communities, and they can help your child learn how to act in social settings. Some schools teach social skills to elementary and even middle-school students. You may want to bring up the idea of sponsoring such an after-school project to the guidance counselor, principal, or PTA.

In short, social skills groups provide a safe setting for children to practice new behaviors and get feedback from their peers about how successfully they do it. Groups can also be very helpful if your child resents or won't listen to your suggestions, which often occurs when children begin to feel more independent, at age nine, ten, or older.

Social skills groups are designed to help children develop a repertoire of behavior and language skills through repetition. As I wrote this chapter, the mother of an eleven-year-old boy I worked with sent me a highly complimentary report from the facilitator of a social skills group her son recently attended. This child had a fantastic experience! He learned to give others a chance in conversational exchanges, to direct conversation more to peers than adults, to share his personal frustrations with the group, and to listen to suggestions from others.

Many children attending these programs have then been referred to me for individual sessions, to review and further practice their newly learned social skills. I have also guided children as they encountered victories and setbacks when applying the social skills in the real world with peers.

14. Encourage good grooming and hygiene.
It's important for your child to take care of her daily hygiene. It may sound incredible, but many parents I have worked with have

found themselves in power struggles with their children over taking showers and brushing teeth. But persistence pays off, and good hygiene is important for all children. Kids who continue to resist basic hygiene will likely suffer strong negative feedback from peers, despite any social skills they are taught.

15. Help your child anticipate what to expect—and what's expected of her—at social gatherings.

It's always helpful to prime the pump before submerging your child into the ever challenging waters of social interaction. Whether she is headed to a friend's birthday party or to a family wedding, give her a preview of who'll be there and what might happen. Reinforce the simple rules of social etiquette. For example, your child may need to be told: Join in the group activity. Let the kid hosting the party open his own presents. Wait your turn.

Talk to your child about what she is likely to enjoy or fear at the event. If you're upbeat about it, she will look forward to going. This is particularly important for children with distraction problems, who often act inappropriately when they are in overstimulating or new situations that make them anxious.

16. Give a signal.

If you directly observe your child interacting with peers or anyone in a manner that is not befitting, you may want to give her a signal to guide her back on track. A subtle hand motion, wink of your eye, or nod of your head can help do the trick. One mother with whom I worked, Rachel, effectively used a yawn gesture to let her ten-year-old daughter, Becky, know to slow down and not come on so strong with others.

17. Reward your child for solid social behaviors.

As I said earlier in this program, and will emphasize even more in "Day 8," encouragement and praise are valuable tools you can use to reinforce your child's appropriate decisions and behaviors. I have found that children like to hear about what they did well with peers. This is especially the case for distracted children, who so often receive negative feedback about their social blunders. The more you highlight your child's social successes, the more likely your child will be to continue behaviors that will help her fit in socially.

18. Allow your distracted child to play with a child a year or two younger.

Given that distracted children have some lags in emotional intelligence, they may feel comfortable with peers who are younger. I have seen this be a positive experience for many children. One thirteen-year-old boy I worked with forged a healthy friendship with a new neighbor who was eleven. In this case, the friendship allowed the older child to function in a leadership role (recommending new video games to play and coaching the younger boy when practicing baseball pitching). However, you should encourage some interaction with same-age peers as well.

19. Listen to and learn from your child's input.

Your child may or may not be able to describe why she doesn't like playing with a particular friend. One overzealous father pushed football on his very resistant nine-year-old son. The father learned quickly that he was the one who fumbled by asking his son to be something that he wasn't.

I also encourage you never to force friendships on your child. If your child says she doesn't like someone, take a break from play dates (for younger children) and hanging out times (for older children) for a while, unless you're willing to be very involved during the time they spend together. If you've observed her play, you may be able to ask her how she felt, by reconstructing an incident you witnessed.

20. Ask school staff for help.

Let the teacher and playground supervisors know that you're trying to address your child's social skills, and ask for their input on how you can work together. If you're working with a psychologist, or your child is attending a social skills group, ask the professional with whom you're working for suggestions on what information and recommendations to share with school staff. I have found it invaluable to personally connect with guidance counselors, teachers, and other educators involved with the kids I see in my psychology practice. These professionals spend six hours a day with these kids and have much wisdom to offer me.

21. Encourage social coaching at school.

Give your child's teacher the green light, if she is willing, to guide your child in her social connections. The school guidance counselor can also help this cause. If your child seems to have trouble reading social cues—body language, tone of voice, timing, and the like—the teacher or guidance counselor may discreetly offer specific and explicit advice, as a sort of social coaching. For example, the teacher might say, "Before you tell your story, ask to hear your friend's permission first," or "He would appreciate it if you look at him when he's talking." You can emphasize to the teacher that many children with distractibility are viewed as indifferent or selfish, when in fact they just haven't learned how to interact properly.

22. Give your child regular feedback about her off-putting habits and behavior.

The younger your child is, the easier it will be for you to give her guidance on how to be accepted by others. As children approach the middle-school years, they are much less receptive to your input, unless you've worked hard to develop an easy rapport with them. Again, this is where being calm, firm, and noncontrolling can help you bypass your child's defensive posturing.

In this spirit of supportive feedback, if your child picks at her nose or acne, or scratches her private parts inappropriately, you should point it out, but not in a shaming manner. The more your child trusts you and hears positive feedback as well as negative, the more she will let you bring up what may be a delicate subject. Remember that there's a fine line between reminding your child of what's appropriate and nagging. Always convey to your child that you appreciate her willingness to receive your feedback.

DAY 6: SUMMING IT UP

Today you have learned about your distracted child's social challenges and what to do about them. Your child's successes with peers are very important. Keep the following points in mind as you continue to support your child's healthy peer relationships:

- Distractible children, who are often internally preoccupied, have a harder time effectively reading the cues of their peers, teachers, and others.
- Parents often want distractible children to direct their energy toward getting good grades and staying out of trouble. Yet helping your distracted child make friends is important and vital to her socialization and overall success.
- The more understanding you are about your child's social challenges, the more likely she will be to follow your advice and encouragement.
- With your support and coaching, your child can build lasting friendships, and in doing so, she will feel better about herself.

Conquering
Coexisting Conditions

Y ou have worked hard since Day 1 to help your child reduce his distractibility. I want to congratulate you on your effort and your dedication to following this ten-day program. By applying these suggestions and strategies in earnest, you will soon see some positive results, and that's a wonderful thing. After all, a less distracted child means less stress for you!

I have asserted throughout this book that, regardless of the underlying cause of your child's distractibility, the strategies in this ten-day program will be effective. However, you may not be seeing the results you are hoping for yet. Or perhaps you're concerned that your child has more problematic distractibility than you anticipated. If this is the case, it's possible that your child suffers from one or more other conditions that are also fueling his distractibility.

Today you will learn about some mental health conditions in children that can co-occur with, and often exacerbate, distractibility. Some of these conditions, such as ADHD, which I discussed in "Day 1," can be either causes of distractibility, co-occurring conditions, or both. For this reason, these conditions are mentioned on both days. (However, since I discussed ADHD in detail in "Day 1," I will not repeat the information here.) I will also briefly discuss some other health conditions that can make lowering distractibility in children more challenging. Understanding the mental and physical health difficulties that can negatively impact your child will enable you to seek out the appropriate help, if needed.

As with all the information in my ten-day program, the knowledge provided to you here is educational in nature. Please bear in mind that the formal diagnosis and treatment of any mental health conditions, including those described in this section, should be made by a qualified mental health professional.

Identifying Coexisting Conditions

By now, it's very clear that distractibility is a challenge for your child to manage. At the same time, there are a number of common conditions that can exist along with, and worsen, distractibility in children. These are called coexisting conditions. I encourage you to keep in mind that every child is different, and that the severity and impact of all coexisting conditions can vary from case to case. In some cases, I have seen kids with several symptoms from more than one condition mixed in with their distracted behavior. But even if your child falls into this challenging category, don't get discouraged. Being patient and employing the calm, firm, and noncontrolling approach and strategies described in this ten-day plan can make the situation much more workable for you and your child.

My hope is that the following information will be useful to you. However, the last thing I want is for you to end up with what I call "vicarious medical student syndrome." Medical students (and overly curious laypeople) have been known to start believing that they have medical problems once they learn about them. Similarly, parents sometimes start to believe that their kids have an illness or disorder after they've read about it. If you suspect your child has one of these conditions, make an appointment with his doctor and let *him* make a diagnosis.

At the same time, the following information may help you see and understand some obstacles that your child faces, of which you have been unaware. Keep in mind that these are only conceptual classifications. In the same way that each distracted child has his own individual strengths and weaknesses, each of these conditions affects children uniquely. And again, even if you suspect that your distracted child has one or more of these problems, rest assured that they can usually be effectively managed. The list of concerns and conditions that can co-occur with distractibility includes:

- Learning disabilities
- Depression or bipolar disorder
- Anxiety
- Health problems such as allergies, gastrointestinal problems, migraine headaches, and sleep disorders
- Oppositional defiant disorder and lesser forms of defiant behavior
- Drug and alcohol abuse
- Asperger's disorder
- Tourette's syndrome
- Stresses such as the arrival of a new sibling, school pressures, peer conflicts, divorce, and relocation

Learning Disabilities (LDs) Are Distracting and Disruptive

All children, even those not plagued with problematic distractibility, can occasionally have problems in school. But there is a huge difference between a child struggling with a particular subject or teacher and a child struggling because he has a certified learning disability. This section addresses some of the general considerations about learning disabilities you should keep in mind. As I have mentioned before, school problems tend to cause a cycle of failure, especially in distracted children, who have a difficult time recovering when schoolwork is neglected or missed. When a learning disability is occurring alongside other distractibility problems, the result is usually more chaos and despair. Further complicating matters, if the learning disability is not addressed, your child may not get the help he needs, his self-esteem will plummet, and as a result he will put forth even less effort.

Earlier, I touched on the fact that some conditions can cause distractibility, co-occur with distractibility and worsen it, or both. For many distracted children, an underlying learning disability is one of those conditions. In many kids, it can be very difficult to determine whether a learning disability causes distractibility or coexists with it.

What we do know is that research has shown that between 5 and 10 percent of kids between the ages of six and seventeen have learning disabilities. More than half of the kids receiving special education in the United States have learning disabilities. For this reason, I have encouraged the parents of many distractible children to have their child undergo educational testing to determine if learning disabilities are part of the problem. The good news is that if a child is found to have a learning disability, the right educational interventions can help him overcome this problem.

Learning disabilities, like ADHD, have a neurological basis. They are disorders that affect the ability to understand or use spoken or written language, do mathematical calculations, coordinate movements, or direct attention (see "Day 1" for a list of descriptions of common learning disabilities). Children with learning disabilities often require the services available through the special education system. As I discussed in "Day 4," there are educational provisions provided through schools to help children with diagnosed learning disabilities. Special education is specially designed instruction to meet a child's unique needs. This instruction may include intensive remediation in reading, math, or other areas of need. In some cases, it can also include services such as psychological counseling, physical and occupational therapy, speech and language services, transportation, and medical diagnosis.

Sixteen-year-old Julie has an inattentive form of ADHD and was diagnosed with dyslexia in seventh grade. As you may recall, inattentive ADHD symptoms represent the key problems faced by distractible children as a whole: careless mistakes in schoolwork, losing schoolwork and homework, trouble paying attention in class, difficulty listening when spoken to by teachers, and failure to follow instructions and finish schoolwork.

With regard to her dyslexia, Julie recalled with me that fateful day in sixth grade when it really hit her that she was different from her classmates. She was doing an assignment where she was copying information from a class handout, and she saw that most of her classmates copied the material word by word, or phrase by phrase. Julie, however, trudged through the assignment painstakingly, going letter by letter. She had a long-term substitute teacher that year, who was caring, but lacked the experience to help accurately identify Julie's academic problems.

In the face of chronic academic struggles, Julie, like many dually diagnosed children, felt very frustrated. Like many children with learning disabilities and ADHD, Julie pegged herself as "just stupid." Fortunately, in seventh grade, after undergoing some in-depth educational testing, Julie was discovered to be dyslexic as well as distractible.

Julie's dyslexia was managed when her educational support team and main teachers applied interventions to help her. They worked together by using a combination of visual, tactile, and kinesthetic teaching tools to improve and facilitate her learning. Julie was seated near the teacher's desk in each class, and this helped address her inattention and dyslexia-related challenges. Julie also had a provision built into her educational plan that a special education instructor would teach her the more difficult math and science concepts. She was also taught decoding skills for

reading, which helped her make great academic progress. Fortunately, Julie's teachers also stressed confidence building, which she
sorely needed, given her negative self-concept. I personally worked
with Julie's teachers to help them encourage Julie to change her
negative attitude toward herself. Julie eventually learned that she
possessed both strong and weak sides, just like the rest of us.

In recent years, teachers have become increasingly understanding and accepting of children with learning disabilities. Still, a
minority of teachers may neglect dyslexia and other learning
difficulties and attribute the school problems of a child like Julie
to laziness, lack of concentration, and absent-mindedness. Fortunately, in Julie's case, a strong team effort between me, her parents,
and the school's educational support services team helped Julie
manage her dyslexia and distractibility.

It comes as no surprise that learning disabilities can be mad-
dening for many students. They can shut down motivation and be
a lifelong challenge. Keep in mind that, in some children, several
overlapping learning disabilities may be present. Other children
may have a single, isolated learning problem that has little impact
on their lives. The good news is that there are many educational
recommendations and resources to help address these issues (see
the Resources section for more information).

Depression Detracts and Distracts

Depression can also be a complicating problem for distracted
children. Sadness and lethargy, which are common elements of
most forms of depression, can greatly compromise your child's
ability to focus.

The origins of depression in children can be genetic and physi-
ological. While only 2 percent of preteen school-age children, and
3 to 5 percent of teenagers, have clinical depression, it's one of

the most common diagnoses of children who have mental health problems, second only to anxiety disorders.

Many children find themselves struggling with depression in response to events such as divorce, relocation, social problems, the death of a loved one, or, for teens, breaking up with a boyfriend or girlfriend. While depression can be similar in adults and children, there are a few differences. Adults more often experience an enduring sense of sadness, while children usually display a more irritable than depressed mood. Adults may tend to lose weight, while children may not gain the expected amount of weight for their age.

Given the repeated academic and social failures encountered by distracted children, their depression threshold may be lower than that of other children. Once distracted children become depressed, they struggle with feeling chronically sad and discouraged. (Remember, though, that often their depression will appear as irritability, rather than sadness.) The combination of distractibility and depression can be devastating.

Distracted children who suffer with depression tend to be loaded with negative self-talk (e.g., "I'm stupid"). Many distracted children who struggle with depression also have considerable anger. This anger is fueled by the longstanding frustration of not measuring up to their peers academically and often socially. Internalized anger can spur further depression. Taken together, the negative thoughts of depression can lead children to being more distracted.

Perry was fourteen years old and, in his mother's words, he "never comes out of his room anymore." Years of awful grades and alienation from his peers left Perry feeling hopeless (a key feature of depression) about his future. During our first few counseling sessions, Perry told me that "life really sucks." Perry's parents were at their wits' end, as they felt very helpless in the face of his depression.

Perry worked with me in counseling, and he also received antidepressant medication from a psychiatrist I collaborated with. He participated in school conferences with his parents and had supportive teachers pulling for him to succeed. With continued counseling and support from those around him, his depression became more manageable, and his social and school functioning gradually improved.

As you observe your child coping with his distractibility, it's important to remember the complexities of depression and consider that this penetrating, enduring funk really could be impacting him. Again, try to stay mindful that distracted children certainly never chose to have such extensive focusing issues. It's not surprising that the academic and social frustrations distracted children must contend with can lead to hopelessness and depression. Depression also swallows up a distracted child's self-esteem, and this is another reason why it's so crucial to address it.

IDENTIFYING THE SIGNS OF DEPRESSION IN CHILDREN

The following are common symptoms of depression in children. If three to five or more of the following symptoms persist for more than two weeks, you should seek out a thorough professional evaluation of your child from a qualified health-care professional. Not all children with depression experience each of these symptoms. The severity of the symptoms also varies from child to child. The diagnosis of depression should only be made by a trained medical or mental health professional.

Distracted children who struggle with depression may:

- Feel sad or cry a lot

- Feel guilty for no reason
- Have low self-esteem
- View life as meaningless or feel as if nothing good is ever going to happen again
- Withdraw from doing the things they used to like— such as music, sports, being with friends, going out—and want to be left alone most of the time
- Have trouble concentrating and making decisions
- Get irritated often and overreact
- Have sleep-pattern changes, which can include sleeping more or having trouble falling asleep at night
- Have either a marked loss or gain of appetite
- Feel restless and tired most of the time
- Think about death, feel like they're dying, or have thoughts about committing suicide

Depression in children should never be brushed aside. Self-injury or even suicide attempts are a possibility if depression is not addressed.

At the time of writing this chapter, I heard about a local high-school student who had fatally shot himself at his school. It was later discovered that this teen had very negative feelings about his sudden decline in grades. Obviously, there were some significant mental health complexities behind this tragedy, and by no means am I trying to alarm you with this example. At the same time, if you have any suspicion that your child is depressed, you must have him evaluated and treated. The typical warning signs of suicide are similar to those of depression. They are:

- Extreme sadness
- Changes in appetite and sleeping patterns
- Increased irritability, anger, or hostility
- Boredom and low energy

- Difficulty with relationships
- Feelings of worthlessness

Depression can be managed, and it's common for distraction-related symptoms to lessen as the depression is treated. Sometimes antidepressant medication helps. I have personally seen that if depression and distracted behavior both go unmanaged, the distraction and the depression will both get worse.

Beyond Positive Thinking

There is a great deal of evidence to suggest that distorted thoughts play a role in depression, in children and adults alike. In helping distracted children who suffer from depression, I find it very useful to help them look at how they think about themselves. I draw from cognitive therapy strategies to help children with depression learn to think in more rational and helpful ways. This is not just about "thinking positive." To make this point clear, I tell kids that no matter how much I think positively, I could never play in the National Football League. I never had or will have that level of brute strength and athletic ability. Don't get me wrong—the power of positive thinking does have value. But all the positive thinking in the world won't change the reality that some people are blessed with the skills to be professional athletes and others to be psychologists and self-help authors.

Instead of focusing on positive thinking, cognitive therapy focuses on helping individuals to think more realistically. In short, the basic assumption of the cognitive counseling model is that there is a strong relationship among thinking, feeling, and behavior. Feelings and behavior are influenced by the thoughts on which we base them. This means that our feelings can be controlled by changing our distorted thinking patterns. Examples of these distorted thought patterns in distracted children are:

- **Black-and-white thinking:** "I'm either a success or a loser."
- **Catastrophizing:** "I'll never amount to anything in life."
- **Overgeneralization:** "I'm dumb in everything I do."
- **Personalization:** "I'm to blame for having this distraction problem."
- **"Should" statements:** "I should have more friends."

You may recall from "Day 6" that I discussed how distorted thoughts can lead distracted children to further problems in connecting with peers. Your distracted child's negative thinking can be changed to healthier, helpful thoughts, as shown in the box below. As you will see, there are different types of negative thinking patterns, but rigid, distorted thoughts are common to them all.

NEGATIVE THINKING PATTERN	NEGATIVE THOUGHT	ALTERNATIVE HELPFUL THOUGHT
Black-and-White Thinking	"I'm either a smart kid or a dumb one."	"I can understand some things in school better than others, and that is okay."
Catastrophizing	"School will never go well for me."	"I'd like things to be easier with school, but as long as I try hard, I won't feel so bad."
Overgeneralization	"I always say dumb things and lose my friends."	"I have made some mistakes with my friends. I am starting to get better at thinking before I speak."
Personalization	"My school problems are my fault."	"I did not choose to have a hard time with some schoolwork, and I have nothing to be ashamed of."

NEGATIVE THINKING PATTERN	NEGATIVE THOUGHT	ALTERNATIVE HELPFUL THOUGHT
"Should" Statements	"I should do better in school like my friends do."	"I would like to get better in my schoolwork, but comparing myself with my friends may just make me feel worse."

I have found that by developing a strong, trusting rapport with depressed, distracted children, I can use cognitive therapy methods with them that are very effective. When working with depressed, distracted children, my goal is to help them:

- Feel safe to explore their thoughts and feelings related to struggles with distractibility
- Identify the relationship among thoughts, feelings, and behavior
- Recognize their own distorted thoughts about academic and social struggles
- Examine the evidence for and against their irrational thoughts
- Learn alternatives to distorted thinking
- Adopt more realistic thoughts that will lead to more stable and positive emotions

Dana was an eleven-year-old depressed and distracted child. Her parents brought her to see me after she began crying more frequently and isolating herself in her room. Dana had a long string of failure-laden thoughts about herself. As we got to know each other, she identified the following distorted thoughts:

> "I hate being so stupid."
> "I'll never be good at anything."
> "My life is horrible."

Dana and I set about disproving these negative thoughts. We made lists of all of the successes in her life (academic and social), and she realized that, while she admittedly had experienced some disappointments and struggles, her overarching negative thoughts just were not true. Within a few sessions, Dana became notably more animated and cheerful as she realized that she was not stupid, that she had talents, and that her life was much better than she realized.

Dana and I then made a list of these alternative, healthier thoughts:

> *"Just because it is hard for me to pay attention, that does not mean I am stupid."*
>
> *"My violin and karate activities are things I do well."*
>
> *"My life is not horrible. My mom and dad are trying to help me. I'm not the only one who has challenges with school."*

As a result of our work together, Dana had far fewer self-deprecating thoughts and started to feel better about herself. I have seen, over and over, that cognitive counseling (and medication, when deemed necessary) can help most depressed children start to feel better in just a few weeks. A critical part of helping distracted children with depression is to help them see that they are not alone. Being supportive and trying to understand what is troubling your distracted child will make a huge positive difference for him.

Bipolar Disorder

Bipolar disorder, also known as manic-depressive disorder, can occur in children as well as adults. Bipolar disorder affects an estimated 1 to 2 percent of adults worldwide. The numbers have not been firmly established in children, yet in recent years increasing attention has been given to how it impacts them. It is often extremely difficult to differentiate bipolar disorder from distraction-related behaviors in children, due to overlapping symptoms. In addition, symptoms of bipolar disorder may be initially mistaken for normal emotions and behaviors of children.

While I have not seen a high number of children formally diagnosed with bipolar disorder, I can tell you that it is very hard to tell it apart from other problems that occur in these age groups. For example, while irritability and aggressiveness can indicate bipolar disorder, they also can be symptoms of attention-deficit hyperactivity disorder, conduct disorder, or oppositional defiant disorder. Drug abuse also may lead to such symptoms.

Bipolar disorder itself is complicated to understand. It also complicates the distractibility picture for kids, because it impairs functioning in school, with peers, and at home with family. Bipolar children may show no clear-cut mood cycles, but rather sustained or rapidly fluctuating periods of high energy, volatility, defiance, grandiosity, irritability, anxiety, and explosiveness. In many ways, children with bipolar disorder can appear to be like other distracted kids. But when a child is distracted and also has to contend with the mood fluctuations of bipolar disorder, life can be even more challenging. In short, children with bipolar disorder are distracted by their own racing thoughts. The vast majority of them meet the diagnostic criteria for ADHD, but they do not have ADHD. They need to be treated with mood-stabilizing medications, which typically reduce the racing thoughts and lower distractibility.

IDENTIFYING BIPOLAR PATTERNS

Children with bipolar disorder will have some symptoms from the list of depression indicators (see pages 182–83) and at least three to five from the following list of manic behaviors, persisting for one week:

- Severe changes in mood, either extremely irritable or overly silly and elated
- Inflated self-esteem
- More extreme distractibility, attention moving constantly from one thing to the next
- Increased energy
- Decreased need for sleep, ability to go with very little or no sleep for days without tiring
- Increased talking, talking too much, too fast; changes topics too quickly; cannot be interrupted
- Hypersexuality, increased sexual thoughts, feelings, or behaviors; use of explicit sexual language
- Increased goal-directed activity or physical agitation
- Disregard of risk, excessive involvement in risky behaviors or activities

I worked with a sixteen-year-old distracted child named Angie who also had increasing mood fluctuations with prolonged high-energy periods. During these "highs," Angie would sleep very little, become promiscuous with boys in her neighborhood, and engage in shoplifting. As I further interviewed her, I realized that Angie had a history of mood cycling, and that her distractibility was complicated by both her depressed and manic mood states. A referral to a psychiatrist colleague confirmed my suspicions that Angie had bipolar disorder. Angie was put on a mood stabilizer and some other medicines that were successful in reducing her mood cycling.

Anxiety Aggravates Distractions

Most children have occasional anxiety. In some cases, modest amounts of anxiety can serve to keep distracted children on track. For example, the anxiety behind the thought "I did not do well on this test, I better work harder" can keep a child honest in meeting his schoolwork demands. A mild to moderate amount of anxiety can be beneficial to distracted children by keeping them motivated to face their responsibilities.

At the same time, a child with an anxiety disorder or just high levels of anxiety experiences the symptoms of anxiety more often, more readily, and more intensely than other kids. Anxiety is considered problematic or a disorder when the symptoms cause significant distress or interfere with a child's functioning in at least one aspect of his life.

The problem with anxious, distracted children is that excessive anxiety can result in impaired concentration and restlessness—leading to even higher levels of distractibility. These anxiety issues are some of the same symptoms that are seen in children with distractibility. In addition, problematic levels of anxiety can cause a child to have problems sleeping, and to become excessively tired, on edge, irritable, and tense. As a group, anxiety disorders in children are more common than any other psychiatric disorder.

Approximately 10 percent of all youth experience anxiety disorders, and most go untreated. I have often seen that underneath the bravado of a distracted child lurks significant anxiety. Anxiety-related problems in distracted children can interfere with school attendance, create problems with peer relationships, lower self-esteem, and drive negative self-perceptions. Children with anxiety have a subjective sense of worry, apprehension, and fear. Again, most kids have these feelings on occasion, so it's important to distinguish between normal levels of anxiety and unhealthy levels of anxiety.

While there are different forms of anxiety problems, which I describe in the next few pages, distracted children who struggle with anxiety tend to have these types of symptoms:

- Nausea
- Sweating
- Stomach pain
- Shortness of breath
- Poor decision-making ability
- Distorted views of others
- Problems with concentration
- Negative perceptions of their environment

Distracted children who struggle with anxiety also feel a lot of shame and frustration. The diagnosis of normal versus abnormal anxiety depends largely upon the degree of distress and its effect on a child's functioning. The degree to which anxiety affects a child must be judged within the context of his age and developmental level. Distracted children whom I have counseled have shared a wide range of fears with me. They include:

- Fear of the dark
- Fear of parents' negative reactions to poor school performance
- Fear of being rejected by peers
- Fear of being stupid
- Fear of doing poorly in sports and activities
- Fear of doing poorly at school
- Fear of not being able to get a good job

Nine-year-old Juan was brought to see me because he was petrified of ghosts. He had auditory learning problems and had been very distractible in his classes. In fact, when observed by a school educational support teacher in his class, he was "on task" only 50 percent of the time (solid on-task behavior is usually at least 70 to 85 percent). It was determined that Juan's poor attention in class was exacerbated by his recent ghost fears, which had been preventing him from sleeping well at night. This fear had been triggered by watching a horror movie about ghosts terrorizing teenagers.

Juan and I looked at the reality that no nine-year-old child had been snatched out of his room in the middle of the night by a ghost. I helped Juan see that he was really just panicking at the thought of ghosts. Juan and I made up a poster listing the number of times that a ghost actually bothered him, compared to the number of days he had been alive. It was helpful for Juan to see the reality in black and white that his fear was not rational. I also suggested Juan use a nightlight and keep his closet light on. While I am no ghost management expert, I encouraged the new perception that ghosts are afraid of the light. Juan learned to verbalize and work through his night fears, instead of letting them get in the way of his sleep and further add to his distractibility.

There are different patterns of anxiety that can plague children. Here are some of the more common ones.

Generalized Anxiety Disorder

Generalized anxiety disorder appears to be the most common form of anxiety in children. Children with generalized anxiety anticipate the worst and often complain of fatigue, tension, headaches, and nausea. Distracted kids with generalized anxiety have excessive worry, apprehension, and anxiety occurring most days for a period of six months or more. The worrying of these children just leads to more distraction. They tend to feel restless, keyed up, irritable, or on edge; they are easily fatigued; they have difficulty concentrating, or their minds go blank; they suffer from muscle tension; and they have difficulty falling asleep, can't stay asleep, or experience restless sleep.

I worked with eight-year-old Betsy, who had symptoms of generalized anxiety disorder. In her parents' words, she "worried all the time." In my counseling sessions with Betsy and her family, I emphasized that while it seemed that Betsy worried "all the time," this was not really true. We identified her strengths: she was very attentive and confident with her four-year-old brother, and she was also a talented young gymnast. Building on these areas of confidence was helpful in getting Betsy to start seeing herself as stronger and more in control of herself. These efforts, combined with individual and family counseling, helped reduce Betsy's generalized anxiety. Over the course of a few months, Betsy's anxiety diminished, and this also served to lower her distractibility.

Panic Disorder

Panic disorder or considerable levels of panic can also occur in distracted children, making their distractibility even more serious. Panic attacks usually average a couple of minutes but can last as long as ten minutes and occasionally longer. Most distressing for distracted children is that panic episodes seem to come out of the blue and feel like they will last forever.

Once true medical causes have been ruled out, distracted children with panic issues need to be educated that the symptoms (e.g., difficulty breathing, heaviness in the chest, trembling) are frightening but not dangerous. This educational component is important for all children with panic, but particularly for distracted kids, because they are so mentally disconnected from their thoughts, feelings, and bodily sensations to begin with.

While it may be counter to their instincts, children can be coached to be less fearful of the panic itself. In my work with children who have panic issues, I use some visual exercises to appeal to their imaginations (e.g., floating on a puffy white cloud). Another strategy is to coach kids to go "outside themselves" and rate the anxiety symptoms on a scale of one to ten. The more kids can quantify their panic, the more they tend to feel in control of it.

The most difficult aspect of panic for children is the panic over being panicked. As with depression and all forms of anxiety, the thoughts and feelings involved in panic can become a vicious cycle. Some children may actually feel that they are about to die or have a serious medical problem (usually stomach- or head-related). Children tend to have less insight than adults and may be less articulate in describing their symptoms. The best thing you can do to support your child when he has panic is to be patient, calm, and reassuring. Letting your child know that he is not "crazy" or a "weirdo" for having involuntary panic will help him gain the confidence to soothe himself and avoid further panic.

WHAT TO DO IF YOUR DISTRACTED CHILD HAS A PANIC ATTACK

Symptoms of a panic attack include shortness of breath, heart palpitations, dizziness, dry mouth, nausea or diarrhea, high levels of muscle tension, and possibly an irrational fear of death. If your child has a panic attack, the following may be helpful:

- Quickly reassure your child that the panic *will* soon end.
- Be calm, firm, and noncontrolling with him. In addition, be sure to speak in a supportive, soothing/ accepting manner. The calmer you are, the faster your child will calm down. Maintain eye contact, listen, and reassure your child that he will be fine.

- Gently encourage slow, deep breaths, while being reassuring and nonjudgmental. Sit with your child. Seek medical attention if the panic worsens and/or if there is significant hyperventilation.

- Listen for irrational ideas, such as "I have no future," "No one will ever like me," "I am the most stupid one in my class." Similar thoughts may include, "I suck in everything I do" or "Everyone in the school is going to say bad things about me for the next ten years." For young children who can't articulate as well, puppets and drawings may help in uncovering anxiety-related thoughts (after the attack has passed, of course).

- Once your child starts to calm down, help him see that irrational self-talk can provoke anxiety. Work to show the lack of evidence for irrational (unhelpful) thoughts, and help your child find evidence for more rational (helpful) thoughts. For example, give fact-based reasons why your child is not a total failure or a total loser or totally unpopular. Pointing out such exceptions to the rule is very helpful. For younger children, age four to six, who have fears that drive their panic, again you can use puppets, drawings, and stories to help them see scary things differently. Eight-year-old Donato moved a few months ago and became panicky at the beginning of the school year. I had Donato sit with the guidance counselor when he arrived at school, for the first few weeks. This prevented Donato from being overwhelmed by the new surroundings, and he no longer felt the panic urge.

- To help prevent future panic, have your child ask himself, "What is the worst that can happen?" when he begins to feel panicked. This may help him calm down and see that panic is not warranted.

Obsessive-Compulsive Disorder (OCD)

Some distracted kids may also have obsessions (intrusive, unwanted thoughts or urges) and/or compulsions (intense uncontrollable repetitive behaviors related to the obsessions) that are unreasonable and excessive. These obsessions and compulsions wreak havoc on an already distracted child's ability to maintain attention at school and with peers. They cause considerable distress and impairment and can be very time-consuming (they often eat up more than one hour a day).

The most common obsessions involve germs, dirt and contamination, repeated doubts, the need to have things arranged in a specific way, fear of aggressive or harmful impulses, and disturbing sexual imagery. The most frequent compulsions involve repetitive washing of hands or using a tissue to touch things; checking drawers, locks, windows, and doors; practicing counting rituals; repeating actions; and requesting reassurance.

Brit, age thirteen, was a boy I worked with who had intense obsessive-related anxiety over germs. Brit would frequently need to count the number of times the kitchen counter and bathroom counters were cleaned off. When I reviewed his family history and spoke to his parents, I noted that neither of his parents had significant anxiety issues. Two of Brit's grandparents, however, one paternal and one maternal, did. Cognitive therapy and relaxation training was very helpful in reducing Brit's OCD symptoms. Interestingly, about twelve years later, I bumped into Brit's parents at a shopping mall. They shared that Brit was doing quite well and was working in the field of accounting. Clearly, Brit was able to overcome his difficulties, yet perhaps some of his need for order actually played a beneficial role in his career ambitions.

Post-Traumatic Stress Disorder

I've worked with some distracted children who had experienced a trauma such as sexual or physical abuse, natural disasters, or extreme violence. They developed post-traumatic stress disorder symptoms, including nightmares, flashbacks, the numbing of emotions, depression, anger, irritability, and being easily distracted and startled.

Fourteen-year-old Danny initially came to see me for school-related problems. We worked together with his parents and school personnel to help better manage his academic situation. Danny and I agreed after our sixth session that things were better and that he would end counseling. About a month later, I received a call from Danny's mother, who informed me that he had witnessed a peer on a skateboard get seriously injured when he was struck by a car. Immediately after seeing this unfortunate event, Danny began to develop severe panic symptoms, as described in the earlier section. He came back to see me and, over the course of our counseling, Danny learned techniques to manage his post-traumatic stress symptoms. I also used cognitive therapy and relaxation training with Danny to help him reduce his panic.

Phobias

I have seen phobias negatively impact some distracted children. A phobia is a disabling and irrational fear of something that actually poses little or no real danger. The fear leads to avoidance of objects or situations and can cause extreme feelings of terror, dread, and panic, which can substantially restrict one's life. "Specific" phobias center on particular objects (e.g., certain animals) or situations (e.g., heights or enclosed spaces).

Taylor was a seven-year-old boy I worked with who was scared of spiders. In reaction to his fears, Taylor refused to go on a family camping trip and stayed with his grandparents instead. I traced his family history to determine that Taylor's uncle (his father's brother) had been hospitalized for different forms of anxiety disorders. Taylor's father also reported being "wound up most of my life," but he had never needed counseling or medication.

I used what are referred to as exposure techniques to gradually help Taylor face his fear and overcome it. He looked at pictures of spiders with me on the Internet and eventually touched a spider that I let crawl on my arm outside of my office.

Social Phobia

Social phobia is a stubborn and persistent fear of one or more social situations in which a child fears being exposed to unfamiliar people or to possible scrutiny by others. I worked with an eleven-year-old named Kelly who had some of the classic symptoms of social phobia. She told me that she felt very uncomfortable when talking with peers because she was preoccupied with the fear that they didn't like her. Interestingly, she was far less socially rejected than most other distracted kids I had worked with.

Children with social phobia have poor social skills. For most of the distracted children I have seen with social phobia, the avoidance, anxious anticipation, or distress in the feared social or performance situation(s) interfere significantly with their lives.

Common symptoms of social phobia are:

- Hypersensitivity to criticism
- Difficulty being assertive and low self-esteem
- Fear of reading aloud in front of the class
- Fear of musical or athletic performances
- Fear of joining in a conversation
- Fear of speaking to adults
- Fear of starting a conversation
- Fear of writing on the blackboard
- Fear of attending dances or birthday parties
- Fear of answering questions in class
- Fear of asking the teacher for help

I have helped distracted children like Kelly manage their social phobia by teaching them how to relax and use appropriate social skills. For ideas, go back to "Day 6," where I provided an extensive overview of ways parents can coach social skill development in distracted children.

I have found that for many socially anxious kids, it's helpful to get them to articulate their specific concerns. These children tend to respond well to learning to identify and change anxious thoughts that increase their feelings of anxiety in social situations. By thinking more positive, rational thoughts, children are typically able to dismantle their fears and enter social situations more easily. Again, I draw from cognitive therapy techniques to help children to reduce distortions in their thinking. I also help children develop lists of successful social situations they have been in. We work together to try to "spread this around" to future social situations. I also stress that expectations are best kept realistic and that the goal of counseling is not to help the child be the most popular kid in class.

Health Problems That Drive Distraction

As if contending with their distractibility weren't enough, some distracted children have health concerns as well that can actually increase their distractibility. There are too many to mention here, but some representative medical problems include:

- Asthma
- Allergies
- Bone diseases
- Cancer
- Constipation/encopresis
- Cystic fibrosis
- Gastrointestinal problems
- Headache/migraine

- Past head injury/trauma
- Heart disease
- Irritable bowel syndrome
- Juvenile diabetes
- Lyme disease
- Mental retardation
- Obesity
- Sleep disorders
- Seizure disorder
- Physical/sexual abuse

Ten-year-old Cassandra came to see me after she was diagnosed with a severe form of Crohn's disease—an unusual diagnosis for a child. The challenge of monthly blood transfusions had left Cassandra and her family feeling very stressed. Cassandra also had ADHD symptoms of distractibility, which her mother also had been diagnosed with. This stressed-out family had many issues, and my focus was to help them learn to take one day at a time in a more organized and calm fashion. I also helped Cassandra and her family address their fears of medical unknowns, going forward.

Another client, sixteen-year-old Scott, had advanced Lyme disease, which added to his baseline distractibility. Lyme disease is an inflammatory disease characterized by a skin rash, joint inflammation, and flu-like symptoms, transmitted by the bite of a deer tick. It was unclear whether the Lyme disease was the underlying cause of Scott's distractibility, as he also had a family history of ADHD.

Fortunately, in both of the above examples, these children's medical conditions stabilized. The point to note, however, is that children have increased distractibility when shouldering medical stressors. In all of these situations, I empower parents to join support groups, tap into spiritual resources, and keep addressing the physical aspects of their children's conditions.

It's common for children with long-term or chronic illnesses to get burned out from managing their condition. These children want to be like everyone else and not have to visit the specialists, take the medicine, or follow a strict diet.

Oppositional Defiant Disorder and Distraction

I have never met a parent who didn't understand that a child can be oppositional from time to time, particularly when tired, hungry, stressed, or upset. When being difficult, kids can argue, talk back, disobey, and defy parents, teachers, and other adults. *10 Days to a Less Defiant Child* addresses the problem of openly uncooperative and hostile behavior that reaches frequent and consistent levels. In this case, your child's defiant behavior is worse than it is for children of the same age and developmental level, and it affects his social, family, and academic life. Distractible children who are frustrated and feel misunderstood by parents and teachers may increase their negative behaviors out of self-defeating frustration and/or as a means to call out for help.

A considerable percentage of misunderstood distracted children end up with serious defiance issues. Again, I can't stress enough the value of being calm, firm, and noncontrolling, which helps to bypass the emotional reactivity and avoid power struggles. The more your distracted child feels understood, the less likely he is to become defiant.

Some kids have more frequent and more intense defiance. This is known as oppositional defiant disorder (ODD), which is characterized by an ongoing pattern of uncooperative, defiant, and hostile behavior toward authority figures that seriously interferes with the child's daily functioning. Symptoms of ODD include:

- Frequent temper tantrums
- Excessive arguing with adults
- Active defiance and refusal to comply with adult requests and rules
- Deliberate attempts to annoy or upset people
- Blaming others for one's mistakes or misbehavior
- Often being touchy or easily annoyed by others
- Frequent anger and resentment
- Mean and hateful talking when upset
- Seeking revenge

The symptoms are usually seen in multiple settings, but may be more noticeable at home or at school. Five to 15 percent of all school-age children have ODD. The causes of ODD are unknown, but many parents report that their child with ODD was more rigid and demanding than his siblings from an early age. Both biological and environmental factors may play a role.

Even nonclinical levels of defiant behavior can be very difficult for parents. One distracted boy I worked with named Dennis, age fourteen, had high levels of defiance, but not ODD. His parents tended to harbor their frustrations about his school problems and then blow up and scream at Dennis. Dennis retaliated by calling them foul names and hiding important possessions, such as their car keys.

I used my calm, firm, and noncontrolling approach to coach Dennis's parents to avoid getting caught on the metaphorical fishhooks he floated their way. I worked with Dennis to get his trust, and then empowered him to express his frustrations more directly with his parents. He became far less defiant and better able to focus on getting help that was offered to him at school.

Drugs Can Add to Distractibility

The pain of chronic school pressure and possible failure can lead distracted children to abuse alcohol or other drugs. Distractibility leads to a circus of confusion, and the "high" of doing drugs can be a very tempting way to avoid all of the pain.

The chronic social challenges explained in "Day 6" and the consequent intense peer pressure to fit in with their friends are another reason why distracted children seek refuge in the wasteland of drugs.

Parents who also struggle with distractibility may use alcohol or drugs to numb the pressure of being mentally scattered as well. Parents and other adults who abuse drugs or alcohol model a very poor example for their children.

There are other parents who just can't—or refuse to—understand what addiction is. In the words of one father I worked with, who had a highly distracted and substance-abusing daughter, "I just don't believe in addiction. People have to take charge of their lives." To this I say, "Easier said than done." There are certainly some people who never use drugs and couldn't care less about them. There are also some people who can occasionally use drugs but have an "I can take them or leave them" attitude. However, for far too many chronically distracted children who lack support and the ability to soothe themselves in a healthy manner, drugs can be a damaging and even fatal escape.

It's particularly troubling that there are more ways today than ever before to obtain chemicals, and that much misinformation about drugs is available on the Internet. The exposure to and availability of addictive chemicals in most communities surprise most parents.

Anthony, age sixteen, had been miserably battling ADHD-related distractibility for years. His parents were adamantly opposed to having him receive medication to help him with his ADHD concerns. (I discuss medication for distractibility in "Day 9.") Anthony shared with me that he was both smoking marijuana and secretly using his friend's stimulant medication. After we established a firm trust and rapport, Anthony gave me permission to speak with his parents, together with him, about his drug concerns. Anthony was then referred for psychiatric follow-up, where he was given medication to help him manage his distractibility. His parents, with a new appreciation for the complexities of the situation, supported the decision for Anthony to use legal drugs versus illegal ones. Fortunately, aside from a few occasional setbacks, Anthony stopped using marijuana. His grades picked up, and the last I heard he was attending community college.

Unfortunately, in many cases, a child will use drugs and alcohol for quite some time before parents notice the signs of a problem. Often by the time a parent sees the signs, the child has a problem that goes beyond occasional use of these substances. In some cases, the child may have developed an abusive pattern of use and may be addicted to drugs or alcohol. The best solution for kids in this situation is to get them out of their immediate environment and away from the peer influences that are enabling their abuse of drugs or alcohol.

Drug or alcohol rehab may be necessary to give your child a chance to get back on his feet and begin a program of recovery from addiction. The bottom line is that if your child has a drug or alcohol problem, or both, the sooner you get him into treatment the better. Denying that your distracted child also has a drug or alcohol problem will only make things worse. You really need to be honest about this—first with yourself and then with someone who can help you get your child into treatment. It's the only way to help him get better and *stay* better.

WARNING SIGNS OF DRUG USE

It's important for you to be aware of the signals that may suggest your child is using drugs. This will help you to more quickly determine if your distracted child has a drug problem.

- Increased moodiness (e.g., anger, sadness, or hyper-manic episodes)
- Alcohol or prescription medicine missing from your cabinet
- Glassy eyes, low eye contact, pasty skin
- Being sick more often, coughing in morning
- Money/valuables missing, music players and cell phones "lost"
- Disappearing for long periods
- Change in sleep patterns/more fatigue
- Running away
- Secretive text messaging and dramatic increase in cell phone use
- Unusual containers, wrappers, tin foil
- Reports of intoxication at school
- Dramatic drop in grades, skipping classes
- Desperation/withdrawal from family
- Switching of friends
- Drug-seeking behavior, such as researching drugs on the Internet
- Seeming mentally preoccupied, easily distracted
- Loss of interest in healthy outlets such as sports, church, and family contact

If you're dealing with drug and alcohol problems in your distracted child, remember that he's not a bad kid trying to become good. He has a disease from which he is trying to recover. Many parents think that drug use is just a phase, or that everybody's got to get their drinking legs. However, the issue is much more serious than that. The development of the adolescent brain and the risk of damage in these formative years is a very serious matter. For example, neurologists can show where marijuana sits in the frontal cortex of the brain and affects development, memory encoding, and even hand-eye coordination. The earlier appropriate intervention stops the progression of an adolescent addiction, the less strain there is on family relationships and community functioning.

If you think your distracted child is using drugs, your natural reaction may be to panic (and shout at him). Wait until you feel calmer, and then talk to your child. Don't come across in a critical or shaming manner.

If your child does have a drug problem, it's important for him to know that you will be there for him—from answering simple questions to helping him through difficult times. It's worth telling him that you trust him, but at the same time feel free to show disappointment if this trust is broken.

It's also vital that you watch what you do as his parent. If you drink excessively or condone drug use, you're just encouraging your child to cope in the same problematic way.

Asperger's Disorder

Asperger's disorder is a pervasive developmental disorder commonly referred to as a form of high-functioning autism. Unlike most children with other forms of pervasive developmental delay, children with Asperger's disorder do not show obvious delays in language development and skills. They often have solid or even strong vocabularies that seem advanced compared to those of other children their age. Yet, despite their large vocabularies, these children are quite literal in their understanding of what others are saying. Children with Asperger's disorder usually acquire self-help skills like potty training and dressing at the same ages as their peers, but their social skills lag far behind. Children with Asperger's disorder also often have an obsessive interest in a particular subject and very little interest in much else. They may obsessively seek information about maps or clocks or some other topic. They may also be very inflexible in their habits and rigidly adhere to certain routines or rituals. Children with Asperger's disorder may show strange mannerisms such as hand flapping, mouth movements, or peculiar postures that make them appear clumsy. These mannerisms unfortunately may alienate them from peers. These children are considered to have a higher intellectual capacity while suffering from a lower social capacity.

The typical symptoms of Asperger's disorder include:

- Being locked into one or more stereotyped and restricted patterns of interest that are abnormal in either intensity or focus
- Having an apparently inflexible adherence to specific nonfunctional routines or rituals
- Showing stereotyped and repetitive motor mannerisms (e.g., hand or finger flapping or twisting or complex whole-body movements)
- Having a persistent preoccupation with parts of objects

I saw a fifteen-year-old girl named Leah who was diagnosed with Asperger's disorder. Of great concern to her parents was the realization that Asperger's is a spectrum disorder. This means that two children with the same diagnosis might have totally different symptoms. Suffice it to say, parents of children with high-functioning-autism-related concerns find the ambiguity of what the future holds for their child justifiably frustrating.

Unlike many other similarly diagnosed children, Leah did not have a monotone voice. She did, however, have problems with a flatness in her emotional reactions (aside from some meltdowns on the tennis court), and she made little eye contact in social situations. Leah was an average student, and her interests outside of school were restricted to tennis, which she mostly played with her mother.

The optimum treatment for children with Asperger's involves educational and social interventions to give them the support and skills they need to be successful in life. Educational interventions that focus on making the environment more predictable are particularly helpful. Graphic organizers and other similar strategies that capitalize on a visual learning style are also beneficial. Since some individuals with Asperger's disorder can have IQs in the gifted range, they need to have learning opportunities commensurate with their skill levels. Therefore, enrichment activities are usually a part of the curriculum for these children.

Tourette's Syndrome

Tourette's syndrome is a neurological disorder characterized by involuntary body movements and vocal outbursts (tics) that last for at least twelve months. Tourette's syndrome occurs in about one in every two thousand children. It is more common in boys.

The tics can be very demoralizing. They are involuntary and sudden, usually occurring in a rapid and repetitive manner. Examples of verbal tics include compulsive barking, grunting noises, frequent throat clearing, coughing, or sniffling. Echolalia (vocal tics characterized by repeating overheard words) and/or coprolalia (vocal tics characterized by repeating or shouting obscene words) can also occur. Contrary to common perceptions, coprolalia is rare.

Nick is a ten-year-old distracted boy I worked with who had been diagnosed with ADHD, OCD, and Tourette's syndrome. Surprisingly articulate given his age and his disabilities, he related to me that his life was falling apart. Nick felt tremendous shame after being teased by peers about his tics. This left Nick further distracted by his feelings of inferiority in the eyes of his peers.

I worked with Nick's teacher, who educated his peers about the sensitive nature of his Tourette's challenges. After a few months of counseling with Nick and his parents, Nick began to feel better about himself and do better in school and with peers. He still came in to see me from time to time, just to keep himself feeling supported in the face of his challenges. Tourette's syndrome currently has no cure, but symptoms can usually be managed with counseling, accommodations at school, and medication.

Stress Worsens Distractibility

Children can face many stressors that can increase their distracted behavior. They include:

- Arrival of a new sibling
- School pressure
- Conflict with a teacher
- Conflict with a peer
- Being bullied
- Relocating
- Divorce
- Health problems of a parent
- Financial strain/unemployment of a parent
- Death of a loved one
- Domestic violence

Distracted kids can get even more disoriented and confused if they are stressed over life situations. For some children, facing uncertainties and pressures may simply add pleasure and vigor to their lives. For distracted children, however, often the variety and unpredictability of stresses can aggravate and overwhelm them. They have real difficulty adjusting to change.

Kurt, age fifteen, was brought in by his parents after he had been increasingly disrespectful to them. The last straw was when he threw his parents' clothes out of a bedroom window and into the muddy yard below. Having just moved from another state, Kurt decided that he hated his newly built new home (the grass had yet to grow, hence the muddy yard). He also "hated" his new school and "all of the crappy kids" he was meeting. Kurt had ADHD and did not do very well with transitions. After only a few months, he was failing his major subjects during his first quarter of school. I provided supportive counseling to Kurt and his family. He eventually overcame his fears and adjusted relatively well to the major changes in his life. This included learning to center himself and focus on his schoolwork and on making new friends.

DAY 7: SUMMING IT UP

Today you have learned a great deal about coexisting conditions that can increase your child's distractibility. Please keep the following points in mind as you move forward:

- Some distracted children may have one or more health issues.
- While many of these conditions can cause distractibility, they can also worsen existing distractibility.
- The more you learn about any of these mental health concerns, the more you can help if you suspect that your child suffers from one or more of them.
- Your commitment to being patient and persistent will help your child overcome any coexisting conditions he struggles with.
- Please consult a qualified mental health professional about any persistent problems, or to gain further information.

Focusing on Reinforcement

Your child's distractibility is draining—not only for your child but also for you. You have both faced many challenges, but hopefully, now that you are applying this ten-day plan and getting positive results, things are becoming easier.

However, there are still ongoing challenges in helping your child manage her distractibility. Making positive changes and keeping them going in a positive direction is crucial. To do this you have to keep yourself and your child filled with positive energy and motivation to bust through any new barriers. Today, I am going to give you a powerful tool to help you and your child keep the motivation going strong as you move forward. This tool is called positive reinforcement.

Positive reinforcement refers to the process of giving rewards to strengthen behaviors in the future. Today I will show you what positive reinforcement is and help you marshal its power to continue to guide your child to success. As you will see, positive reinforcement involves using powerful rewards that can influence your distracted child to *want* to make changes and stick to them, almost instantly.

While it's important to reward all kids for positive behavior, distracted kids especially need to be rewarded. Given the "noise" in their heads from being so internally preoccupied, distracted children need the extra positive incentive to get their work started, get it done, stick to a schedule, and reach out to peers.

Today, you will hear me praise the benefits of giving praise and encourage the importance of providing encouragement. By learning how to use positive reinforcement, you will gain valuable tools to reinforce your child's progress, as well as your own efforts and achievements as a parent.

The Power of Positive Reinforcement

When managing your child's distractibility, it's more effective to notice and develop her strengths and positive behaviors than to dwell on her weaknesses and problems. When the relationship between a parent and child is basically positive, it provides a very important source of motivation. Parents who are savvy about motivating their children to behave appropriately give them positive consequences for doing so (i.e., privileges or rewards). Parents who are overly critical and harsh run the risk of sabotaging the impact of whatever positive motivation they try to offer their children. I make this case very clear in this book's companion volume, *10 Days to a Less Defiant Child*.

I encourage you to take a closer look at where you stand on the praise/criticism continuum. I'm asking you to take a good, honest look at yourself right here and now. Please consider these powerful questions:

- How often do you let your child know when she does the right thing?
- How often do you remember to reinforce her efforts when she puts forth effort?
- How often do you let her know that you are proud of her when she settles down and gets things accomplished?
- How often do you praise your child's progress as she works toward her goals?
- How often do you provide encouragement and support in the face of her setbacks?

Your answers to these questions will show how and if you provide positive reinforcement to your child. Sadly, I have seen many parents lose track of one huge parenting principle: Most behaviors are controlled by their positive or negative consequences. So if you focus on reinforcing your child's positive behaviors, you'll be more likely to see positive behaviors. If you focus on criticizing her negative behaviors, you'll probably see more negative behaviors. It's just that simple.

Searching for Positives Requires an Ongoing Commitment

I can understand if you feel that it's hard to consistently find opportunities to give positive reinforcement to your distracted child. Even though your child has likely made some huge positive strides forward as you have been applying the strategies in this book, distracted kids act impulsively and can be highly disorganized. For example, many parents have shared with me that when they ask their distracted children to do something, they have to ask more than a few times. These exasperated parents say things like, "It's like she pretends she has no homework and then actually forgets she has it in the first place" or "Why won't she just pick up her shoes left in the middle of the floor?" or "I ask her to put the milk away and I feel my words fall on deaf ears."

I do understand how situations like these can be frustrating. But I also encourage you to be careful of what these frustrations consequently lead you to focus on. Once you zero in on a child's lack of ability to focus or absentmindedness, you will find it difficult to focus on what she actually does well. This leads to impatience and mutual frustrations, which can make it hard to talk things out and guide your child to making better choices. Often the end result of focusing on your child's negative behaviors is that your "telling becomes yelling." You may recall that in "Day 3," I provided many strategies to help you avoid overreacting to your distracted child. Feel free to refer back to that now if you need a refresher course.

As you continue to apply the strategies in this ten-day program, I encourage you to commit to seeing your child and her behaviors in a positive manner. Be encouraging and provide rewards to keep cultivating and maintaining her positive behaviors.

Positive Reinforcement Is Not about Bribery

Many parents are concerned that positive reinforcement involves manipulating and even bribing their distracted children. I consider positive reinforcement as coaching for success, not manipulating or bribing a child. Positive reinforcement is manipulation or bribery only when applied the wrong way. For instance, if you were to use rewards as a positive consequence to stop an inappropriate behavior, such as offering a reward to stop a tantrum or whining, you would be applying it incorrectly. No matter how desperate you're feeling (believe me, we've all been there), never use rewards such as toys, candy, or new privileges to end bad behavior. This tactic almost always backfires and winds up encouraging her to continue the inappropriate behavior. You will see examples of this precarious parenting method later today.

In contrast, positive reinforcement is about rewarding distracted kids for their positive behaviors. This technique is much more productive. For example, suppose your child spontaneously (yet responsibly) asks you to help her study for a test. It would be helpful to take this opportunity to praise her responsible behavior and resist any desire to point out what she did not do well in her studies. Your goal is to make sure that you are not using rewards to stop self-defeating behavior, but rather to encourage appropriate behavior.

I can't impress upon you enough how effective it is to use the power of positive reinforcement to help your distracted child learn, and continue to use, more effective skills. This applies to every aspect of her life, including essential ones such as schoolwork, peers, and relative harmony within your family.

Sadly, many distracted children confide in me that they are reluctant to be open with their parents about their academic or social problems, for fear of being criticized. Therefore, I encourage you to give lots of support and positive reinforcement to your child. This will create a sense of emotional safety and security that will allow her to open up to you. In many cases, positive reinforcement can be accomplished by merely giving recognition to your child's effort. It's important to bear in mind that your distracted child does not learn skills to better herself easily. It takes time for her to learn how to do new things and feel good about doing them. When your child improves at any newly acquired skill, you get to help her pick the next one to work on.

Two Types of Reinforcement

Reinforcement, when used effectively, is designed to increase desired behaviors. There are two types of reinforcement: positive and negative. Positive reinforcement increases behavior when you add or give something following a desired behavior. So buying your child a desired article of clothing in recognition of desired behaviors would be positive reinforcement. Negative reinforcement is a reward created by the removal of painful or stressful conditions or events. Telling your child she won't have to do the dreaded chore of cleaning up the dog excrement if she starts her homework on time is an example of negative reinforcement. As you can probably tell, I am not a big fan of negative reinforcement. Negative reinforcement holds a punitive vibe for most children. Plus, if the goal behavior is not met, negative reinforcement often leads distracted children, who already have shaky self-esteem, to feel pressured, criticized, shamed, and most importantly—demotivated.

Punishment Is Usually Not Helpful

The bottom line is that the punishment mentality does not teach or support your child to make important positive changes. Instead, a punishment mind-set uses shame, control, and intimidation to influence your child to behave differently. Nothing will fail more quickly when trying to encourage positive changes in your defiant child than blindly and rigidly adhering to this approach. Many defiant children learn to avoid punishment by hiding their misbehavior from you or other authority figures. If you overdo the unpleasant consequences for misbehavior, your child (and possibly you) may end up feeling excessively guilty. Kids often end up with damage to their self-esteem, which actually increases the likelihood of continued misbehavior.

Punishment Produces More Distraction

Many parents have tried punishing their distracted kids as a way to motivate them to do their schoolwork or accomplish things in other areas of their lives. The problem is that punishment is punitive in nature, and it breaks down motivation rather than enhances it. I am all for accountability and solid discipline in parenting, but your child did not chose to have distractibility problems, and making her pay for her shortcomings really isn't fair.

Unfortunately, I find that some punishment-oriented parents become extremely hungry for consequences. But heavy-duty consequences for punishment are not productive. Consider the following statements:

> *"I fixed her good this time by taking away her computer for the next few months. That will get her to buckle down and do her work."*
>
> *"Since she never remembers to do things around the house, she won't be surprised when she finds out she is not being allowed to sign up for soccer."*
>
> *"She never listens to me. I have had it. Now I just won't listen to her."*
>
> *"That's it! You don't have any motivation to do anything. You're grounded for the next four weeks."*

No parents are perfect. Most of us have tried some form of the above punishments. The problem with parents having a punishment mentality is that children often feel overly controlled and resentful. Distracted kids get even more distracted by dwelling on their consequent negative feelings, and the situation just further deteriorates.

Positive reinforcement is the better way to go, to support and foster motivation in children, especially distracted ones who need the additional emotional support. Read on to find out how to best understand positive reinforcement and make it work for you and your child.

Getting the Situation in Order

To properly use positive reinforcement to influence your child's behaviors, you need to understand the circumstances and pattern of events that occur in relation to her misbehaviors. A few sections earlier, I described how you can unwittingly fuel inappropriate behaviors in your distracted child by rewarding her for poor choices. You are more likely to be able to help your child learn new skills if you have an understanding of what caused her past difficulties and what can potentially cause them to persist.

I'm going to give you a brief lesson in behavioral psychology, to give you a framework for understanding what triggers your distracted child's problematic behaviors. The main point here is that your child's actions can be broken down into what are referred to as *antecedents, behavior,* and *consequences.* Each is described following the illustration below, which shows the order of antecedents, behaviors, and consequences.

ANTECEDENTS, BEHAVIORS, AND CONSEQUENCES

A   B   C

(A) **Antecedents:** Antecedents are what occurs before a behavior. It's important to remember to examine the antecedents of a behavior. This is because sometimes the context of a situation needs to be altered in order for the behavior to change. Say, for example, your child has a procrastination problem. For you to really understand why she is procrastinating, it would be helpful to look at what she experiences or does before she procrastinates. Ask yourself, "What led up to the behavior?" and "What was the situation or context in which the behavior occurred?"

(B) **Behavior:** When looking at behaviors, you are really asking yourself, "What is the behavior of concern?" Staying with the example above, the answer would be procrastination. As you will see, it's crucial to specify exactly the kind of procrastination that occurred. So when you consider your child's behaviors, you need to be specific.

(C) Consequences: I'm not talking here about "consequences" as they relate to discipline. Rather, in the realm of positive reinforcement, the *results* of your child's behaviors are referred to as consequences. Consequences are what happens in response to the behavior. When trying to understand the consequences of your child's behavior, ask yourself, "What was my response, the response of my child, or others who were impacted by the behavior?"

As you can see from the illustration above, breaking down your child's behaviors into a sequence of events can be very enlightening. It will also help you figure out how to optimally employ positive reinforcement.

Please realize that I am not asking you to keep a notebook or worksheet in your pocket and classify all of your child's actions into antecedents, behaviors, and consequences. Rather, I'm asking you to remember the circumstances of the challenges and difficulties that you and your child face. Let's now consider the example below of fourteen-year-old Al and his mother, Louise. For the purposes of illustration, we will use this example to explain antecedents, behavior, and consequences.

ANTECEDENTS	BEHAVIOR	CONSEQUENCES
Al is told to do homework.	Al argues/refuses.	Al storms off, homework not done.

As you will see below, Al and his mother, Louise, do a "patterned dance" that follows a sequence leading to Al being rewarded for *not* doing his homework. Here is the nightly saga that occurs, as related to me during a counseling session.

LOUISE: "Al won't ever sit down and do his schoolwork."

JEFF: "What do you mean by that? Can you give me an example?"

LOUISE: "He gets home and has all this time to get his work done, but he lets time slip away. When I get home, I ask him to show me what work he has completed, and he tells me he will get to it. When I question him further, we start arguing."

JEFF: "What does Al say to you?"

LOUISE: "He just gets more and more upset, tells me I am on his case and how all his friends' parents are less strict than I am. He says I am not fair and that he hates me."

JEFF: "What do you do?"

LOUISE: "Well, I have to admit, he is a master at pushing my buttons. And believe me, I do make many attempts to try to reason calmly with him and explain why he has to get going on his work. But, like clockwork, my husband and I end up becoming upset with Al's apathetic attitude. And he never seems to see, or wants to see, our position."

JEFF: "What happens next?"

LOUISE: "Well, we start arguing back at him because Al has an answer for everything we say. After a while, we become sick of all the nonsense and verbal ping-pong. So we just say do whatever you want. I mean, c'mon, this kid really wears us down."

In this example, if Al listened to his parents, he would do his homework. However, by aggravating them and refusing to give an inch, he is able to avoid his homework. The reason this avoidance behavior occurs—and continues—is that it works! Does this sound familiar to you? If so, don't feel bad. Now you can see why it doesn't work and start to do things differently.

In Al and Louise's situation, you can see that the *behavior* was Al's unwillingness to get the homework done. The *antecedent* was the arguing, and the consequence was avoidance. Examining the sequence of events can show how reinforcement can work against you as a parent.

Let's look at another example. Gary, seeking to keep order in the house, would see his eight-year-old son Trent's shoes in the middle of the floor and ask him to pick them up. Much to Gary's chagrin, Trent would ignore him and keep watching TV. Gary would repeat his request (this time in a louder tone), and Trent would ignore him again. Then Gary would get angry and intensify his demand for the shoes to be picked up. Trent, who initially had not been deliberately defiant, but rather just distracted and self-absorbed, would then really become defiant and throw a tantrum. This arguing would go on for a few more cycles, leaving Trent and Gary both very frustrated and angry. Finally, seeing red and not wanting to explode, Gary would drop his demand and tell Trent to go to his room. Gary, by then emotionally spent, would pick up the shoes himself because "I'm not going to drive myself nuts" trying to make Trent do what he is supposed to do.

My guess is that you have had your share of Al- or Trent-like situations with your own distracted child. Unfortunately, what your child learns from this type of exchange is that if she keeps refusing to do what you want, she will eventually get her way. Even though it may not feel this way, your child's avoidance or refusal to do what she needs to do actually gets rewarded. If you consider the events that shape such problems, you can avoid unwittingly reinforcing inappropriate behaviors.

Putting Positive Reinforcement into Action

Now that you know what not to do, it's time for some pointers on how you can make positive reinforcement work for your distracted child. I am aware that your child will probably not drop everything, give you a big hug, and say, "Mom, I can't wait to see how your rewards motivate me." So if you get some smart remarks or resistance, don't be discouraged. Stay calm, firm, and noncontrolling to avoid getting sucked into a power struggle with your child—and keep trying.

Let's take a look at what might have happened if Al's and Trent's parents had used positive reinforcement in the above examples. When Al refused to do his homework, Louise could have pointed out to Al the times that he *did* do his homework. (All children have successes in their lives, even in areas where they typically struggle. Using past successes can be a very effective tool in positive reinforcement.) She also could have calmly and supportively told him to consider the fact that he gets more privileges when he does his homework. This would have created a more positive interaction, avoided the power struggle, and leveraged Al's past successes to spur current motivation. If Louise had wanted to take it a step further, she could have empathized with Al that homework is not easy for him to tackle. This "joining" mind-set would encourage Al to feel that Louise was on his side, rather than a nagging adversary.

Similarly, when Trent avoided picking up his shoes, Gary could have told Trent that being responsible for his personal property would motivate Gary to give Trent more privileges. This might include more computer time, television time, or time to play with friends. In an effort to anchor the interaction in success rather than failure, Gary could have pointed out to Trent how responsible he has been in other areas of his life, such as brushing his teeth and getting to school on time. Even if Trent did not comply with putting his shoes away in this instance, Gary still would have been more successful by speaking to Trent in a positive, motivating manner. Trent would be more likely to pick his shoes up off the floor next time if the current situation did not escalate into a power struggle.

Be Specific

To help your child make improvements in her behavior, you need to be clear about what you are expecting. Be very specific when defining the behavior that you are planning to change. Keep in mind how vague and diffuse distracted kids are. So when setting behavior goals to reinforce, it's very helpful to break larger behaviors into smaller definitive parts and work on them one at a time.

Dominic, the father of nine-year-old Derek, observed that getting Derek to do his homework in ten- to fifteen-minute segments was more successful than expecting Derek to remain seated for an uninterrupted half hour. Dominic kept a timer by the table to help Derek do his work for these shorter, more manageable time intervals. In addition to giving him praise, one day Dominic surprised Derek with a new gift card to his favorite toy store. In this case, the parent specifically targeted what worked best for his child to help make a positive change occur. The positive reward of the gift card helped the new behavior stick.

Remember to keep your child striving toward measurable behaviors, and choose behavior goals that you and your child can truly assess in terms of change. In order to successfully see changes in behavior(s), you need to have a clear sense of what is "normal" for your child. Otherwise, you could be setting your child up for failure.

Be open to looking at what works and what does not work. Ask yourself, "How often does the desired behavior occur now?" This may involve the number of times something occurs, or how long it lasts. Here are some examples of other specific, measurable goals you can help your distracted child work toward:

- Starting homework at a mutually agreed-upon time

- Discussing her homework frustrations in a calm tone, instead of yelling or crying
- Volunteering to show her teacher's marks and comments to you
- Completing homework and other assignments
- Getting ready for school on time
- Following requests after only one reminder

Put a Positive Spin on It

Helping your child achieve a homework goal so that she will have more time to play is probably going to be more appealing to her than telling her she just has to get her work done. Showing your child how to "sweeten the pot" when reaching goals will help her learn how to best reward and motivate herself. Remember that in the end, your goal is to help your child learn to set her own goals and feel good about them.

Karin, another client of mine, helped her thirteen-year-old daughter, Leanne, become more motivated to clean her room. Karin did this by showing Leanne that cleaning her room would make it a lot easier to find her favorite hair bows and lip gloss. These prized possessions tended to get lost beneath what had been piles of clothes on the floor. Leanne began to think of cleaning her room as a benefit and not a chore.

Don't Try to Change the World

Be selective in identifying the changes you're facilitating your child to strive toward. Many overambitious parents (and consequently beleaguered children) try to change too many behaviors at one time—this is likely to fail. And, if your child gets increasingly overwhelmed and frustrated, it's a recipe for disaster. I encourage you not to take on too many behaviors at once.

Donna, the single parent of twelve-year-old Michelle, learned this lesson the hard way. Michelle had major organizational issues, which Donna had set out to help her overcome. Michelle had made wonderful progress in remembering to go through her backpack every night. This required Michelle to take about fifteen minutes to go through and sort out her assignments and organize them into piles of past, current, and upcoming work. Donna initially was lavish with praise to reinforce Michelle's progress, but then became upset that Michelle was doing this task independently *only* for about three out of five days, and still needed some reminders. One day in a counseling session, Michelle turned to Donna and said, "You want me to be perfect and I just can't be." Michelle made a valid point, and Donna, to her credit, heard it. The organizational goals became more realistic and accordingly modified.

Try to set things up so your child has a good chance to taste some early success. You want to strive for progress, not perfection. Even a small improvement is still an improvement.

Keep Priorities Clear

Prioritize your child's goals according to the real needs. For example, Fred's goal for his ten-year-old daughter, Rhea, was to remember to make her bed every morning. Ostensibly, this was a justifiable and worthy goal, except that a more pressing matter—Rhea brushing her teeth—was falling by the wayside. This lack of oral hygiene certainly was not a good thing for Rhea's faltering peer relationships. Fred and Rhea readjusted the emphasis of desired goals accordingly. A month later, once she began reliably brushing her teeth, for which Fred provided a cool-looking new toothbrush as a reward, they began to focus on getting the bed made.

Similarly, Jill realized that encouraging her sixteen-year-old son, Eric, to be more independent in completing his homework and turning it in was a top priority. Prior to this, she had been fruitlessly hounding Eric to do recreational reading. Eric's incentive for handling his homework responsibilities was more driving time in the family car. To soundly accomplish the most pressing goal, Jill had to put her initial priority of having Eric read an extra recreational book each month on hold.

Keep It Real and Practical

The realities of time and your ability to monitor your child's behaviors should be taken into consideration when targeting a behavior for change. For example, if the behavior you choose to improve or change occurs mostly in school, you will not be able to monitor it directly. At the same time, while you may not be able to leave your job and directly observe your child in her classes at school, you can still stay on top of your child's progress. Perhaps you can establish an e-mail loop with your child's teachers and get daily or weekly reports on how she is doing with regard to your concerns. Weekly check-ins by phone may also be an option.

Ginger, a single mother of four whom I worked with, realized that it was not possible for her to sit down each day after school for extended time periods to help Jerome, her thirteen-year-old learning disabled son, with homework problems. Ginger brought this issue up at the next school meeting for Jerome's individualized education plan. I reminded Ginger that her realistic role was to oversee Jerome getting his homework started. His teachers were more than willing to reteach the concepts that he had difficulty grasping.

Give Thought to Selecting Rewards

In choosing rewards for your child, don't neglect those that already motivate your child. Also, make sure that your choice of rewards not only "feels good," but is "good for" your child.

During the course of our work together, Christine helped her nine-year-old daughter, Rebecca, practice her violin more consistently by rediscovering Rebecca's love of baking cookies. Christine had baked cookies with Rebecca more often a few years earlier, when she went through her divorce from Rebecca's father. Christine now used this soothing experience as a positive reward for Rebecca's violin practice. Both Rebecca's violin recital and the freshly baked cookies served afterward were a hit a few months later.

Judi was a parent I worked with who realized that giving her thirteen-year-old, obese son, Sam, candy or ice cream as a reward for doing his homework in a timely manner was not healthy for him. Judi wisely realized that Sam valued extra television time, phone privileges, sleepovers with friends, and a Saturday at the mall—all of which he enjoyed and perceived as powerful incentives—and used them instead.

Time Tells All

The concept of time is a very important consideration in using positive reinforcement with children. Younger kids tend to do better with a very short delay between the behavior and the reward. As kids mature, parents can use longer delays between behavior and reinforcement.

Distracted children tend to require shorter intervals between the behavior and the reward. The longer the delay, the less the reward will weigh in the mind of your child. In other words, overly delayed rewards have a smaller impact on motivating more desirable behaviors. Naturally, you may unwittingly delay a reward too long or even miss a few praiseworthy moments, especially in the beginning. It's still okay to bring it up by saying, "I meant to tell you that I noticed how you got ready on time for school today. You really are making progress on this."

Andy, the father of twelve-year-old Dennis, had initially promised Dennis a weekend reward (going canoeing) for having no more than one argument with his parents during the week. This reward system failed, however, and I helped Andy see that the reward was too far in the future to function as an effective motivator for Dennis. While keeping the weekly reward for Dennis, Andy also made a conscious effort to praise Dennis for his more cooperative behaviors. Hearing this praise from his father kept Andy mindful of the overall goal of reduced conflict with his parents.

As illustrated in this example, daily rewards, or even more frequent opportunities to earn privileges, will often be helpful. Providing younger children (age ten and younger) with points or "tokens" for good behavior that can be used to purchase more tangible rewards (e.g., TV time, video game time, getting to rent a video) can also be useful in helping children reach desired goals.

Variety Is the Spice of Reinforcement

Not surprisingly, distractible children tend to need frequent changes in rewards, to stay motivated by reinforcement. So keep offering new and innovative rewards instead of the same old ones over and over. The possibilities are endless. You could offer a reward of varied time for playing a video game or more choices of places to go with friends. The important thing to remember is that what motivates children one day may not motivate them the next.

Dan, the father of eleven-year-old Cheryl, found that she would often get off to a great start with her punctuality goal and then lose interest in earning any rewards. Dan then discovered that the best way to combat this was to change the reward program to keep it feeling new. He experimented with changing the rewards, such as extra TV time one day and getting to stay up an extra half hour the next. This helped Cheryl improve in getting ready for school on time.

Joy was a client of mine who was very innovative in keeping the creative reward juices flowing for her four-year-old son, Diego. Diego had problems intruding on peers at preschool. Joy used drawn smiley faces one week, the next week animal stickers were used, and the next week Joy introduced Diego to the joy of bouncy balls. This commitment to helping Diego achieve goals was effective, and soon he learned to engage peers and preschool teachers without interrupting them.

Obviously, when being innovative in varying the rewards, the age of the child and her current interests need to be carefully taken into account. Keeping kids invested in rewards takes plenty of awareness and creativity, but the reward for you is a better shot at promoting changes in your child.

It's All in the Contract

Getting your child to "buy in" to a reward plan can be a challenge in some cases. To help get your child invested in making some positive changes, show her you will follow through (and that you expect her to do the same) by making a contract.

I have found parent-child contracts to be very helpful in my practice. Many children like the idea that their parents, not only they, are being held accountable. Brian was initially doubtful that his father, Steve, would "get off his case" about his homework if he did it before dinnertime. In a father-son counseling session, they wrote up a contract that gave each party a sense of accountability. Steve let Brian use his own language in the contract. Steve followed my advice that the greater his son's involvement in setting up the agreement, the more likely it was for the system to succeed, which it did.

On the following pages I have provided sample contracts for you to use (one is for younger children and one for teens). Feel free to customize them to your own needs with your child. Please note that contracts work best when there are only one to three objectives. I have included more objectives on these sample contracts for illustrative purposes only.

SAMPLE CHILD/PARENT CONTRACT

Child is to meet the following expectations at least _____ out of 7 days a week.

1. Mom and Dad will help make sure child does not take things out of sibling's room.
2. Child will sit down and do homework between hours of 4:00 PM and 5:00 PM.
3. Child will be ready to leave the house on time but will be given a five-minute warning. She will not keep others waiting. On school days she is to be ready by 8:15 AM.
4. Child will follow parent's request to pick up shoes with no more than one reminder after the request.
5. Child will answer parents' questions right away but can have up to three repeat questions.
6. Child is to complete her homework calmly without being nagged.

If child meets all _____ (number of) objectives _____ out of 7 days per week, she will be awarded _____ per week.

_____   _____
Signature of Child   Signature of Parent(s)

_____
Signature of Witness

SAMPLE TEEN/PARENT CONTRACT

1. Mom or Dad will help teen to get up by putting on a radio station the teen likes.
2. Teen will call parents when out with friends after 8:00 PM and discuss options for remainder of plans for the evening and reach agreement with parents.
3. Teen will argue for no more than five minutes, no more than two times a day.
4. Teen will follow parents' request with no more than one reminder after the request.
5. Teen will answer parents' questions respectfully but can have up to three counter points.
6. Teen will seek parents to intervene instead of yelling at younger siblings.
7. Teen will get job during summertime and agree to pay one-half of car insurance.

If teen meets _____ of the _____ (number of) criteria above, she will be rewarded with _____ .

_____   _____
Signature of Teen   Signature of Parent(s)

_____
Signature of Witness

Six More Important Considerations When Using Positive Reinforcement

1. Keep the praise flowing.

I can't emphasize enough that kids of all ages benefit from positive verbal feedback. Positive changes are much more likely to occur when you help your child take pride in her accomplishments. The more your child feels good about her positive changes, the more she will carry the behavior forward in the future. Research shows that all children, particularly distracted ones, actually perform better when they are given frequent feedback about their performance.

Alice found this proved true when she helped her son Toby learn to carefully read and follow his homework directions. She had been trying to reinforce Toby with praise each week for following directions, but she found that her feedback had more impact when she gave it each night. On nights when Toby felt unsure of his homework requirements, Alice found that offering supportive encouragement and praise a few times that evening was well received.

Remember that distracted children require more frequent reminders about what is expected of them. They also need to be reminded of what they can earn for meeting those expectations. They may forget what their behavior goals are, but positive feedback can help them remember what they are working toward. I often suggest that parents use frequent reminders about the goals and rewards. Judi, a mom I worked with, found it helpful to make a note and put it where she could see it often. One of her notes simply stated, "Point out the positives." The point here is that distractible children need frequent feedback, for behavioral programs to be effective.

As I discussed in "Day 4," it's also important that teachers give liberal positive feedback to your distracted child at school. This helps your child feel that the teacher is on her side, rather than being a demanding adversary who is trying to make her life difficult.

2. Make failure hard to find.

A major reason that children fail to change or that changes do not last is that their parents get frustrated and give up too early. Be sure to be patient and give your child every opportunity to succeed.

Whether it's a homework contract, an agreement to do chores, or encouragement of a new morning routine, if a technique is not working, do some troubleshooting. Ask yourself what circumstances are interfering. Look at whether you are being realistic in the goals you are trying to reward. When changes go smoothly, give positive feedback. Don't target a new behavior until you're confident that your child has succeeded at the one you're currently working on.

Charlene wanted her ten-year-old daughter, Tessa, to do a better job of keeping her room neat. Working together (with me facilitating), they made a list of three things that they each agreed would constitute Tessa having a neater room: her clothes should be picked up off the floor, the garbage can should be emptied, and the bed should be made. Notice that this mother and daughter kept it simple, with only three tasks.

I encouraged Charlene to ease into the program rather than rushing to the finish. To get her involved, Charlene asked Tessa to pick just one thing that she was capable of—not necessarily willing—to do. Tessa picked making the bed. They then came up with a list of things that would be good rewards for Tessa—activities that were no-cost or low-cost and had some other benefit, such as taking a walk together, playing a game of Scrabble together, and baking something together.

Within a week, Charlene had encouraged Tessa to do all three steps to keeping her room neat. Charlene asked Tessa how many nights she thought that she could keep her room neat. At first Tessa gave her a sarcastic "till I die" response. To her credit, Charlene stayed calm, firm, and noncontrolling and did not get sucked into a power struggle. Charlene reached an agreement with Tessa that she would neaten her room four out of seven days each week. Charlene also extended Tessa some good will and flexibility by offering to keep Tessa company while she straightened up her room.

3. Apply praise effectively.

I know this sounds obvious, but I encourage you to be mindful of applying praise in ways that work. For example, when giving praise, it's important that you let your child know what exactly she did that was different than before, and why it was helpful, as shown in the examples below.

> *"Thanks for starting your homework before I needed to remind you."*
>
> *"I really appreciated how you walked the dog after I only asked you one time to do this."*

4. Stock up your storehouse of rewards.

On the next page is a chart of positive behaviors that deserve praise. Feel free to photocopy it and place it somewhere for easy reference. It should serve as a helpful reminder for you to identify and reward your child's positive behaviors. Blank lines are provided at the bottom so that you can include any behaviors specific to your child.

Following the chart of positive behaviors that deserve praise are two charts that illustrate rewards for elementary and younger kids and teens, respectively.

SAMPLE POSITIVE BEHAVIORS OF DISTRACTED CHILDREN TO PRAISE AND REWARD

Writing down assignments	Starting homework	Complaining less about schoolwork
Inviting a friend over	Finishing homework	Starting homework on time
Not rushing homework	Asking teacher for help	Speaking quietly
Walking softly	Being patient with siblings or friends	Doing chores without rushing
Getting a good quiz/test grade	Making a new friend	Not calling out in class
Being considerate with a friend or sibling	Remembering school supplies	Getting to school in a timely manner
Observing good hygiene	Joining a school activity	Being calm/relaxed
Admitting school problems	Being patient	Being friendly
Cooperating with teacher	_____	_____
_____	_____	_____

REWARD POSSIBILITIES FOR PRESCHOOL/ ELEMENTARY AGE KIDS

Playing with clay or Play-Doh	Going someplace alone with Dad or Mom	Helping plan the day's activities
Helping Mom or Dad	Having a longer time in the bathtub	Riding on a bicycle with Dad or Mom
Going out for ice cream	Playing with friends	Feeding a pet
Going to the park	Playing in the sandbox	Making noises with rattles, pans, or bells
Playing a board game with Dad or Mom	Going to the library	Drawing with crayons
Bouncing on the bed	Playing outside	Sitting in the front seat
Staying up later	Going on a trip to the zoo	Renting a video game
Going to the movies	Riding on Dad's shoulders	Eating out
_____	_____	_____
_____	_____	_____

REWARD POSSIBILITIES FOR PRETEENS/TEENS

Talking additional time on the telephone	Playing the stereo	Making a trip alone that is deemed safe
Finding a part-time job	Taking the car to school for a day	Getting to stay out later than usual
Going to summer camp	Getting a special haircut or hair style	Going to Disneyland or some other amusement park
Being allowed to stay home when the family goes out	Inviting a friend to eat out	Getting to sleep in late on the weekend
Having their own checking account	Receiving a magazine subscription	Going shopping with friends
Computer time	Playing a video game	Renting a new video game
Watching a video	Buying a CD	Skateboarding
Redecorating their own room	Participating in activities with friends	Receiving money for a new purchase
_____	_____	_____
_____	_____	_____

5. Don't forget to focus on their effort.

Tough we've talked a lot about behavior and accomplishments, your child's efforts are just as important. Praise and other rewards are powerful positive reinforcement tools to help increase any demonstrated positive behaviors. Encouragement focuses on your child's efforts. Praise focuses on results. Both are valuable in reinforcing appropriate behaviors.

Lillian found that her fourteen-year-old son, Cole, thrived when he was given encouragement. Lillian had been brought up by stern parents and previously did not believe much in being warm and fuzzy. "Let Cole first show me he made an improvement, then I'll make a fuss," was originally her take on the idea of encouraging with positive support. I worked with Lillian to help her see that her stern mentality was not helping Cole deal with his distract- ibility at school. When Lillian switched to a more encouraging, nurturing approach, Cole responded positively.

6. Look for past examples of strengths to encourage your child.

We benefit from recalling our past successes. Anchoring yourself in past successes can provide motivation for tackling new chal- lenges. Distracted children tend to dismiss what they did well in the past. You can encourage your child by reminding her in a calm, firm, noncontrolling way about what she has done well in the past. Here's a good example: *"You did a great job with your math problems yesterday. I know you can tackle this new sheet of equations."*

Keep Your Own Tank Full of Positive Energy

The focus of this book so far has been on skills that you can use to help your child, but it's just as important that you praise and reinforce yourself as well.

I want to congratulate you right now for making it this far in my program. You have learned many ways to manage your distracted child. Take a few moments and give yourself credit for the wonderful things you have been doing to help your distracted child. Go through the list of positive behaviors below and pat yourself on the back for all the ones you can check off.

Met with teachers   _____

Educated myself by reading books on distractibility   _____

Organized school materials   _____

Was emotionally supportive to my child when upset   _____

Attended extracurricular school events my child
is involved in   _____

Coached and encouraged peer relationships   _____

Bought notebooks and school supplies   _____

Helped with homework   _____

Attended teacher conferences   _____

Listened to my child's concerns each day   _____

Loved my child despite frustration directed at me   _____

No matter how many or few of the above supportive parenting behaviors you have done, let yourself feel good about them. Remember that you are taking big steps to help your child. Stay mindful of all of your efforts and feel good about them.

DAY 8: SUMMING IT UP

Today you have learned about the power of praise and other rewards to reinforce positive behaviors in your distracted child. Remember how much progress you have made since you started. Keep in mind the following key points about reinforcing positive behavior in your child:

- Praise, if given in the correct manner, can significantly increase your distracted child's positive behaviors.
- The more you reward your child's focused behaviors, the more you will lessen her distracted ones.
- Other rewards can be combined with praise to recognize your child's positive behaviors.
- Reinforcing yourself for your positive parenting efforts and actions is very valuable to both you and your child.

Medication and Alternative Treatments

Congratulations—you've almost finished this ten-day program, and you have learned many powerful strategies to help your child lower and manage his distractibility in different settings. I hope you feel good about how far you have come in such a short time.

If you have applied the strategies presented so far in earnest, then you and your distracted child probably feel more in control. If so, your child is well on his way to more effectively managing life's challenges. I am very confident that this ten-day program will continue to be helpful as you go forward.

If you have been applying the suggestions in this book and have seen only minimal or no improvement in your child, then today's discussion about medications and alternative treatments for distractibility may be helpful. Even if you feel that your child's distractibility problems do seem much more manageable at this point, I still encourage you to read this chapter. Learning about medications and alternative treatments will be valuable if your child's distractibility ever takes a turn for the worse in the future.

What's hot and what's not with regard to medications and alternative treatments for distracted children changes over time. Therefore, my purpose in this chapter is not to provide an exhaustive or in-depth review of them. Rather, I discuss important general considerations that you should be aware of. Please be aware that I am a psychologist, not a physician, and the information presented here is not a substitute for discussing questions and concerns with your child's doctor or other qualified health-care professional.

Medication and Your Distracted Child

So far this book has focused on behavioral interventions to be used in school, with peers, and at home. If these interventions have significantly lowered your child's distractibility, then it makes sense to avoid using medications. At the same time, it's well known that medication (particularly stimulants) can be highly beneficial to many distracted children. The efficacy of medication to lower problematic distractibility has been shown by many studies. Yet, most parents that I have worked with are quite cautious, and often apprehensive, about putting their distracted children on medication. While I have found that most parents are eventually willing to allow their distracted children to take medication, they understandably want to make sure that taking this step is really necessary.

Medication is seen by most physicians as the most viable treatment option when a child's distractibility stems from a moderate to severe case of ADHD. In many cases, I have seen firsthand— particularly with children who have moderate to severe levels of distractibility—that medicine does in fact make a huge positive difference in their lives. I can also echo the same findings for children with clinical levels of depression, anxiety, and other mental health concerns that are, at times, not solely responsive to counseling interventions.

Let me be clear, however, that medication is no magic bullet that will end all of your child's problems with distractibility or any other mental health issues. It has been widely demonstrated that the optimum treatment of ADHD usually involves a combination of educational/behavioral strategies such as described in this book, counseling, and medication, when deemed appropriate and as prescribed and monitored by a physician. It's also important to bear in mind that recent research has shown that educational and behavioral interventions, when effectively implemented and used in combination with medication, result in significantly lower doses of medication than when medication is used alone.

A NOTE OF CAUTION

Physicians, distracted children, and their families need to work patiently together to find the right medication at the right dose. The reality is that children, by definition, are growing, and their fluctuating body weights and changing tolerances to medications warrant close follow-up. A distracted child's responsiveness to medication needs to be monitored over time through the collective input of the child, his parents, and his teachers.

Please see the Appendix for the ADHD Monitoring System by David Rabiner, PhD. This tool is a helpful teacher resource for monitoring medication effectiveness over time. It can be used with children of any age. In practice, however, it's easier to implement with elementary-school children. There is nothing about the system that makes it inappropriate for older kids, but once kids get to middle school and have multiple teachers, it may be more challenging to get the information reported in a timely manner . The ADHD Monitoring System is available as an electronic document at www.helpforadd.com.

Reflections from the Trenches

As I was writing this chapter, I asked some distracted children and parents I see in my practice to describe their views and experiences with the medication they take. Here are some of their responses:

> *"My mom leaves it on the counter and I take it in the morning. My teacher told my mom that it helps me do better, but I don't really know."—Ryan, age ten, on taking his medication and whether or not it helps him*

> *"It helps me pay attention more to what everyone is saying. If I don't take it I space out and have trouble listening to what other people are saying."—Grace, age fourteen, on how her medication helps her with peers*

> *"It helps me learn to control myself on my own. Now I don't really get in trouble at school and I can get my homework done better."—Ricky, age thirteen*

> *"Without his medicine he is unable to focus and he has uncontrollable outbursts. And with the medicine he is more able to stay on and complete tasks and is more focused in school. When he is on the medicine he also makes better decisions, peerwise. When this kid is off the medicine he makes bad decisions with peers, and acts like too much of a clown."—Karen, mother of a twelve-year-old boy on medication*

> *"It makes the day go by faster. And it makes me have energy to take notes in class. If I don't take it, it feels like the day won't come to an end."—Allen, age sixteen, on taking a well-known prescribed stimulant medication*

> *"Since Jeanie went on medication she has gone from a*
> *C/D student within four weeks to an A/B student. And,*
> *my son Josh became so much less stressed-out and the joy-*
> *ful happy child again that we remembered from when he*
> *was young.—Lisa, mother of two distracted children, ages*
> *eleven and thirteen*

As exemplified above, medications can be helpful for distracted children. Yet, it's important to keep in mind that children benefit from medication to varying degrees. While medication is generally helpful to most children with ADHD, I have also found that some children with ADHD can have their symptoms managed effectively without medication. This latter group, however, usually consists of children whose ADHD symptoms are relatively mild.

I have seen few children who outwardly object to taking medication, though some do. In these cases, I certainly don't advocate forcing medication down a child's throat. When children do refuse to take medication, even in the comfort and privacy of their homes, trying to force the issue can create even more problems. More often than refusal, distracted children have difficulty remembering to take medications. Parental monitoring and supervision can help solve this problem.

Newer, longer-lasting medications have reduced the need for children to feel singled out or "weird" for having to visit the school nurse each day to take another dose. For many children, these longer-acting medications have helped reduce the embarrassment factor that results from having to stand in line at the school nurse's office.

Parents understandably have a strong protective instinct about their children. This can make them fearful when first venturing into the realm of medication for their distracted children. In the next section, I will address some common myths about medication for distracted children that can fuel such fears. Please note that the overall focus of this forthcoming discussion is on ADHD, as this is the most common distractibility condition for which medication is prescribed.

Myths about Medication for Reducing Distractibility

Medication for children with ADHD issues, including distractibility, is a hotly debated topic. I empathize with parents who struggle with the decision of whether or not to place their distracted child on medication. It seems that many parents get upset not over the medications themselves, but over the rampant misconceptions about them. To help clarify some important points, I will debunk the common inaccurate beliefs about medication for ADHD-related distractibility.

MYTH: Medicine can't really help lower distractibility for children with ADHD.

A vast number of children have benefited from medication, but I still come across many parents who doubt the efficacy of medication for ADHD. Maybe this is because many parents learn, after reading the relevant literature, that it's still not absolutely clear why stimulants and some other medications do work. Researchers believe that medications lower distractibility because they alter activity within certain brain regions, which leads to more focus, less hyperactivity, and less impulsivity. I have seen children of all ages make dramatic improvements seemingly overnight in important areas of their lives, when placed on medication. This includes better attention in class, with improvements in the quantity and quality of the work they complete. Another benefit of medication is less impulsivity on the playground. Peer relationship problems often show dramatic improvement as medication helps these kids be perceived as less intrusive and annoying. Medication for distracted kids who are impulsive can also help reduce problems at home, such as defiant behavior. In short, while it may not be easy for many parents to accept, medication does tend to work—often very well—to lower distractibility and hyperactivity/impulsivity in children.

MYTH: *Giving my child medication will turn him into a drug addict.*

There is a popular misconception that medicating a child for ADHD is essentially preparing him to continue on to full-fledged drug abuse. Recently, I had one concerned parent tell me, "I just worry that by giving my son this medicine I'm not only saying that drugs are okay, I am teaching my child how to take drugs."

The truth is that kids who have untreated ADHD are much more likely to abuse illicit drugs than children who are properly taking medication. The bottom line is that problematic levels of ADHD can lead to bigger problems later in life, if the ADHD is not medically treated. In fact, research shows that children with ADHD who need and do not receive medication are more likely to have academic and social problems, as well as to use illicit drugs.

At the same time, having a doctor prescribe stimulant medication to a teen who has an active drug addiction is quite risky. I have seen teens abuse and sell stimulants to other teens, who can abuse them. Children with substance abuse issues need to be under the care of a qualified mental health professional. If there is any concern that a child has a proclivity for substance abuse, his prescribed medications must be judiciously monitored.

MYTH: *Stimulants and other medications for ADHD have major side effects and are not safe.*

Seemingly countless parents have relayed to me their fears about the possible side effects of medication. They are mostly referring to stimulant medications such as Adderall and Concerta.

Most studies on the long-term use of stimulant medication agree that stimulants have been safely used to treat ADHD for millions of children and adults over the past sixty years. To date, there have not been any apparent long-term side effects. However, it's always important to keep in mind that any medication, including those bought over the counter, can have potential side effects in some individuals.

Research shows that approximately 20 percent of children on psychostimulant medication may have transient, mild, short-term side effects that can usually be alleviated by careful drug dosage or timing adjustments. Within this group of kids, some may experience problematic side effects that prevent them from taking medication on a long-term basis. These side effects include tics, sleep difficulties, stomachaches and other gastrointestinal issues, headaches, appetite reduction, drowsiness, irritability, nervousness, and excessive staring, among others. In very rare cases, stimulant medication can lead to nervous tics, hallucinations, and bizarre behavior. Please keep in mind, however, that serious side-effect-related concerns are far more the exception than the rule.

I do appreciate that the above description of possible side effects can be very scary when you are considering the use of medication for *your* child. Again, research findings from many carefully controlled studies show that, when properly employed, stimulant medication is safe and the side effects are minimal. When side effects do occur, they are frequently short term and generally disappear when the dosage is reduced. Despite knowing this data, I encourage you to discuss your questions and concerns with your child's physician.

MYTH: Medication will change my child's personality or make him into a zombie.

I recall Sarah being fearful that her fourteen-year-old son, Sergio, "will end up walking around like a zombie." In no way minimizing the fears of this concerned mother, I assured her that I have not seen children experience radical, unfavorable personality changes when put on medication. Some children do become sluggish and withdrawn when on medication, but these symptoms generally indicate that the dose is too high, or that a coexisting condition such as a mood problem has not been identified. Studies have generally shown that, far from turning kids into "zombies," treatment with stimulants causes an increase in positive social behaviors in ADHD children.

MYTH: Stimulants are the only class of medications that helps distracted children.

While stimulants appear to be the most widely used medications for ADHD, other classes of medications (antidepressants, anti-anxiety medications) may help distracted children, as well. This is particularly the case if there are other mental health conditions affecting the distracted child. In short, the source of the distractibility is very important to consider when physicians are making medication-related decisions. I have seen many children with distraction issues who also have clinical depression and anxiety disorders, for example, become far less distracted when treated with appropriate medications.

Stimulant Medication and Growth Issues

For obvious reasons, the idea that stimulant medications hinder physical growth is a huge concern for parents. Given the widespread attention to this issue, I am addressing it separately from the other side effect/health concerns mentioned above.

The best knowledge so far regarding whether or not stimulants stunt growth in children comes from researchers who conducted a National Institute of Mental Health (NIMH) study. They concluded that the growth-restricting effects of ADHD drugs are relatively mild. Another study has shown a mild growth suppression rate of nearly a half-inch per year in children who took stimulants such as Ritalin. Their findings got a bit fuzzy, however, when the researchers compared these figures to the national growth averages of children in the same age group. It was determined that those treated with medication lagged behind by only one-eighth of an inch in height, making the research findings inconclusive.

In short, the use of medication is an individual decision best made in consultation with your child's doctor. The difficult reality is that even if medication has some risk for height suppression, this may not offset the risk of untreated ADHD. In a considerable number of ADHD children who do not get properly medicated, the range of problematic outcomes includes school failure, difficulty getting along with peers, problems with self-esteem, substance abuse, possible juvenile delinquency, and more.

Medications Commonly Used with Distracted Children

Stimulants

Stimulant medication has been the preferred class of prescription drug for children with ADHD. Although most children with ADHD will be helped by stimulants, it's impossible to predict the individual response of any one child. I have seen many instances where children are prescribed one type of stimulant with a range of doses and experienced no significant benefit. In such cases, a different stimulant usually works instead.

Research shows that, on average, 80 percent of children with distractibility due to ADHD and other neurological conditions respond to stimulant medication. This means they show a significant improvement in the core symptoms of ADHD, which are inattention, hyperactivity, and impulsivity.

The most commonly prescribed medication used to treat ADHD is Concerta, although a number of other stimulant medications are also used, including Ritalin, Adderall, Focalin, Metadate, and Dexedrine. Recently, Daytrana, a new medicine patch containing the same stimulant that's in Ritalin, was developed to help children with ADHD. Daytrana is also associated with the mostly transient side effects of stimulant medications, but the flexibility of a skin patch may be a valuable benefit of this new product.

Antidepressants

Some tricyclic antidepressants are also used in treating kids with ADHD. These drugs have been well studied and are completely safe. Commonly prescribed tricyclic medications include Imipramine, Desipramine, Amitriptyline, Nortriptyline, and Clomipramine. Doctors will typically use tricyclics if stimulant medications are unsuccessful, or if they produce unfavorable side effects that can't be tolerated.

In addition to the tricyclic antidepressants, newer antidepressants such as Lexapro, Prozac, Zoloft, and Wellbutrin may be used to directly target coexisting symptoms of anxiety or depression. These drugs may also be helpful in treating distractibility, although less evidence documenting their effectiveness in treating ADHD has been gathered.

Strattera is a selective norepinephrine reuptake inhibitor (SNRI) that has also been used more recently to treat ADHD with success.

As is the case with many medications out there, Strattera's exact mechanism of action is not known.

In sum, when it comes to problems of distractibility, there is no one magical elixir that will solve all of your distracted child's problems. Stimulants appear to be quite effective, but no matter what medicine is prescribed, your distracted child will still need help from you and others to teach him effective behavioral coping strategies. These will help him to manage frustration and effectively tackle academic challenges, such as time management and breaking tasks down into more manageable parts.

Follow Up with Responsible Follow-Up

Parents of distracted children understandably want their child to be on medication only as long as it is helpful and necessary. As I mentioned earlier, follow-up is key in determining medication needs as children go forward. For some children with ADHD, symptoms appear to dissipate as they get older, and continued use of medication is no longer necessary. Many other children, however, continue to struggle with ADHD symptoms into adolescence and young adulthood. Because the need for stimulant medication may change over time, most experts recommend that this issue be reevaluated on an annual basis.

I have seen an increasing number of parents and children decide to stop or resume medications without consulting their physician. This is obviously not a good practice. All medication decisions must be made in conjunction with a supervising physician.

Questions to Consider When Deciding If Medication Is Right for Your Child

Here are some important questions to ask yourself as you try to determine whether medication is right for your child. All of these can be discussed with your qualified health-care professional.

- When did distractibility start becoming a problem for my child?
- How long has my child been distractible?
- Have distraction-related problems been constant or erratic for my child, and to what degree?
- In what settings is the distractibility of most concern (school, home, community activities)?
- What level of distractibility does my child struggle with (mild, moderate, severe)?
- What is the opinion of past teachers, physicians, and others involved with my distracted child regarding the extent of his distractibility?
- Can I see a benefit to my child trying medication?
- Will my child cooperate with taking medication?
- How will the effectiveness of the medication be monitored?

Alternative Treatments

Alternative treatments are treatments used in place of conventional medical treatments (such as prescription medication), in an attempt to cure or treat a condition. There is considerable debate about whether alternative treatments such as dietary changes, herb formulations, fish oil, biofeedback, and counseling (with distracted kids many consider counseling as an alternative treatment) can help distracted children. Many parents share with me how overwhelmed they feel when considering alternative treatment options. In fact, I bet you could spend the rest of your life exploring the staggering number of proposed natural cures for ADHD on the Web. Generally, however, the efficacy of the products out there has not been convincingly supported by rigorous research.

At the same time, I am aware that a growing number of alternative and natural remedies to treat ADHD are being touted. Twenty years ago, fresh out of graduate school, I was much more likely to readily dismiss the effectiveness of anything that hadn't appeared in an esteemed scientific journal. However, since that time, my thinking has changed somewhat. If, for example, a parent and child tell me that a simple dietary change, like no longer eating bananas, has done wonders for the child's distractibility, who am I to argue? It does appear that for milder distractibility cases, some alternative therapies may help control symptoms. In more severe cases, they can possibly support conventional medicine treatment. The important thing to remember about alternative treatments is that they are usually supported only by anecdotal reports and testimonials, and have not been proven effective by scientific trials. If any of the alternative methods I discuss next appeal to you, talk to your health-care practitioner about their safety and how you might use them to lower your child's distractibility. As with any health-care products and practices, never use alternative treatments without consulting a qualified physician.

DIETARY SUPPLEMENTS

Keep in mind that dietary supplements do not require approval from the Food and Drug Administration (FDA) before they are made available to the general public. This means that there are currently no FDA regulations specific to dietary and herbal supplements to establish a minimum standard of practice for manufacturing them.

The somewhat unsettling reality is that the company making the product is responsible for establishing its own manufacturing practice guidelines. Basically, it falls on the manufacturing company itself to ensure that the dietary supplements it produces are safe and contain the ingredients listed on the label. So if you do purchase supplements, do your best to find a company that is established and reputable.

Supplements

Since they are not monitored by the FDA, the identity, purity, quality, strength, and composition of the dietary supplements discussed here may or may not meet the expectations of you or your child. At the same time, I have had a considerable number of clients claim modest to significant benefits from supplements. Below is a list of supplements that their manufacturers suggest can help lower distractibility.

Omega-3 Fatty Acids

There has been increasing attention recently on the use of omega-3 fatty acids (commonly called "fish oil" because they're found in fish) to lower distractibility. In fact, of all the supplements claimed to help manage distractibility, omega-3 fatty acids appear to be the most promising.

The rationale behind omega-3 fatty acid supplements is that the brain is approximately 60 percent fat, and it needs certain fatty acids to function properly. Kids with ADHD may be deficient in these fatty acids, and therefore a supplement would theoretically restore balance. According to the manufacturers of omega-3 fatty acids, they support cell membrane fluidity, neurotransmitter function, and several aspects of brain development.

Some research has shown that supplementing a child's diet with the omega-3 fatty acids can help manage ADHD symptoms. Theorists suggest that, compared to youngsters with normal levels, children with lower omega-3 fatty acid levels have significantly more temper tantrums and problems with behavior, learning, health, and sleep. Omega-3 fatty acids are inexpensive and have no known side effects (in proper doses), so they may be worthwhile to pursue. I still advise that you talk to your doctor before giving your child supplements of any kind.

Megavitamins and Minerals

Few people would dispute the fact that vitamins are helpful for promoting general health. There have been some bold claims, however, that giving a child with ADHD large amounts of certain vitamins (such as B6 and B12), minerals (such as zinc or magnesium), trace elements, and other nutritional elements can alleviate symptoms. Currently, and much to the dismay of many vitamin advocates, very little reliable research exists to support this theory. In fact, giving your child large doses of certain vitamins and minerals can be dangerous. I encourage you to speak to your child's doctor if you are concerned about his nutrition. While some kids and parents may see a benefit from using megavitamins and minerals, these generally do not appear to be worthwhile.

Herbs

From health food stores to the Internet, there are abundant and increasing amounts of herbal formulations targeted at kids with ADHD. To date, there really is little evidence supporting herbs as a consistently effective treatment for ADHD.

The most popular herbal products for ADHD include herbs such as ginkgo and ginseng with herbal sedatives (such as valerian and lemon balm). Ginkgo increases circulation to the brain and has been shown to significantly improve memory and other cognitive functions in healthy adults. Ginseng is reportedly helpful for enhancing both mental and physical functions under stress. Ginseng extracts have been shown to improve memory and attention in healthy adults.

Children with ADHD do tend to have trouble sleeping, regardless of whether or not they are on stimulant medication. This of course only worsens problems with attention, learning, and behavior. One reported herbal remedy for sleep problems is valerian. Again, always speak with your child's doctor before giving your child any over-the-counter product, whether natural or synthetic.

Dietary Changes

Years ago, pediatrician and allergist Dr. Ben Feingold became very popular by asserting that the reactions to certain types of food additives accounted for approximately half the cases of ADHD. He further claimed that when children with ADHD were placed on his prescribed diet, 50 percent showed such dramatic improvement that they were able to discontinue stimulant medication. However, Dr. Feingold's diet plan lacks the research to validate it in the eyes of the scientific community.

But the lack of consistent evidence of a causal relationship between food additives and ADHD symptoms does not mean it doesn't occur in some children. I have had many parents suggest that certain food dyes, and possibly preservatives as well, can aggravate their children's distractibility. When I have a parent swear to me, for example, that excluding foods that have Red 40 and Yellow 5 from her child's diet leads to better attention span, I encourage her to tell her child's physician. Red 40 is used mainly in junk foods. Yellow 5 is an artificial coloring typically found in gelatin desserts, candy, and baked goods. It could also be that these foods contain more sugar than most.

On the flip side, many parents have told me that the amount of time and energy needed to maintain their children's diet restrictions is usually highly challenging, and the payoff of reduced distractibility is minimal. One mother I worked with was a trained natural healer with extensive knowledge of diet and nutrition, and a close relationship with her thirteen-year-old distracted son. Even so, she could not prevent his self-defeating binges on chocolate, which, suffice it to say, was not on the "okay to eat" list.

Food allergies are also cited by some as a cause for ADHD symptoms. Commonly discussed dietary culprits include dairy, wheat, corn, citrus fruits, strawberries, eggs, chocolate, and peanuts. If you suspect that your child may be allergic or behaviorally sensitive to any of these foods, talk to a nutritionist or allergist before removing them from his diet, to ensure that your child is still getting all the nutrients his growing body needs.

Limiting Sugar

While many studies have examined a possible link between sugar and hyperactivity, none has found a significant relationship. Still, some parents swear that their children act out more after eating foods that contain a lot of refined sugar. I recall one teenage girl who became highly hyperactive and very sick after she ate ice cream and candy one day, after years of avoiding sugar.

It can't hurt to reduce the amount of sugar in your child's diet. According to the U.S. Department of Agriculture, children consume an average of twice the amount of sugar recommended. It's just not clear how much of this is responsible for distractibility in children.

Limiting Carbohydrates

Some people also believe that a diet too rich in carbohydrates can cause cyclical spikes and drops in blood sugar levels and can consequently exacerbate the symptoms of ADHD. There is, in fact, some evidence that kids with ADHD crave carbohydrates, particularly refined or simple carbohydrates such as sugar and fruit. In a small percentage of cases, eating these foods does seem to make the symptoms worse. Proponents of this theory recommend avoiding simple carbohydrates and replacing them with protein and fiber-rich foods, such as meats and vegetables. Overall, however, carbohydrates receive much more attention for sabotaging waistlines than attention spans.

Homeopathy

Some years ago, I had a client who was doggedly determined to avoid having his twelve-year-old daughter receive stimulant medication. He went to a well-respected homeopathic physician, who had the child try various remedies. The theory behind homeopathy is that certain potentially toxic substances, when taken in an extremely diluted form, can trigger the body's natural healing process. The daughter had some modest success in reduced distractibility, but it only lasted for about two months.

I have seen a few distracted children who purportedly benefited more from homeopathic treatments than medication, but the number of children who have benefited from medication is vastly larger. I do value the input of my clients and people I have met at seminars, and I listen with curiosity to those who maintain that homeopathic remedies can significantly improve the symptoms of ADHD. At the same time, there are currently no reliable studies showing that homeopathy is reliably effective for treating ADHD.

Biofeedback

Some people claim that biofeedback, also referred to as neurofeedback, helps manage ADHD symptoms, including distractibility. The goal of biofeedback is to teach an individual how to calm down and increase his ability to focus. There are different types of biofeedback machines available, but they all help control the body's responses to stress, including pulse rate, breathing rate, and muscle tension. Over the years, a few of my child clients have received biofeedback over several sessions, to lower anxiety. I have seen some positive results, which is consistent with some research supporting the efficacy of biofeedback for treating anxiety-related concerns.

To receive biofeedback, a child is "hooked up" to a machine that first registers some baseline measurements and then shows the child when his pulse rate is up, for example, indicating that he's upset or excited, and when it's coming back down, indicating that he's succeeding in calming himself. Eventually, biofeedback teaches the child to calm himself without using the machine.

While it may be helpful in reducing anxiety, biofeedback has not been consistently shown to reduce the symptoms of ADHD. Biofeedback takes a number of sessions to show results, and the results may not last beyond the sessions. In short, there is not yet enough good research to prove that biofeedback actually treats the underlying ADHD.

Counseling

When I counsel children, I do not guarantee that any child I work with will have lower distractibility as a result. However, I do use many of the strategies in this book when counseling parents and children, and I promote the use of them. I also try to help parents and children develop mutually agreed-upon distractibility management goals.

You know by now that I am all about children being understood by their parents. When I counsel distracted children and their parents, I stress that understanding the child's challenges helps parents make informed decisions. One of the biggest difficulties for parents (and children) is differentiating between what a distracted child can and cannot reliably do. Too many distracted children suffer with low self-esteem in response to their parents' erroneous belief that they are bad, stupid, or lazy. I help bridge the gap of misunderstanding between parents and children.

I also coach children to appropriately attribute their problems to their distractibility. At the same time, I discourage them from using ADHD as an excuse. It's important that children take responsibility for their behaviors.

Another major counseling goal with distracted children is to repair broken relationships. ADHD can impair the relationships a child has with his parents, siblings, teachers, and peers. To this end, I try to educate a child's siblings about ADHD. This helps them better understand the problem and be more of an ally during treatment.

ADHD can also strain the marital relationship between the parents. It's essential that the parents be able to work together as a cooperative team in order to cope better with the problems. Parents might need marital therapy if the problems continue to affect their marriage.

Exercise

A common misconception is that children with ADHD just need more exercise to lessen distractibility. I worked with one thirteen-year-old hyperactive girl with distraction issues who rapidly paced all around my office during our counseling sessions. I joked with her mother that if she was put on a treadmill that was wired to a generator, then she could power the whole community.

I do believe that exercise in general and involvement in specific sports can, to some extent, give ADHD-diagnosed children a way to blow off steam, build self-confidence, improve focus and concentration, and make friends. I have also seen that sports that require high levels of focus, such as karate, can sometimes modestly increase attention span in distracted children. The more kids move around, the more the activity can produce positive changes in attention span, concentration, coordination, dexterity, and social behavior. However, whether this translates to the classroom or leads to better social judgment and restraint is unclear.

Using the Arts

Some believe that engaging in creative activities such as drawing, listening to music, or dancing helps children with ADHD calm down and focus better. Art utilizes the part of the brain that controls emotions. Children with ADHD often have trouble controlling their emotions, and these activities may help calm them.

How long these positive effects last is more debatable than whether they occur in the first place. If nothing else, some distracted kids do have an affinity for music and other kinds of artistic expression. For any child, finding a creative outlet that allows him to excel and express himself can be a great self-esteem booster. Of course, you may need some caution (and noise-canceling headphones) if your child has a trumpet or drum set on his wish list.

Other Alternative Treatments

There are many other treatments that claim to help relieve the symptoms of ADHD, such as magnet therapy, sound treatment, visual training, chiropractic care, and yeast eradication. While all of these treatments have supporters, there simply are no solid studies that prove that they lower distractibility over the long run.

I also want to encourage you not to dismiss the value of commonsense measures, such as making sure your child gets a good night's sleep, eats well, and feels connected to you. They will go a long way in helping your child feel and function better.

Points to Bear in Mind When Considering Alternative Treatments

Stay vigilant as you explore alternative types of treatments to help your distracted child. Whether you read about a "hot new discovery" of a new plant extract from the far reaches of China or you see some riveting new procedure on TV, stay cautious. I recommend you stay away from any product or procedure if any of the following applies to its promotional message:

- There is a miraculous, universal, one-size-fits-all claim that the product will work for everyone with ADHD and/or will also cure other health problems.
- You have to call 1-800-Buy-NOWW within two minutes to get this life-changing product.
- There are only case histories or testimonials from "everyday people just like you and me" giving proof of effectiveness (and no well-recognized scientific research).
- There is no list of ingredients or directions for proper use provided.
- There is no information to warn about side effects.
- The product is described as harmless because it's "natural" (most drugs are developed from natural sources).
- It's available from only one source, such as a mail-order company.
- The product is promoted through infomercials featuring highly animated, unrealistically optimistic actors (or paid participants).

DAY 9: SUMMING IT UP

Today you learned about medications and alternative treatments as further options to lower your child's distractibility. Please keep the following points in mind:

■ Medication, particularly stimulants, can provide significant benefits to the majority of children with ADHD.

■ Even though a child may benefit from stimulant medication, there can often be remaining academic and/or behavioral difficulties that need to be addressed with other forms of intervention.

■ Most children do not experience any prolonged adverse side effects from taking stimulant medication when it is administered properly. It is very important, however, for parents to discuss their questions and concerns with their child's physician.

■ A child's response to medication can change over time, as can the child's need for medication. Reevaluating these issues on a periodic basis is very important.

■ Alternative treatments such as dietary changes and natural remedies can be helpful in some cases to lower distractibility. Fish oil supplements appear to be the most promising. However, keep in mind that for most dietary and herbal supplements, there is currently little solid scientific evidence proving their effectiveness in treating ADHD.

■ The strategies I've provided in this book can be used alone or in addition to medication.

Reducing Distractibility for the Long Run

My overarching goal in this book has been to give you the most effective tools and strategies I can to create positive and long-lasting changes in your distracted child. It is my hope that by earnestly applying the strategies I have provided in this book, you have created significantly less disruptive distractibility in your child. As you complete the program today, I encourage you to continue to use all of the ideas and strategies I have shared with you, going forward. They are timeless.

I realize that you want your child to learn these coping skills and empowering strategies so that she can take care of herself as she faces life's current and future challenges. The best way to encourage your child's receptivity to the strategies in this book is to foster her cooperation and enthusiasm to strive for success. Whether the goal is helping your overwhelmed child break down larger tasks into more manageable ones or giving her feedback for handling peer difficulties, using the calm, firm, and noncontrolling approach is key to getting these skills to stick in your child's mind. The more you can understand, join with, and support your child, the more receptive she'll be to your help and support.

Today I offer you some final thoughts on how to best manage your child's distractibility in the long run. You started this program with a commitment to coach your child to manage her distractibility. Through the use of this program, you now have many ways to facilitate your child's success in educational, emotional, and social settings. I encourage you to keep thinking of yourself as a coach for your child, going forward. As such, remember that continued progress comes from continued practice.

Empower Your Child by Being Proactive

I have seen too often that just when distracted children start to get themselves clear of problems, they end up falling back into old routines. For example, many lagging distracted kids who do catch up with their schoolwork can easily get overwhelmed and rapidly fall behind all over again. So, for the big picture, remember that staying proactive means staying mindful of how easy it may be for your child to fall behind or to reencounter difficulties. Please never take your distracted child's easier times and progress for granted.

Some key ways to be proactive are:

- Having a routine time to talk with your child about upcoming school assignments and projects (I find that Sunday nights can be a good time to do this).
- Providing ongoing messages of encouragement and support to your child.
- Remembering to stay calm, firm, and noncontrolling as you communicate with your child about school and other parts of her life. The more you do this, the more your child will likely confide in you while her problems are still molehills and not yet mountains.
- Staying positive and tuned in to what is working well. For example, your child may be more effective getting her schoolwork done after taking an hour to blow off steam. Forcing the issue of her starting her schoolwork right away may work best for you, but it may not ultimately be best for her.

- Realizing that sometimes the best way to check up is to check in—with your child's teachers, other parents, coaches, or anyone else involved in your child's life. Keep up with her schoolwork and other activities to make sure she is keeping up with and feeling positive about them.

Setbacks are Not Setups for Failure

Despite all the progress your child has made and your commitment to being proactive in the future, the road ahead will likely have some bumps. As your child meets upcoming challenges at school, with peers, at home, or in the community, she may face some setbacks. Just remember that setbacks do not have to be setups for failure. Instead, they can be valuable opportunities for further learning and self-improvement.

Be aware that distractibility is especially likely to reemerge when your child is frustrated, stressed, or dealing with any negative emotions due to difficulties and challenges. It's important to remember, when your child is having a setback, that these backslides are only natural. When either one of you is feeling disappointed, think about all the hard work you've put into this ten-day program and how very far you have both come.

When your child's focus seems to unravel, the following tips will help you keep her from continuing down the slippery slope:

- Stay mindful of all the positive changes you and your child have made so far, and talk about them. She may act indifferent, but deep down she loves hearing the good stuff.
- When you and your child discuss concerns, stick to the relevant issues. Discuss all concerns in a calm, nonaggressive, concrete, and specific way. Avoid using words such as "always," "never,"

and "should," which tend to create defensiveness. Staying calm, firm, and noncontrolling will keep you connected to your child—and keep her connected with herself.

- Stay mindful of any negative parenting behaviors you may be sliding back into, such as being overly demanding, making rigid comments, throwing out unrealistic and harsh ultimatums, acting in a threatening manner, and slinging shame to try to influence change.
- If you become frustrated and "lose it," sincerely apologize to your child.
- Empathize with (but don't enable) your child's problem behaviors.
- "Catch" your child's positive behaviors and praise them.
- Listen to your child's frustrations and understand them.
- Stay optimistic in the face of setbacks.
- Be loving and respectful.
- Talk to a friend or trained mental health professional, if necessary, to sort out what is pushing you into some problematic, counterproductive parenting behaviors or decisions.

Don't Be Overly Attached to the Results

I have found that too often, well-meaning parents decide to throw in the towel because their child is not making as much progress as they expected. If you start to feel this way, try to remember that the results will take care of themselves as long as you stay committed to helping your child.

Of course you want to continue to see your distracted child manage her challenges more effectively and learn to make her own life easier. But, as the Alcoholic's Anonymous (AA) slogan so aptly goes: "Seek progress, not perfection." Keep doing the best you can, and don't obsess over results. Maybe your child won't make honor roll anytime soon, but if she gets B's, B-'s, or C's and she's really trying, then that's okay. Stop pushing yourself and your child so hard, and just keep encouraging, rather than demanding, that she do her best with what she has to work with.

Forget about "Other Kids"

It's very important to help your child strive to be the best she can be on her own merits, and not to compare her to other children or let her compare herself to others. Distracted children often have a history of feeling inferior to peers. In order to truly succeed, your child needs your support, not the fear-based motivation to succeed that comes from being compared to other kids.

Remember the Walt Disney animated cartoon about the tortoise and the hare? Max Hare and Toby Tortoise are having a foot race. Max has much more style and is generally cocky. During the race, he pauses for a short nap, and then stops to chat with the bunnies outside a girls' school, where he also shows off in several sports. When he hears the crowd roar, indicating that Toby is approaching the finish line, he takes off. But a last-minute sprint and a long neck give Toby the victory (Reeves, John. "Plot Summary for *The Tortoise and the Hare*." Available online at www.imdb.com/title/tt0027126/plotsummary). I often think of this cartoon when working with distracted children, because it really rings true. They might have to work longer and harder to reach a goal, but they usually do get there, and sometimes they even get there first.

Celebrate what your child stands for by helping her realize that she is not a victim. She may have to work harder than some other kids, but this doesn't mean she should give up. Help her see that even if she doesn't come in first, like the tortoise, she is still a winner because she stayed in the race.

Relish the Resources

Many parents of distracted children woefully underutilize the help that the school or other third parties can offer. Along these lines, I encourage you to:

- Keep building positive relationships with your child's teachers and other school personnel. Encourage your child's caring new teachers to speak with her invested teachers of the past.
- Use the strategies in this book to the fullest. If necessary, use medication as recommended by your child's doctor.
- Keep good records. Medical evaluations, behavior counseling, and previous school records are all helpful when developing educational programs for your child.
- As needed, encourage the open—and frequent—exchange and flow of important information about your child between school officials, teachers, your child, your child's doctor, and any involved mental health professionals.

Make a "Positives" List

There is magic that occurs when you put a pencil to paper. Writing things down helps you concretely see and appreciate efforts you have made and steps you have taken. In this spirit, I encourage you to review all the positive changes you and your child have made so far. In the introduction of this program, I suggested that you keep a running log of successes. If you did this, keep it going. If you didn't do this, consider starting one now. If you list examples of your child showing less distractibility, you will continue to feel inspired. A mother of a distracted teen client of mine kept a log that she found helpful. A random three-day sample of that log looked something like this:

Monday: Brian was honest that he still had work that he had to complete. He began doing it when I calmly and yet firmly prompted him.

Tuesday (the following week): Brian shared how he felt frustrated by his teachers getting impatient with him. Yet, Brian did not let this get in the way of starting his homework.

Friday: Brian told me about a peer conflict, but he was open to looking at his role in it.

Forgive Yourself for Mistakes

Distracted kids have the capacity at times to bring out the worst in parents and teachers. It's easy to lose your patience and become frustrated and angry instead of calm, firm, and noncontrolling. If this happens, cut yourself some slack. Give yourself the gift of forgiveness. This does not mean that you should stop striving to improve your efforts to guide and support your child's growth toward independence. It means you shouldn't beat yourself up when you fall short of your own expectations. Forgiveness means letting go of self-deprecation, shame, humiliation, resentment, or anger that you may feel when things did not go well with your child. Today is a new day where you can embrace areas to improve and renew a personal commitment to do the best you can, while being less critical of yourself in the process.

Keep Your Batteries Charged

To avoid being depleted by your child's distractibility and her other related needs, I encourage you to take care of yourself. Making a positives list and forgiving yourself, as described above, are an important part of doing this. Other ways to keep yourself full of positive energy include:

- Keeping helpful, positive people around you. Talk to parents with similar concerns, at CHADD meetings, for example. Be open to their praise when they offer it.
- Remember to set up and enjoy good times with your child, other family members, and friends.
- Avoid becoming your child's adversary by not becoming defensive or creating defensiveness in your child. Again, staying calm, firm, and noncontrolling keeps you positive.
- Stay balanced in meeting the needs of other children in the family and your spouse. (If you are not currently married, stay connected to anyone special in your life.)
- Tap into your spiritual support system.
- Stay active with friends and draw support from them.
- Keep a healthy perspective on what you have to be grateful for.
- Take up new hobbies such as gardening, quilting, or joining a local gym.
- Attend a lecture in a topic you are interested in (other than how to help your distracted child).

As Your Child Goes Forward

Remember that distracted children are often surrounded with negativity and begin to expect failure. It may not be clear how much your child will grow out of her distractibility, down the road. For some children, the symptoms get better as they grow older and learn to adjust. Others may have the genetic propensity and/or continued tendencies for distraction. Just keep in mind that those children prone to distraction who have the best chance of becoming well-adjusted adults are those who have loving, supportive parents who work together with school staff, mental health workers, and their doctor (when needed).

Many parents make the mistake of telling their children how hard the future's going to be, as a means of motivating them. This can backfire and fuel feelings of inadequacy and shame. It won't help her succeed. What will help is having you explain how proud you are of how hard she has worked to achieve success, even though she has been challenged with distractibility.

Going forward, your continued commitment to this ten-day program should help you counter the forces of negativity. The following points will help your child keep moving forward:

- Put your child in situations where she will succeed. Whether they occur at school, with peers, in dance lessons, on the debate team, or on the soccer field, celebrate small victories and build momentum. This will help your child to believe in herself.
- Help your child discover and set goals. Once she has attained them, remind her of her larger goals in life.
- Reinforce that she has a bright future ahead of her.
- Stress that with persistence and effort, she can overcome obstacles.

As You Go Forward

I know that distractible kids are not easy to parent. Start fresh each day with a clean slate for you and your child. Build success one day at a time. You child is very fortunate to have a parent (or parents) that strongly cares about her and wants to help her. She already has a huge advantage in life. Keep the following points in mind as you move into the future:

- **Provide structure.** In a calm, firm, and noncontrolling way, work with your child to set specific times for waking up, eating, playing, doing homework, doing chores, watching TV or playing video games, and going to bed. Keep revisiting the schedule to see what works best. Stay flexible in the process of providing structure. Explain any changes to the routine in advance.

- **Remind your child to keep breaking down large tasks into smaller parts.** The more she reduces seemingly overwhelming tasks into more manageable ones, the better she will do.

- **Focus on effort, not outcomes.** Reward your child with praise when she tries to finish schoolwork, not just for good grades. You can give extra rewards for earning better grades.

- **Talk with your child's teachers.** Show solid respect for your child's teachers and try to forge a close alliance with them. The more they feel apprised of concerns and appreciated, the more apt they are to go the extra mile for your child.

- **Keep things simple.** It's important to clearly explain your expectations. Tell your child in a clear, calm voice specifically what you want. Keep directions simple and short. Ask your child to repeat the directions back to you.

- **Give your child adequate supervision.** While she has hopefully improved considerably, your distracted child may still have a tendency to be impulsive. Remain vigilant about events and circumstances going on in her life.

A Final Word

Remember that you are not only parenting a child who has struggled with distraction. You are also parenting a child with many gifts, many other exciting parts of herself, and all these make up that unique, dynamic whole that is uniquely her. Embrace your child's individuality. Her creativity, spontaneity, and views may differ from yours, and that's okay. Your job is to give your child both roots and wings, as the old saying goes. Her roots are the safety and self-confidence to tackle life's challenges and even obstacles. Her wings, which you have just strengthened by completing this ten-day program, are the ability to soar to new places and manage her life. Your ongoing love and encouragement are just more air beneath her wings.

I always look forward to and deeply value feedback from readers. I can be contacted through my Web site at www.drjeffonline.com.

The ADHD Monitoring System

by David Rabiner, PhD
Duke University

The ADHD Monitoring System is intended to help parents and health-care professionals monitor the ongoing effectiveness of treatment(s) a child is receiving for ADHD.

Dear Parent, Health-care Professional, or Educator:
One of the most important things one can do to help promote the healthy development of a child with ADHD is to carefully monitor how he or she is doing at school. The ADHD Monitoring System will help make it easy for you to do this. By using this program, you will be able to carefully track how your child, student, or patient is doing in school, and will be alerted when any adjustments or modifications to the child's treatment need to be considered. The directions below are written specifically for parents, but are applicable for use by teachers and health-care professionals as well.

Although the program was originally developed to monitor the ongoing effectiveness of medication treatment, it can be used to monitor the success of whatever treatments your child is receiving.

This material contains a comprehensive set of instructions that explain how the ADHD Monitoring System is used, along with the rating form that is to be completed each week by your child's teacher. (This form can be found at the end of the Appendix.)

In my own experience, I have found that this program works best with elementary-school children who have only a single teacher. This program can also be quite helpful for children who are in middle school or high school, although sometimes teachers in these grades do not spend enough time with a student to provide ratings that are as reliable. You will have to see how this works in your own situation.

I have used this program in my own practice for a number of years and have found that it is an extremely helpful tool for parents to have available. I sincerely hope that you begin to use it regularly and find it to be as helpful to you as it has been to many of the parents that I work with.

Sincerely,
David Rabiner, PhD
Senior Research Scientist
Duke University

The ADHD Monitoring System provides an easy and systematic way to monitor how a child with ADHD is doing each week at school, in several important areas. This will alert you to difficulties that may develop so that timely changes or additions to the treatment your child is receiving can be made. Guidelines for using this program effectively are presented below.

For this system to be of the greatest benefit to your child, the cooperation and support of your child's teacher is *essential*.

You will be asking your child's teacher to complete the rating form at the end of each week, and should provide the teacher with a sufficient number of copies. Although completing this form should not require more than five to ten minutes of the teacher's time, you should discuss this with him or her and make sure the teacher understands the importance of the information to be provided. Rather than just having your child give the forms to the teacher along with a note, it is better if you discuss this with the teacher on the phone or in person. (*Note:* The form you will print out and copy is at the END of the instructions.)

The teacher needs to understand that the information he or she provides will help to determine when any changes/additions to treatment need to be made, and that without this input, it will be difficult to know how well your child's ADHD symptoms are being managed.

Important

Some teachers may object to filling out this form on a weekly basis. If this is the case, then having the teacher complete the form on a monthly basis can still be quite helpful. I believe that weekly feedback is preferable because it helps you to really stay on top of things, but if this is not possible, receiving this feedback on a monthly basis will still be valuable. You may also wish to begin by getting the feedback each week, then switch to a monthly basis when things seem to be going well on a consistent basis.

There are two versions of the rating form at the end of this material. The first version, titled "Weekly Monitoring Report," asks the teacher to provide ratings based on what he/she observed during the prior week. The second version is titled "Monthly Monitoring Report" and asks for the same information based on observations made over the prior month. Use whichever form is appropriate for the frequency with which the teacher will provide ratings.

In your discussion with the teacher, be sure that arrangements are clearly made to ensure that you will be getting the completed form each week, or each month, depending on the rating period you have decided upon.

The information won't do you or your child any good if it sits in the classroom for weeks before you receive it.

If your child has multiple teachers, you can provide copies to each teacher who spends a significant amount of time with your child each week.

What Information Is Provided?

The ADHD Monitoring System is designed to provide you with information on:

- How well ADHD symptoms, specifically, are being managed
- Your child's behavioral, social, and emotional functioning at school
- Your child's weekly academic performance

These different areas are discussed in the following sections.

How Well Are ADHD Symptoms Being Managed?

Questions 1–12 deal specifically with symptoms of ADHD. Items 1–6 ask for teacher ratings of hyperactive/impulsive symptoms, and items 7–12 provide information on inattentive symptoms.

For children without ADHD, the vast majority of the ratings on these items will be either 0 or 1. For a child with ADHD whose symptoms are being managed effectively—via medication or some other means—you would also expect to see a majority of 0's and 1's being circled.

Note: Not all children with ADHD display both inattentive symptoms and hyperactive/impulsive symptoms. For example, children diagnosed with ADHD Predominantly Inattentive Type display primarily problems with attention (i.e., items 7–12) and do not show many of the hyperactive/impulsive characteristics (i.e., items 1–6). Conversely, children with ADHD Predominantly Hyperactive/Impulsive Type show the reverse pattern. Thus, should your child have one of these subtypes of ADHD, you would look specifically at the appropriate symptom group to determine how well the difficulties are being managed.

Behavioral, Social, and Emotional Functioning

Items 13–15 provide a basic screening for behavioral, social, or emotional difficulties. In addition to seeing mostly low scores for items 1–12, you want to see high scores (i.e., 3's or 4's) for these items. If your child receives low scores (i.e., 0's or 1's) on any or all of these items, you will want to contact the teacher to obtain more detailed information about the difficulties that were observed.

Note: It is important to emphasize that these items provide only a simple screen for behavioral, social, and emotional difficulties, and are not intended to be a comprehensive assessment. Although teachers are generally in an excellent position to comment on how a child is following classroom rules, they can be less aware of how a child is doing socially or how a child is feeling. Thus, the absence of any teacher-reported difficulties in these latter two areas does not necessarily mean that your child is not experiencing any such difficulties. Learning about this in a more comprehensive way requires feedback from the child as well.

Academic Performance

The second page of the rating form provides important information on your child's academic performance during the school week. Information is provided on the amount of assigned work completed, the general quality of the work completed, and whether this varies by subject; it also alerts you to homework assignments that may not have been turned in. Obviously, the ideal is for your child to be completing all assigned work, for it to be of good to very good quality, and for no homework assignments to have been missing.

Suggested Guidelines for Using the Information

The information contained in the weekly monitoring form is designed to provide you and your child's physician with the data you need to make informed decisions about the effectiveness of your child's treatment and the possibility that additions or modifications may be necessary.

It is important to stress, however, that any child can have an occasional bad week. If your child has been doing well, and then one week the monitoring form indicates difficulties in one or more areas, this should not necessarily cause alarm, and does not necessarily indicate the need for changes in treatment. In general, this would not be suggested unless the problems persist for several weeks in succession, or if troublesome weeks start to occur with increased frequency (i.e., instead of one bad week every couple of months, you start to see several bad weeks each month).

Important: If your child's teacher is making monthly ratings rather than weekly ratings, a single bad month would be cause for concern. Thus, I would recommend the information be shared right away with your child's physician so that he or she can determine whether modifications to your child's treatment(s) need to be made.

With these guidelines in mind, a simple and reasonable framework for evaluating the information contained in the weekly monitoring form is to consider the ADHD symptom ratings (i.e., items 1–12) and the other information separately. When done in this way, several different combinations are possible. These are discussed below.

Everything Going Well

This is what we hope to see each week. In this scenario, ratings of ADHD symptoms in items 1–12 are primarily or exclusively 0's and 1's; ratings for items 12–15 indicate that your child is following rules, getting along with peers, and appearing happy; and your child is completing all or almost all assigned work, and the work is of good quality. When this is the case, it is clear that your child is doing a great job at school, and that whatever treatments and/or support are in place are working well. No changes or adjustments are indicated.

Everything Going Poorly

At the other extreme is a situation where nothing is going well. Ratings of ADHD symptoms are high; problems with behavior, peer relations, and/or mood are also evident; and both the quantity and quality of assigned work being completed are problematic. In almost all cases, this indicates a situation where changes and adjustments (i.e., to medication, behavioral plan, etc.) need to be implemented. The only exception would be if, as noted above, your child has been doing consistently well and then has a single bad week. If this is the case, it is still important to speak with your child and his or her teacher, to try to learn what may have accounted for the difficult week. Should things get back to normal the following week, there is probably no need to change anything. If the difficulties persist, however, it will be important for the appropriate modifications to be made. Consult with your child's physician about the most appropriate steps to pursue.

As noted above, if ratings are being provided monthly, this situation would definitely warrant a discussion with your child's health-care provider.

ADHD Symptoms under Control, but There Are Problems with Behavior, Peer Relations, Mood, or Academics

This would be the case when ratings of ADHD symptoms on items 1–12 are fine (i.e., mostly 0's and 1's), but problems are indicated in one or more of these other areas. When ADHD symptom ratings are low, these other problems are unlikely to be direct results of ADHD, but may reflect additional difficulties. Such difficulties can occur for a variety of reasons, and it is very important to try to learn what factors may be contributing to the difficulties occurring for your child. Once again, consulting with your child's physician is recommended.

Note: When children are in middle school or high school and have multiple teachers, teachers often do not spend enough time with the child each day to observe problems with regards to ADHD symptoms. At these ages, it is more common for these symptom ratings to look okay, but for the difficulties to show up in a child's academic performance or behavior. It is important to be aware of this because, from the teacher's ratings, it may look as if primary ADHD symptoms are being effectively managed when they may not be, and adjustments in medication may be necessary.

Other Areas Look Good, but Rating of ADHD Symptoms Are High

This would be the case when ratings on items 1–12 include lots of 2's and 3's, but no other real problems are reported. This is probably the most unusual combination because, generally, when a child's ADHD symptoms are not being managed well, significant problems in behavioral, emotional, social, and/or academic functioning are also evident.

Should this pattern persist for more than one week, some adjustment in treatments used to manage primary ADHD symptoms is likely to be necessary (e.g., medication adjustment, revising behavior plan). Of course, if a child continues to do well academically, socially, and behaviorally at school despite high levels of ADHD symptoms, it may not be necessary to change anything. Generally, however, one would expect problems in these areas to emerge if ADHD symptoms are not being managed well for any sustained period. Again, consulting with your child's physician is strongly recommended.

Note: The last question on the page two of the form asks for the teacher's rating of how morning and afternoon periods compared. If your child is taking medication, and is receiving a longer-acting stimulant or is taking a second dose during the day at school, morning and afternoon behavior would not be expected to differ.

If your child is receiving only a single dose of a stimulant that is not intended to provide coverage across the entire school day, however, and the teacher's ratings indicate that mornings are consistently better than afternoons, it may indicate that the medication is wearing off during the day and that a single dose is not sufficient. If this pattern emerges in the teacher's ratings, you should discuss this issue with your child's physician. It is possible that a second dose or the use of a longer-acting medication would be helpful.

Note: You'll find the weekly and monthly versions of the monitoring form on the next pages. I hope this is helpful to you.

Weekly Monitoring Report

Child Name: _____   Date: _____

Teacher: _____   Class: _____

0	Not at All
1	A Little
2	Pretty Much
3	Very Much

Teacher: Please answer the items below on your observations of this child during the past week by circling the number that best applies.

Question	Scale			
1. Fidgets with hands or feet or squirms in seat	0	1	2	3
2. Difficulty remaining seated	0	1	2	3
3. Difficulty waiting turn	0	1	2	3
4. Talks excessively	0	1	2	3
5. Interrupts others	0	1	2	3
6. Always "on the go"	0	1	2	3
7. Easily distracted	0	1	2	3

8. Fails to complete assigned tasks	0	1	2	3
9. Trouble paying attention	0	1	2	3
10. Careless/messy work	0	1	2	3
11. Does not seem to listen when spoken to	0	1	2	3
12. Difficulty following directions	0	1	2	3

Note: For the following three items, higher scores indicate better functioning by the child.

13. Follows class rules	0	1	2	3
14. Gets along with peers	0	1	2	3
15. Seems happy and in good mood	0	1	2	3

Please indicate how the behaviors rated above compared during morning and afternoon times for the prior week by circling one of the choices below. Note: If you only have this child in class during morning or afternoon, this does not apply.

Morning better than afternoon	No clear difference	Afternoon better than morning

Circle the value below to indicate the approximate percentage of assigned classwork that this child completed during the past week:

0	10	20	30	40	50	60	70	80	90	100

The quality of work completed by this child this week was:

Very poor	Poor	Satisfactory	Good	Very good

If the quality of this child's work varied significantly between academic subjects, please indicate this in the next column.	
Did this child turn in all assigned homework? If not, please indicate the missing assignments:	
Please indicate any other comments or observations that you believe are important:	

Thank you for your help!

Monthly Monitoring Report

Child Name: _____   Date: _____

Teacher: _____   Class: _____

0	Not at All
1	A Little
2	Pretty Much
3	Very Much

Teacher: Please answer the items below on your observations of this child during the past month by circling the number that best applies.

Question	Scale			
1. Fidgets with hands or feet or squirms in seat	0	1	2	3
2. Difficulty remaining seated	0	1	2	3
3. Difficulty waiting turn	0	1	2	3
4. Talks excessively	0	1	2	3
5. Interrupts others	0	1	2	3
6. Always "on the go"	0	1	2	3
7. Easily distracted	0	1	2	3

8. Fails to complete assigned tasks	0	1	2	3
9. Trouble paying attention	0	1	2	3
10. Careless/messy work	0	1	2	3
11. Does not seem to listen when spoken to	0	1	2	3
12. Difficulty following directions	0	1	2	3

Note: For the following three items, higher scores indicate better functioning by the child.

13. Follows class rules	0	1	2	3
14. Gets along with peers	0	1	2	3
15. Seems happy and in good mood	0	1	2	3

Please indicate how the behaviors rated above compared during morning and afternoon times for the prior month by circling one of the choices below. Note: If you only have this child in class during morning or afternoon, this does not apply.

Morning better than afternoon	No clear difference	Afternoon better than morning

Circle the value below to indicate the approximate percentage of assigned classwork that this child completed during the past month:

0	10	20	30	40	50	60	70	80	90	100

The quality of work completed by this child this month was:

Very poor	Poor	Satisfactory	Good	Very good

If the quality of this child's work varied significantly between academic subjects, please indicate this in the next column.	
Did this child turn in all assigned homework? If not, please indicate the missing assignments:	
Please indicate any other comments or observations that you believe are important:	

Thank you for your help!

SOURCES

The following list contains sources I used in writing this book. Please note that several of these sources are Web sites that were active at the time of this writing. Web sites can change or expire on the Internet, so not all listed below may be active at the time you are reading this book.

Abikoff, Howard, PhD. "Ongoing Follow-Up Findings from the Multimodal Treatment Study of ADHD (MTA)." Available online at www.aboutourkids.org/aboutour/articles/mta_findings.html.

Anderson, Marlene. "Parenting ADHD Children, Surviving the School Years." Available online at www.suite101.com/lesson.cfm/17287/672.

Bailey, Eileen. "Vision therapy for ADHD." Available online at, http://add.about.com/od/alternativetreatments/a/altvision.htm.

Bainbridge, Carol. "Helping Gifted Children Cope with Intense Emotions." Available online at About, Inc., http://giftedkids.about.com/od/socialemotionalissues/qt/emotion_coping.htm.

Baumel, Jan, MS. "Individualized Education Program (IEP)—An Overview," November 20, 2000. Available online at www.schwablearning.org/articles.aspx?r=73.

Birnbaum, Howard G., Ronald C. Kessler, Sarah W. Lowe, Kristina
    Secnik, Paul E. Greenberg, Stephanie A. Leong, and Andrine
    R. Swensen. "Costs of Attention Deficit-Hyperactivity Disorder
    (ADHD) in the US: Excess Costs of Persons With ADHD and
    Their Family Members in 2000," February 2004. Abstract
    available online at www.ncbi.nlm.nih.gov/entrez/query.fcgi?
    cmd=Retrieve&db=PubMed&list_uids=15801990&dopt=A
    bstract Medscape. Article available online at www.medscape
    .com/viewarticle/500028.

Centers for Disease Control and Prevention. "Peer Relation-
    ships and ADHD," September 20, 2005. Available online
    at www.cdc.gov/ncbddd/adhd/peer.htm.

Defective Drugs—Adrugrecall.com. "ADHD Drugs Stunt
    Growth," May 5, 2006. Available online at www.adrugrecall
    .com/news/adhd-stunt-growth.html.

Educational Resources Information Center. Online at www.eric
    .ed.gov.

Educational Resources Information Center. "Providing an Appropri-
    ate Education to Children with Attention Deficit Disorder." ERIC
    EC Digest #E512, February 24, 1997. Available online at www
    .kidsource.com/kidsource/content2/appropriate.add.html.

Eide, Brock, and Fernette Eide. "Brains on Fire: The Multimodality
    of Gifted Thinkers," December 2004. Available online at www
    .newhorizons.org/spneeds/gifted/eide.htm.

Elias, Marilyn. "So much media, so little attention span." USA
    Today, March 30, 2005. Available online at www.usatoday.
    com/news/education/2005-03-30-kids-attention_x.htm.

Fowler, Mary. "Attention Deficit Hyperactivity Disorder." Avail-
    able online at www.kidsource.com/NICHCY/ADD1.html.

Henry J. Kaiser Family Foundation, Program for the Study of Entertainment Media and Health. "Generation M: Media in the Lives of 8–18 Year-olds," March 9, 2005. Available online at www.kff.org/entmedia/entmedia030905pkg.cfm.

Kambayashi, Takehiko. "More Talking, Less Typing," March 2, 2006. Available online at www.japanmediareview.com/japan/stories/060301kambayashi/.

Karras, Tula. "Alternative Therapies for ADHD." Available online at http://parentcenter.babycenter.com/refcap/bigkid/gspecialneeds/67364.html.

Mauro, Terri. "25 Ways to Make This the Best School Year Ever." Available online at About, Inc., http://specialchildren.about.com/od/schoolissues/a/bestyearever.htm.

Mauro, Terri. "How to Focus Attention on Math Worksheets." Available online at, http://specialchildren.about.com/od/learningissues/ht/focus.htm.

Moorman, Chick, and Thomas Haller. "How to Motivate Your Kids to Do Homework (without having a nervous breakdown yourself)." Available online at www.newsforparents.org/expert_motivate_kids_homework.html.

Mrug, Sylvie, Betsy Hosa, and Alyson C. Gerdes. "Children with Attention-Deficit/Hyperactivity Disorder: Peer Relationships and Peer-Oriented Interventions." *New Directions for Child and Adolescent Development* (Spring 2001): 51-77. Available online at www.ldonline.org/article/6347.

National Center for Learning Disabilities. 2006. "Knowing Your Child's Rights." Available online at www.ldonline.org/article/8023.

National Institute of Mental Health. "Attention Deficit Hyperactivity Disorder." 2006. Available online at www.nimh.nih.gov/publicat/adhd.cfm#symptoms.

Needlman, Robert, MD. "Alternative (Non-medical) Treatments for ADHD," January 25, 2001. Available online at www.drspock.com/article/0,1510,5747,00.html.

Nobile, N., G. M. Cataldo, C. Marino, and M. Molteni. "Diagnosis and treatment of dysthymia in children and adolescents." *CNS Drugs*17, no. 13 (2003): 927–46. Available online at www.ncbi.nlm.nih.gov/entrez/query.fcgi?cmd=Retrieve&db=PubMed&list_uids=14533944&dopt=Abstract.

Oracle Education Foundation, ThinkQuest. "Motivating Students." Available online at http://library.thinkquest.org/C005704/content_teaching_motivating.php3.

PBSParents.com. "Talking with Kids." Available online at www.pbs.org/parents/talkingwithkids.

Pelham, William, et al. "Medication Combined with Behavior Therapy Works Best for ADHD Children, Study Finds," March 4, 2007. Available online at www.buffalo.edu/news/fast-execute.cgi/article-page.html?article=72800009.

Rabiner, David, PhD. "ADHD: Increased Medical Costs for Families," February 2004. Available online at www.helpforadd.com/2004/february.htm.

Rabiner, David, PhD. "Behavioral Treatment for ADHD: An Overview." Available online at www.athealth.com/Consumer/farticles/Rabiner.html.

Reeves, John. "Plot Summary for *The Tortoise and the Hare*." Available online at www.imdb.com/title/tt0027126/plotsummary.

Schmidt, Peggy. "When Your Child Has Trouble: 5 ways you can help when your child has difficulty relating to peers." Available online at, http://content.scholastic.com/browse/article.jsp?id=1464.

Stokes, Susan. "Structured Teaching: Strategies for Supporting Students with Autism," page 2: "Visual Schedules." Written by Susan Stokes under a contract with CESA 7 and funded by a discretionary grant from the Wisconsin Department of Public Instruction. Available online at www.specialed.us/autism/structure/str11.htm.

Testingtakingtips.com. "Testing Taking Tips." Available online at www.testtakingtips.com.

University of Illinois Extension, Resources for Working with Youth with Special Needs. "Learning Disability." Available online at www.urbanext.uiuc.edu/specialneeds/lrndisab.html.

U.S. Food and Drug Administration, Center for Food Safety and Applied Nutrition, "Dietary Supplements: Overview." Available online at http://www.cfsan.fda.gov/~dms/supplmnt.html.

Whitten, Elizabeth, MD. "Behavior Management Strategy Index." Available online at http://homepages.wmich.edu/~whitten/champaign_project/behavior.html.

Wright, Diana Browning, MA. "Avoiding Homework Wars," September 12, 2001 (modified April 16, 2004). Available online at www.schwablearning.org/articles.asp?r=352.

ADHD

Children and Adults with Attention-Deficit/Hyperactivity Disorder (CHADD)
8181 Professional Place, Suite 15
Landover, MD 20785
Toll-free: 800-233-4050
Phone: 301-306-7070
Web site: www.chadd.org
CHADD is a nonprofit organization that offers support to individuals with AD/HD and their families, as well as teachers and other professionals.

Attention Research Update
Web site: www.helpforadd.com
This Web site will enable you to subscribe to Dr. David Rabiner's free e-mail newsletter, *Attention Research Update,* which helps parents, professionals, and educators stay informed about important new research on ADHD.

Anxiety

Anxiety Disorders Association of America

11900 Parklawn Drive, Suite 100

Rockville, MD 20852

Phone: 301-231-9350

Web site: www.adaa.org

ADAA is a national, nonprofit organization dedicated to educating the public, health-care professionals, and legislators about the nature and treatment of anxiety disorders.

Depression

Child and Adolescent Bipolar Foundation

1187 Wilmette Ave., P.M.B. #331

Wilmette, IL 60091

Phone: 847-256-8525

Web site: www.bpkids.org

CABF is a parent-led, nonprofit, Web-based membership organization of families raising children diagnosed with, or at risk for, pediatric bipolar disorder.

Depression and Related Affective Disorders Association

Meyer 3–181

600 North Wolfe Street

Baltimore, MD 21287-7381

Phone: 410-955-4647

Web site: www.drada.org

DRADA is an educational organization providing support to individuals affected by a depressive illness, family members, health-care professionals, self-help groups, and the general public.

Depression and Bipolar Support Alliance
730 North Franklin Street, Suite 501
Chicago, IL 60610-7224
Toll-free: 800-826-3632
Web site: www.ndmda.org
DBSA is a nonprofit organization that provides information, educational materials, programs, exhibits, and media activities about mood disorders.

Dr. Jay Carter
Web site: www.jaycarter.net
This Web site is dedicated to offering commonsense explanations of bipolar disorder, prefrontal lobe, and topics like ego, arrogance, and entitlement. It features books and animation on the subject of bipolar disorder.

Drugs and Alcohol

The U.S. Department of Health and Human Services
Substance Abuse and Mental Health Services Administration
200 Independence Avenue SW
Washington, DC 20201
Toll Free: 877-696-6775
Phone: 202-619-0257
Web site: www.samhsa.gov

Herbs

Herbs for Health
1503 SW 42nd Street
Topeka, KS 66609-1265
Web site: www.herbsforhealth.com

Learning Disabilities

All Kinds of Minds

1450 Raleigh Road, Suite 200

Chapel Hill, NC 27517

Toll-free: 888-956-4637

Web site: www.Allkindsofminds.org

All Kinds of Minds is a nonprofit institute that provides programs for students with learning disabilities.

Education Resources Information Center (ERIC) Clearinghouse on Disabilities and Gifted Education

ERIC Project

c/o Computer Sciences Corporation

655 15th St. NW, Suite 500

Washington, DC 20005

Web site: http://eric.hoagiesgifted.org/

The ERIC Clearinghouse for Disabilities and Gifted Education was disbanded by the US Government in December 2003. This Web site is an archive of the material available on that site at that time.

International Dyslexia Association

8600 LaSalle Road

Chester Building, Suite 382

Baltimore, MD 21286-2044

Toll-free: 800-ABCD123

Phone: 410-296-0232

Web site: www.interdys.org

IDA is a nonprofit organization serving individuals with dyslexia, their families, and their communities.

Learning Disabilities Association of America

4156 Library Road, Suite 1

Pittsburgh, PA 15234-1349

Phone: 412-341-1515 and 412-341-8077

E-mail: info@ldaamerica.org

Web site: www.ldaamerica.org

LDA is a nonprofit volunteer organization that advocates for and serves those with learning disabilities, their families, and professionals in the field.

LD OnLine

Web site: www.ldonline.org

LD Online is a service of public TV station WETA, Washington, D.C., in association with The Coordinated Campaign for Learning Disabilities. The Web site provides information and advice about learning disabilities and ADHD.

National Center for Learning Disabilities

381 Park Avenue South, Suite 1401

New York, NY 10016

Toll-free: 888-575-7373

Phone: 212-545-7510

Web site: www.ld.org

National Dissemination Center for Children with Disabilities

P.O. Box 1492

Washington, DC 20013

Toll-free: 800-695-0285

Web site: www.nichcy.org

NICHCY is a center for information on children and youth with disabilities, laws concerning disabilities, research, and special education.

Office of Special Education and Rehabilitative Services
> U.S. Department of Education
> 400 Maryland Ave. SW
> Washington, DC 20202-7100
> Phone: 202-245-7468
> Web site: www.ed.gov/about/offices/list/osers/index.html

University of Illinois Extension, Resources for Working with Youth with Special Needs
> Web site: www.urbanext.uiuc.edu/specialneeds/lrndisab
> .html

Schwab Learning
> Web site: www.schwablearning.org
> Schwab Learning is a nonprofit organization, dedicated to providing reliable, parent-friendly information about learning disabilities from experts and parents.

School Rights

Council of Parent Attorneys and Advocates (COPAA)
> P.O. Box 6767
> Towson, MD 21285
> Phone: 443-451-5270
> Web site: www.copaa.net
> COPAA is a nonprofit advocacy group of attorneys, nonattorney educational advocates, and parents who are dedicated to securing quality educational services for children with disabilities.

Wrightslaw

Web site: www.wrightslaw.com

Parents, educators, advocates, and attorneys visit Wrightslaw .com for accurate, reliable information about special education law and advocacy for children with disabilities. Wrights law includes thousands of articles, cases, and free resources about dozens of special education topics.

Organizations with General Child and Teen Mental Health Information

American Psychological Association

750 First Street NE

Washington, DC 20002-4242

Toll-free: 800-374-2721

Web site: www.apa.org

American Psychiatric Association

1000 Wilson Boulevard, Suite 1825

Arlington, VA 22209-3901

Phone: 703-907-7300

E-mail: apa@psych.org

Web site: www.psych.org

Federation of Families for Children's Mental Health

1021 Prince Street

Alexandria, VA 22314-2971

Phone: 703-684 7710

Focus Adolescent Services
Phone: 410-341 4216
Web site: www.focusas.com/index.html
Focus Adolescent Services is an Internet clearinghouse of
information and resources on teen and family issues, to help
and support families with troubled and at-risk teens.

**National Institute of Child Health and Human Development
(NICHD)**
National Institutes of Health, DHHS
31 Center Drive, Room 2A32, MSC 2425
Bethesda, MD 20892-2425
Phone: 301-496-5133
Web site: www.nichd.nih.gov

National Institute of Mental Health (NIMH)
National Institutes of Health, DHHS
6001 Executive Boulevard Room 8184, MSC 9663
Bethesda, MD 20892-9663
Web site: www.nimh.nih.gov

www.wrongplanet.net
A Web community designed for individuals (and parents of
those) with Asperger's disorder, autism, ADHD, and other
pervasive developmental disorders. It provides a forum,
where members can communicate with each other; an article
section, where members may read and submit essays or
how-to guides about various subjects; and a chat room for
real-time communication with others who have Asperger's
disorder.

Recommended Books
on Child and Teen Mental Health Issues

Barkley, Russell A., PhD. *Taking Charge of ADHD*. New York, NY: The Guilford Press, 2000.

Barkley, Russell A., PhD, and Christine M. Benton. *Your Defiant Child*. New York, NY: The Guilford Press, 1998.

Bernstein, Jeffrey, PhD. *10 Days to a Less Defiant Child*. New York, NY: Marlowe & Company, 2006.

Brooks, Robert, PhD. *The Self-Esteem Teacher*. Loveland, OH: Treehaus, 1991.

Canter, Lee. *Homework Without Tears*. New York, NY: Harper Collins, 2005.

Carter, Jay. *Bipolar: The Elements of Bipolar Disorder*. Wyomissing, PA: Unicorn Press, 2006.

Edward, Hal. *Scream-Free Parenting*. Duluth, GA: Oakmont Publishing, 2005.

Friedberg, Robert D., and Jessica M. McClure. *Clinical Practice of Cognitive Therapy with Children and Adolescents*. New York, NY: The Guilford Press, 2002.

Greene, Ross W. *The Explosive Child*. New York, NY: Harper Paperbacks, 2005.

Hallowell, Edward M., and John J. Ratey. *Driven to Distraction*. New York, NY: Touchstone, 1995.

Kurcinka, Mary Sheedy. *Raising Your Spirited Child: A Guide for Parents Whose Child Is More Intense, Sensitive, Perceptive, Persistent, Energetic*. New York, NY: Harper Paperbacks, 1998.

Levine, Mel. *The Myth of Laziness*. New York, NY: Simon and Schuster, 2004.

Mennuti, R. B., A. Freeman, and R. W. Christner. *Cognitive-Behavioral Interventions for Educational Settings: A Handbook for Practice*. Oxford, UK: Routledge, 2006.

Nolte, Dorothy Law. *Children Learn What They Live.* New York, NY: Workman Publishing Company, 1998.

Pantley, Elizabeth, and William Sears. *Kid Cooperation: How to Stop Yelling, Nagging and Pleading and Get Kids to Cooperate.* Oakland, CA: New Harbinger Publications, 1996.

Papolos, Demitri and Janice Papolos. *The Bipolar Child: The Definitive and Reassuring Guide to Childhood's Most Misunderstood Disorder.* 3rd ed. New York, NY: Broadway Publishing, 2006.

Power, Thomas J., James L. Karustis, and Dina F. Habboushe. *Homework Success for Children with ADHD: A Family-School Intervention Program.* New York, NY: The Guilford Press, 2001.

Rief, Sandra. *The ADHD Book of Lists.* San Francisco, CA: Jossey-Bass, 2003.

Schaefer, Dick. *Choices and Consequences: What to Do When a Teenager Uses Alcohol/Drugs.* Center City, MN: Hazelton, 1987.

Shaywitz, Sally, MD. *Overcoming Dyslexia.* New York, NY: Knopf Publications, 2003.

Sutton, James. *101 Ways to Make Your Classroom Special: Creating a Place Where Significance, Teamwork, and Spontaneity Can Spread and Flourish.* Pleasanton, TX: Friendly Oaks Publications, 1999.

Wender, Paul H., MD. ADHD: Attention-Deficit Hyperactivity Disorder in Children and Adults. Oxford, UK: Oxford University Press, 2002.

Wilens, Timothy E., MD. *Straight Talk about Psychiatric Medications for Kids.* New York, NY: The Guilford Press, 1999.

Wright, Pam, and Peter Wright. *From Emotions to Advocacy: The Special Education Survival Guide.* 2nd ed. Hartfield, VA: Harbor House Law Press, 2005.

ACKNOWLEDGMENTS

In order to complete this book, I owe the following people so many thanks:

Joe Colace, Certified School Psychologist; Ivan Katz, EdD; Geri Toland, MSW; Chuck Pugh, JD; Bonnie Socket, PhD; Marie Paxon; Dr. Bill Morgan; Anthony Nordone, PhD; Ari Tuckman, Psy.D., MBA; Judith Roth, MSW; and Tony Rostain, MD, are all fine colleagues who shared their valuable wisdom. Many of my clients have offered me valuable ideas for this book. To honor their confidentiality, they remain anonymous, but their contribution to this project has been huge.

Many thanks to Katie McHugh and Sue McCloskey for their wonderful editorial support. My heartfelt thanks also go to the following people:

Ralph—Having a best friend since kindergarten has been a special honor. You are all heart and a wonderful friend.

Ed Washington—You're such a courageous, wonderful friend. Thanks for all the times you have said, "Hey Jeff, can I do anything for you?"

Barbara—For treasured times and for showing me what it is like to pay superb attention to detail.

Tony—Your friendship helps keep me moving to great places. I deeply value our ongoing conversations in which we seek to discover the meaning of life.

To my caring extended family—It's always heartwarming to know that you are there for me.

To all of my wonderful colleagues who have supportively spurred me to keep on learning.

I also owe thanks to the many families and children seen in my practice who have inspired me over the years. Their willingness and courage to explore and overcome difficult issues and obstacles are amazing, and I am honored to have had their trust and faith in me. I have learned so much from them and hope that they have also learned from me.

INDEX